SOCIOLOGY
ON
TRIAL

Edited by

Maurice Stein and Arthur Vidich

PRENTICE-HALL, INC.

Englewood Cliffs, N. J.

Current printing (last digit):

12 11 10 9 8 7 6 5 4

Library of Congress Catalog Card No.: 63-19420
Printed in the United States of America—C

In Memory of C. Wright Mills

CONTENTS

Introduction, 1

INTRODUCTION

Sociology has as its task the analysis and understanding of the organized structure and operations of society *and* the basis in values and attitudes on which individual participation in social life rests. The carrying out of this task presupposes sociologists capable of doing the work and a society capable of tolerating their results. There are a number of reasons why neither of these presuppositions is easily achieved.

Grant us first that any "objective" social analysis or social commentary —that is, any analysis or commentary that does not start from accepted or established points of view—is critical either directly or in its implications. Simply by presenting radically different perceptions of a world that is otherwise taken for granted, society is irked, irritated, and perhaps threatened as well. Analysis exposes the glue that holds the joints of society together and it forces people to view themselves within what is at best a fairly precarious social order. To the extent that society even notices the critical sociologist, it can be expected to make a negative judgment on his work.

The critical sociologist requires at least two qualities (a) an ability to get outside the world of his own experience and to project himself into the centers of life and institutions with which he does not in the ordinary course of events have direct experience, and (b) an ability to detach himself from the prevailing values and attitudes of the organized groups in society in order thereby to gain a level of understanding that goes beyond conventional perspectives. For this some measure of alienation is necessary, however it is achieved, and whatever idiosyncratic point of view it represents. However, the very structure of the social world of the sociologist as constituted professionally makes it difficult to achieve these requirements.

Sociological practitioners live and work in universities and other bureaucracies as jobholders whose time and attention is regulated by the requirements of the occupation. They have come to think of sociology as a "field" which possesses jurisdictional rights on a subject matter which can be used as a basis for making claims for budgets and fees from administrators who control the purse strings. They form professional associations organized to perform the classical functions of the guild—regulation of admissions, monopolization of jobs, control and expansion of markets, and the development of occult terminologies. Under this academic and professional dispensation, the same academic and professional experience easily becomes the exclusive touchstone for defining the sociologist's phenomenal world. Thus the tasks of sociology easily get lost in the more immediate "practical" and pecuniary involvement of the middle-class jobholder. Sociology loses its critical sense and willingly forfeits both its capacity to carry out the sociological task and its capacity to judge itself from a sociological perspective.

If critical sociology is destined to be rejected by society and despised by those sociologists who have been unable to resist society's affluent blandishments, it is not worth putting sociology on trial, because the case is already closed. Such would be our conclusion were it not for the few sociologists who have been willing to leave their work to make an analysis of sociology itself. The sociology of sociology by these sociologists stands as an expression of conscience for sociology as a whole. While it is clear that no trial has been held, these essays have made the sociologists' world more trying than it would otherwise have been.

The authors of the essays in this book are substantive sociologists who have primarily devoted themselves to the analysis and understanding of social life. For them, sociology as such as well as its methods have been secondary considerations important only in relation to the substantive problems with which they are concerned. It would not be necessary to make this point in defense of our authors and ourselves except that we wish to distinguish this book from a number of recently published projects whose purpose is the celebration of topics like: the progress of a decade, sociology today, theories of society, and the foundations of sociology. It is our opinion that these efforts mainly contribute to the professionalization of sociology and to the legitimation of academically marketable "bodies of knowledge."

In our experience as teachers at Brandeis University and at the Graduate Faculty of the New School for Social Research, these are the essays we have found to be particularly helpful in liberating our students from the intimidation they feel when they confront the official tomes. These days, even small amounts of irreverence have exceptional regenerative effects on youthful imaginations.

It is clear, however, that criticism has its limits and that the sociological imagination must find its own productive enterprises. What these enterprises might be and who will be their entrepreneurs is always a matter of personal decision. The editors of this book have indicated their own choices and preferences in other essays and books easily available to the interested reader.

M. S.
A. V.

Part I

THE ETHOS OF
AMERICAN SOCIOLOGY

AMERICAN SOCIOLOGY
Karl Mannheim

I consider it my task to convey to you the ideas awakened in a German sociologist by the reading of the "case book" on methods in social science edited by Stuart A. Rice. Of course I do not mean to say that German sociology is a single, homogeneous unit. On the contrary, the most antagonistic schools of thought are lined up against each other in that country. However, even their differences reveal something common in all German conceptions of sociology, a common train of ideas which might profitably be compared with the typical American approach to the subjects of social science. I believe that *Methods in Social Science* furnishes a welcome occasion to confront our different mental habits.

In so limited a space, however, only the fixing of a first impression is possible, without any pretension to finality. Questions of detail must be left aside. The only purpose of this review is to show the difference in the fundamental attitudes of German and American scholars towards the problems of social science.

To speak of the *Methods* of Rice, I must begin with the confession that a European sociologist is bound to feel agreeably surprised by the vast and comprehensive plan of the work and even more by the successful realization of this plan, aiming at a methodological survey by eminent scholars of the latest products of social research in America as well as of

"American Sociology." From *Essays in Sociology and Social Psychology* by Karl Mannheim, edited by Paul Kecskemeti (London: Routledge and Kegan Paul, Ltd.), Chap. 4, pp. 185-94. Copyright 1953 by Routledge and Kegan Paul, Ltd. Reprinted by permission of Routledge and Kegan Paul, Ltd. and the Oxford University Press. A review of *Methods in Social Science,* edited by Stuart A. Rice (Chicago: University of Chicago Press), 1931. This review first appeared in 1932. Copyright 1953 by Julia Mannheim.

historically or theoretically important European works. This example of scientific cooperation reminds us of the excessive individualism prevailing in German sociology. In Germany, almost every author believes it necessary to start from a new beginning, and most scholars take pride in having systems of their own, overlooking the fact that division of labor and organization of scientific research are perfectly feasible in sociology and that central guidance could be of very great profit.

A second fact calling for approval is that the methodological subject matter of the work is treated in close connection with concrete examples of practical study. The problem of method is not examined *in abstracto,* but all methodological questions are exposed as they present themselves to the practical worker. A similar book written by Germans would probably begin with a general treatise on the difference between natural and social sciences, between "understanding" and "explanation," and on other such questions of principle, while the American work soundly confines itself to the methodological requirements of concrete tasks. Methodology of this kind embraces in the first place problems like these: "What should one do to find out this or that? How should this or that problem be set forth? Where are the possible sources of error, and what was done, and must yet be done, to eliminate them?"

As I said, this approach to methodology from the practical aspect is very sound and effective. There is nothing ambiguous about it; all criticism assumes the form of conferences in a workshop where the opinion of a foreman on a piece in construction is immediately understood by everyone.

However, not only methodological criticism has this character of directness, but the sociological research work under examination also shows a similar quality. Each work starts from a practical problem, from a social task calling for immediate solution. The sociologist is called upon to help in finding this solution.

The typical problems of American sociology arise from the immediate necessities of everyday life. They assume the form of convergent planning and concerted action aiming at overcoming the difficulties threatening the progress of collective work. This explains the fact that most of the subjects treated fall under the heading of what in Germany is called "social policy." Such problems are those of juvenile delinquency, juvenile gangs, ghettos, immigration policy, etc., to which excellent studies are devoted. This sort of work brings help where help is needed without devoting much time to elucidating intricate problems of evolution and to defining exactly the historical place of the phenomena in the process of social evolution. It is also characteristic of this kind of research that it is based on ready documentary evidence, focusing on just those matters on which life itself accumulates such evidence. Thus the authenticity of factual observation is guaranteed in advance.

Limitation to practical problems of this kind tends to segregate single phenomena from the social fabric with which they are interwoven, thereby disintegrating the whole of social life. An endeavor toward clarity and exactness, evidenced by the choice of well-defined and concrete subjects, is accentuated by the use of notion-patterns ready for use by anyone. Every phenomenon will be subjected to an analytical treatment laying bare its correlations with these notion-patterns. Thus the variety of problems and aspects will be reduced to a single set of terms. The appreciation of a scholar will depend on his skill in handling the technique of research and on his ingenuity in experimentation.

In fact, nothing else could be expected. Collective research, that is to say, research which may be continued by anyone from the point where it has been interrupted, demands a certain simplification of the phenomena. The embarrassing multiplicity of living facts must be broken up and articulated so as to lend itself to a mental treatment from which all ambiguity and subjectivity is banished and by which the exactness of all terms is guaranteed.

The above seems to me to be typical not only of the contributions to Rice's compendium but also of most of the representative specimens of American sociology. However, after having rendered justice to the high merits of this scientific attitude, I feel obliged to point out some of its shortcomings. It seems to me that the scientific outlook which I have characterized above necessarily misses some essential points, not so much in the treatment of its problems as in its fundamental conception of social life and social science.

The more one approves the empirical outlook of American science—agreeing with its motto that science, after all, is not called upon to reassert the supremacy of all the irrational factors which tend to thwart an effective and intelligent control of social phenomena—the more significant is the uneasiness with which one reads some, though not all, specimens of this kind of scientific research.

To confine ourselves to Rice's compendium, we must admit a very marked and painful disproportion between the vastness of the scientific machinery employed and the value of the ultimate results. The subject and title of most of the contributions evoke the highest expectations; yet, after having reached their conclusions, one is tempted to ask, disappointedly: "Is this all?"

It need not be repeated that this does not apply to all papers contained in the book. However, in order to make our attitude clear, we have to overemphasize a little all the typical traits, meritorious as well as defective, which in our opinion distinguish American sociology from our own.

Now it may be worth while to ask what is wrong in a scientific attitude which, on the whole, is so sound and well founded. What is to blame for the inability of works of such flawless methodical integrity really to satisfy us?

The essential seems to me to be this: American social science of the kind which I regard as typical has the defects of its qualities; indeed, the defects which we have to point out are almost inseparable from the qualities which we praised.

1. The first reason why we are left unsatisfied by this type of science is the limited scope of the questions to which it confines itself and the character of the social knowledge toward which its efforts are directed.

It is certainly worth while to examine the conditions responsible for the neglect and delinquency of juveniles. It is equally useful to know which type of immigrant will adapt himself best. A couple of the best contributions are devoted to these themes. However, if such problems are treated in isolation while the totality of social problems remains neglected, if the scholar examining details does not aspire toward a comprehensive view of social reality or shrinks from generalizing hypotheses out of mere caution or owing to methodical asceticism, then the most excellent work of detail is bound to remain in a vacuum. Society at a given stage of its evolution is no mere agglomeration of exactly observable individual data, of sparse events and relationships all of which, added together, in some way produce the picture of the whole, but a combination of interdependent phenomena, and even more: a structured whole or Gestalt (a term used here in a general, not merely psychological, sense). If we divide this whole into its parts, and focus attention on the individual functioning of each part, then we shall necessarily overlook a very important aspect of the functioning of the parts, namely, their relation to the whole to which they belong. An individual event or a social phenomenon is adequately described only if it be characterized as a manifestation of the life and functioning of society as a while. The observation of individual tasks and their analysis are both necessary to attain scientific truth, but once this task is done, the scholar must turn to the whole of social life and interpret the detail from the aspect of the whole.

Nothing could be learned on the economic laws of exchange if one were to confine oneself to the psychological and empirical analysis of so many hundreds of thousands of individual acts of barter without formulating the principles of economic circulation. These principles are never exactly represented by facts; yet they form the mental pattern to which the individual facts are referred. The same applies to all empirical observations. They must be confronted with constructive principles. Empirical data are only useful if they are enlightened by a constructive hypothesis, by a theory of social processes in general.

It seems to me that American sociology suffers from an excessive fear of theories, from a methodological asceticism which either prevents the putting forth of general theories or else keeps such theories as exist isolated from practical research.

To have nothing but theories without verifying them, to discuss theoretical dicta as a kind of mental sport, serves no useful end whatsoever. On the other hand, it is a misunderstanding of positivism to try to know reality without having theories. Finally, to have theories but not to apply them to reality may be attributed to an excessive love of security which must lead to sterilization.

2. This ascetic attitude toward theories seems to be based on a mistrust of "philosophy" or "metaphysics." Unwillingness to discuss basic questions, however, does not benefit positive research. In conversations with American scientists one often hears the criticism that German sociology is still lingering at the "philosophic" stage, and has yet to make some progress before attaining the "scientific" one. Correct as this criticism may be as regards many German authors who indulge in metaphysical escapades under cover of sociology, it would still be a mistake to overrate the antagonism between philosophy and science, and to brand as "philosophy" in a defamatory sense every theory, every constructive hypothesis penetrating beyond immediate and tangible experience and outlining a comprehensive system of social and historical phenomena. We must distinguish between "speculative" and "constructive" mind; the latter is as indispensable to any empirical research as the former is detrimental. To think speculatively is to sit at a desk and conceive casual and uncontrolled ideas on all things on earth and in heaven. To think constructively means to build up, by an effort of constructive imagination, a structure which is embedded in the phenomena themselves but cannot be detected by direct observation of any individual fragment of reality.

It is possible that many American scholars will admit the importance of theoretical construction. However, the main thing, in the field of methodology, is not to have a right opinion but to act according to it. Now, it seems to me that the most valuable specimens of "empirical" sociology show a curious lack of ambition to excel in the quality of theoretical insight into phenomenal structures. They reveal a greater anxiety not to violate a certain, very one-sided, ideal of exactness. One almost ventures to say, such works aim in the first place at being exact, and only in the second place at conveying a knowledge of things. Now, as to this, I believe that it is much better first to seek to have some knowledge of a vitally important matter, and only afterward to worry about the method assuring the highest possible degree of exactness.

American sociology seems to yield too much to the fascination of natural science. Although it is admitted that all social phenomena are not measurable, still numerical proportions are the ideal of exactness toward which most scholars are striving. However, before adopting a specific ideal of exactness, one should inquire which ideal suits best the particular field of phenomena to which research is to be devoted. In the field of philological and historical science where interpretation plays a foremost part, the criteria of exactness are quite different from those prevailing in experimental psychology, physics, etc.

Exaggerated "methodological asceticism" often results in the drying-up of the sources of scientific inspiration and invention. In order to know social reality one must have imagination, a particular brand of imagination which I should like to call "realistic" because it does not create fiction but exerts itself in binding together apparently unrelated facts by means of a vision of structural correlations which alone enables us to see the framework into which every fact, even the most casual one, is fitted. Like other qualities required for science, such as self-criticism, control of methods, etc., this realistic imagination must be cultivated through generations.

Harmful as the excessive philosophical tradition dominating intellectual life in Germany may be (such tradition is always harmful when it dominates exclusively, without confronting speculation with the facts), philosophical training is useful whenever it is tinged with the yearning for the knowledge of real things. Then it may evolve into a realistic imagination which makes for increased constructive power. Such philosophical training, acquired in many generations, is responsible for a greater capacity of recognizing connections between things, for the development of a comprehensive view of the social process as a whole, instead of mere isolated treatment of sporadic facts which can be mastered in a division of jobs. Comprehensive vision will put every fact in its place within the framework of a broad hypothesis embracing the whole of society.

It is true that, according to Comte's fundamental conception, the survivals of the old philosophical and metaphysical stage must be eliminated once the empirical stage is reached. However, these survivals cannot be eliminated by simply sacrificing everything reminiscent of philosophy, or of a philosophical conception of history, but only by applying to the facts and fructifying in empirical research that gift of consistent questioning and comprehensive vision which humanity for the first time developed in its philosophy.

3. While on the one hand American sociology lacks a certain courage in outlining broad theories, or rather shrinks from inquiring into the structural aspects of social life as a whole at a given stage, out of fear engendered by the common identification of theory as such with theory in the sense of pure, causal, metaphysical speculation—on the other hand there is another reason why our claims on social science are not satisfied by typical American contributions to this science, interesting and valuable as they may be in themselves. This reason is that typical American studies start from questions in nowise connected with those problems which arouse our passions in everyday political and social struggle.

In one respect, American sociology is nearer to reality than German —namely, as regards the solution of everyday problems. The American scholar is no bookish person; he maintains contact with criminal courts and social welfare institutions, lives with gangs, in slums and ghettos. However, as soon as political and social problems impose themselves we notice an immense reserve, a lack of social atmosphere. It looks as if science had no social background; as if groups devoted to social research cultivated no exchange of ideas on matters social and political; as if no conventicles existed in which the practical attitude of science toward such problems were discussed.

Science, in these parts, serves the purpose of reforming or reorganizing society. Scientific interest centers on the dynamic forces determining the process of transformation of society, although, of course, political viewpoints differ very widely. As to myself, I shall always regard it as one of the most important questions to know how human consciousness is shaped and determined by the social struggle; a question which may not only be asked in connection with the present situation, but also applied to history and to the psychic and intellectual changes wrought in the past by social revolutions and by the shift in class dominance. It may be objected to this that such enormous questions do not lend themselves to empirical analysis. Our reply is that, naturally, these problems cannot be solved by one or two works; if, however, every study of detail is carried out in clear consciousness of these comprehensive questions (whether they directly guide the research or merely act as a background), then even such central themes might successfully be tackled.

Just as there is a certain arrogance in the attempt of pure speculation to solve the Gordian knot of big problems at one stroke, there exists a certain false modesty of the empirical scholar whom his "exactitude complex" prompts to ignore the genuine basis of his own questioning, which alone makes a scientific occupation worth while. In our opinion, methodological criticism of sociological studies (as it was undertaken in Rice's compendium) should in each case inquire whether the work in question is devoted to a genuine problem. In America, the inverse method seems to be practised: one concludes from the existence of ready documentary evidence, of statistical material, etc., that social research is worth while. This is nothing but an 'exactitude complex' which canonizes every fact, every numerical certitude just because they are factual and controllable.

In view of the growing amount of the material of science it would be dangerous further to accumulate facts without choice. The loss of command over the material at this juncture has become a serious menace to science as such. The desire to bring order into this chaos is at least as justified as the attempt to isolate and exactly to define individual fragments of it. Genuine problems, real scientific tasks are only those which impose themselves on the basis of the general trend of science; that is to say, questions which emerge from the group consciousness of society struggling for its existence and its livelihood.

In the introduction to the volume under discussion (p. 10), the question is asked whether Marx and Carlyle would have been unable to envisage their problems had they known the statistical method. If the answer is in the affirmative, then we do not hesitate to confess that we would rather renounce statistical exactness than forego seeking answers to those questions which seem important to us. Should it not be possible to save these questions, then the cruel name of a "science of that which is not worth knowing," which was originally applied to academic, dry classical philology, would befit our science.

4. We know that a closer contact with central political problems involves the danger that judgments of value creep into science, reducing it to mere political propaganda. In fact, this danger constantly threatens German sociology just because it is closely in touch with political problems. However, if we know about this danger, we can take precautions against it, evolving methods which help to detect and eliminate political bias. One of the greatest German sociologists, Max Weber, has shown how we can discuss the political *nervus rerum* without making propagandistic judgments of value. The desire to treat politically important problems without being a victim to bias was responsible for the development in Germany of a new branch of social science, *Wissenssoziologie*. This new branch of research, intended to be an organ of critical self-control, has already succeeded in detecting and subjecting to control important groups of sources of error.[1]

The absence of the viewpoint of *Wissenssoziologie* from a methodological analysis seems to us to be a defect, inasmuch as this branch of sociology claims to have discovered that science itself is embedded in the stream of social and historical reality, wherefore even in cases when the sincere effort toward unbiased objective knowledge cannot be denied, the available supply of terms, the technique of questioning, the articulation and grouping of problems may be responsible for distortions which can only be detected by means of an intimate historical acquaintance with the correspondence between the development of science and the evolution of society. Only a scholar well acquainted with these facts of human evolution is able to construct those systems of perspective which necessarily introduce an element of partiality into all human consciousness.

Thus, we miss in Rice's compendium, in which we recognize a serious effort toward objectivity and toward the perfecting of the methods of observation, an element of self-control. A critic who himself shared the American approach to social science would not miss it. If, however, there is any reason for asking for the opinion of foreign critics, the reason is not that the foreigner might make suggestions regarding this or that detail but that he should unreservedly and with all possible frankness convey his impression of the work as a whole.

It is possible that such a general survey will not do justice to every detail, and that it expresses contrast too sharply. However, it may have the merit (if it has any) of making us look from a new angle at things to which daily intercourse and too much familiarity have dulled our senses.

In this review I have abstained from the usual compliments regularly bestowed by foreigners on foreign works. I have done so, in full awareness of the risk that I may shoot wide of the mark in my criticism; however, I deliberately run this risk because I think that the future of American sociology means something to us, just as America is not indifferent to the fate of German sociology. One thing shown by such a discussion more than anything else is that there were hardly ever two different styles of study so fit to supplement each other's shortcomings as are the German and American types of sociology. These two schools can become very useful to each other, just because their approach to their subject is so fundamentally different. We must learn from American sociology that science must remain in contact with real life and its exigencies; on the other hand, American sociology may gain if its studies on questions of practical detail are alive to the great theoretical problems which pervade and coordinate with each other all the scattered empirical facts.

NOTE

1. Cf. the author's article "Wissenssoziologie" in Alfred Vierkandt's *Handwörterbuch der Soziologie,* which also contains a bibliography of the subject.

THE BUREAUCRATIC ETHOS

C. Wright Mills

During the last quarter of a century, there has been a decisive shift in the administrative uses and political meanings of social science. The older liberal practicality of "social problems" still goes on, but it has been overshadowed by newer conservative uses of a managerial and manipulative sort. This new and illiberal practicality assumes various forms, but it is a general trend affecting the human disciplines as a whole. I may as well introduce my discussion of its ethos with an example of its major rationalization: "One final word of caution is needed to the student who plans to become a sociologist," Paul Lazarsfeld has written.

> He is likely to be worried about the state of the world. The danger of a new war, the conflict between social systems, the rapid social changes which he has observed in his country has probably made him feel that the study of social matters is of great urgency. The danger is that he may expect to be able to solve all current problems if he just studies sociology for a few years. This unfortunately will not be the case. He will learn to understand better what is going on around him. Occasionally he will find leads for successful social action. But sociology is not yet in the stage where it can provide a *safe basis for social engineering.* . . . It took the natural sciences about 250 years between Galileo and the beginning of the industrial revolution before they had a major effect upon the history of the world. Empirical social research has a history of three or four decades. If we expect from it quick solutions to the world's greatest problems, if we demand of it nothing but immediately practical results, we will just corrupt its natural course. [1]

What in recent years has been called "The New Social Science" refers not only to abstracted empiricism but also to the new and illiberal practicality. The phrase refers to both method and use, and quite correctly so: for the technique of abstracted empiricism and its bureaucratic use are now regularly joined. It is my contention that, so joined, they are result-ing in the development of a bureaucratic social science.

In each and every feature of its existence and its influence, abstracted empiricism, as it is currently practiced, represents a "bureaucratic" devel-opment. (1) In an attempt to standardize and rationalize each phase of social inquiry, the intellectual operations themselves of the abstracted em-pirical style are becoming "bureaucratic." (2) These operations are such as to make studies of man usually collective and systematized: in the kind of research institutions, agencies, and bureaus in which abstracted empiri-cism is properly installed, there is a development, for efficiency's sake if for no other, of routines as rationalized as those of any corporation's ac-counting department. (3) These two developments, in turn, have much to do with the selection and the shaping of new qualities of mind among the personnel of the school, qualities both intellectual and political. (4) As it is practiced in business—especially in the communication adjuncts of ad-vertising—in the armed forces, and increasingly in universities as well, "the new social science" has come to serve whatever ends its bureaucratic clients may have in view. Those who promote and practice this style of research readily assume the political perspective of their bureaucratic clients and chieftains. To assume the perspective is often in due course to accept it. (5) Insofar as such research efforts are effective in their declared practical aims, they serve to increase the efficiency and the reputation— and to that extent, the prevalence—of bureaucratic forms of domination in modern society. But whether or not effective in these explicit aims (the question is open), they do serve to spread the ethos of bureaucracy into other spheres of cultural, moral, and intellectual life.

I

It might seem ironic that precisely the people most urgently concerned to develop morally antiseptic methods are among those most deeply en-gaged in "applied social science" and "human engineering." Since work in the abstracted empirical manner is expensive, only large institutions can readily afford it. Among these are corporation, army, state, and also their adjuncts, especially advertising, promotion, and public relations. There are also the foundations, but the personnel in charge of these often tend to act under the new canons of the practical, that is to say, the bu-reaucratically relevant. As a result, the style has become embodied in definite institutional centers: since the twenties in advertising and mar-keting agencies; since the thirties in corporations and syndicated polling agencies; since the forties, in academic life, at several research bureaus; and during World War II, in research branches of the federal government. The institutional pattern is now spreading, but these remain its strong-holds.

The formalism of these costly techniques makes them especially serviceable in providing the very kind of information needed by those capable and willing to pay for it. The new applied focus has typically been upon specific problems, designed to clarify the alternatives for practical—which is to say, pecuniary and administrative—action. It is not at all true that only as "general principles" are discovered can social science offer "sound practical guidance"; often the administrator needs to know certain detailed facts and relations, and that is all he needs or wants to know. Since the practitioners of abstracted empiricism are often little concerned to set their own substantive problems, they are all the more ready to abdicate the choice of their specific problems to others.

The sociologist of applied social research does not usually address "the public"; he has specific clients with particular interests and perplexities. This shift from public to client clearly undermines the idea of objectivity-as-aloofness, an idea which has probably rested upon responsiveness to vague, unfocused pressures—and thus more on the individual interests of the researcher, who, in a small way, could divide and hence not be ruled.

All "schools of thought" have meaning for the career of the academic man. "Good work" is defined in terms agreeable to given schools, and thus academic success comes to depend upon active acceptance of the tenets of a dominant school. As long as there are many or at least several differing "schools," and especially in an expanding professional market, this requirement need not burden anyone.

Very little except his own individual limitations has stood between the individual craftsman of social science and work of the highest order. But such unattached men cannot pursue abstracted empirical research on a suitable scale, for such work cannot proceed until an agency of research is sufficiently developed to provide the appropriate kind of material, or perhaps I ought to say, work-flow. To practice abstracted empiricism requires a research institution, and, academically speaking, large funds. As the costs of research increase, as the research team comes into being, as the style of work itself becomes expensive, there comes about a corporate control over a division of labor. The idea of a university as a circle of professorial peers, each with apprentices and each practicing a craft, tends to be replaced by the idea of a university as a set of research bureaucracies, each containing an elaborate division of labor, and hence of intellectual technicians. For the efficient use of these technicians, if for no other reason, the need increases to codify procedures in order that they may be readily learned.

The research institution is also very much a training center. Like other institutions, it selects certain types of mind, and by virtue of the rewards it offers it places a premium upon the development of certain mental qualities. Two types of men, rather new to the academic scene, have arisen in these institutions, alongside more old-fashioned scholars and researchers.

There are, first, the intellectual administrators and research promoters —about whom I cannot say anything that is not, I suppose, familiar in academic circles. Their academic reputations rest upon their academic power: they are the members of The Committee; they are on The Board of Directors; they can get you the job, the trip, the research grant. They are a strange new kind of bureaucrat. They are the executives of the mind, public relations men specializing in the foundations. For them, as for promoters and executives elsewhere, the memorandum is replacing the book. They can set up another research project or institute in a most efficient manner, and they administer the production of "books." The span of time in which they say they work is "a billion man-hours of technical labor." In the meantime, we should not expect much substantive knowledge: first there must be many methodological inquiries—into the methods and into the inquiry—and then there must be all the "pilot studies." Many foundation administrators like to give money for projects that are large-scale and hence easier "to administer" than more numerous handicraft projects; and for projects that are Scientific with a capital S— which often only means made "safe" by being made trivial—for they do not want to be made the subjects of political attention. Accordingly, the larger foundations tend to encourage large-scale bureaucratic research into small-scale problems, and to seek out intellectual administrators for the job.

Second, there are the younger recruits, better described as research technicians than as social scientists. This is, I am aware, a quite large assertion, but I make it with due care. To understand the social meaning of a style of thought, we must always distinguish the leaders from the followers, the innovators from the routine workers, the "first generation" which sets it up, from the second and third generations which carry it out. All schools, if they are successful, contain both types of men; that this is so is indeed one criterion of a "successful" school. It is also an important clue to the intellectual consequences of success.

There is often a difference between the qualities of mind characteristic of the run-of-the-mill followers and of the innovators and founders. On this point, schools of thought differ rather profoundly. To a considerable extent, the differences depend upon the type of social organization that each school's style of work permits or encourages. At least several of the inventors and administrators of the style we are examining have highly cultivated minds. In their youth, before this style flourished, they absorbed the leading models of thought of Western society; such men have had years of cultural and intellectual experience. They are in fact educated men: imaginatively aware of their own sensibilities and capable of continuous self-cultivation.

But the second generation, the young men who come from what, I suppose it will be agreed, is the intellectually impoverished background of the American high school, have not had comparable experience. As often as not they have not had adequate college work; at least there are reasons to suspect—although I do not know—that there is a selection of not quite the brightest for such research institutes.

I have seldom seen one of these young men, once he is well caught up, in a condition of genuine intellectual puzzlement. And I have never seen any passionate curiosity about a great problem, the sort of curiosity that compels the mind to travel anywhere and by any means, to remake itself if necessary, in order *to find out*. These young men are less restless than methodical; less imaginative than patient; above all, they are dogmatic—in all the historical and theological meanings of the term. Some of this is of course merely part of the sorry intellectual condition of so many students now in American colleges and universities, but I do believe it is more evident among the research technicians of abstracted empiricism.

They have taken up social research as a career; they have come early to an extreme specialization, and they have acquired an indifference or a contempt for "social philosophy"—which means to them "writing books out of other books" or "merely speculating." Listening to their conversations, trying to gauge the quality of their curiosity, one finds a deadly limitation of mind. The social worlds about which so many scholars feel ignorant do not puzzle them.

Much of the propaganda force of bureaucratic social science is due to its philosophical claims to Scientific Method; much of its power to recruit is due to the relative ease of training individuals and setting them to work in a career with a future. In both instances, explicitly coded methods, readily available to the technicians, are the major keys to success. In some of the founders, empirical techniques serve an imagination which, it is true, has often been curiously suppressed, but which one always feels to be there. When you talk with one of the founders you are always dealing with a mind. But once a young man has spent three or four years at this sort of thing, you cannot really talk to him about the problems of studying modern society. His position and career, his ambition and his very self-esteem, are based in large part upon this one perspective, this one vocabulary, this one set of techniques. In truth, he does not know anything else.

In some of these students, intelligence itself is often disassociated from personality, and is seen by them as a kind of skilled gadget that they hope to market successfully. They are among the humanistically impoverished, living with reference to values that exclude any arising from a respect for human reason. They are among the energetic and ambitious technicians whom a defective educational routine and a corrupting demand have made incapable of acquiring the sociological imagination. One can only hope that when sufficient numbers of these young men reach the associate professor level of their careers, they will by some intellectual mutation become aware of the fact that they are no longer dependent upon emperors without clothing.

The abstracted empirical manner, the methodological inhibition it sustains, the focus of its practicality, the qualities of mind its institutions tend to select and to train—these developments make questions about the social policies of the social sciences all the more urgent. This bureaucratic style and its institutional embodiment are in line with the dominant trends of modern social structure and its characteristic types of thought. I do not believe that it can be explained, or even fully understood, without recognizing this. These same social trends, in fact, affect not only the social sciences, but the whole intellectual life of the United States, and indeed the very role of reason in human affairs today.

What is at issue seems plain: if social science is not autonomous, it cannot be a publicly responsible enterprise. As the means of research become larger and more expensive, they tend to be "expropriated"; accordingly, only as social scientists, in some collective way, exercise full control over these means of research can social science in this style be truly autonomous. Insofar as the individual social scientist is dependent in his work upon bureaucracies, he tends to lose his individual autonomy; insofar as social science consists of bureaucratic work, it tends to lose its social and political autonomy. I do want to emphasize the "insofar as." For clearly I have been discussing one tendency, although a major one, and not the complete state of our affairs.

II

If we are to understand what is going on in any area of cultural and intellectual work, we must understand its immediate social context. I must accordingly now make a brief excursus on academic cliques. Of course it it true that to the extent that an idea is durable and significant, any given personality or clique can be but its temporary symbol. Yet the whole business of "cliques" and "personalities" and "schools" is rather more complicated than that; their importance in shaping the development of social science deserves more awareness on our part. We must confront them, if for no other reason, because any cultural activity requires financial support of some kind and also a public of some sort to give it the help of criticism. Neither the money nor the criticism is given solely on the basis of objective judgments of worth; and besides, there is usually argument about the objectivity of the judgments themselves as well as about the worth.

The function of the academic clique is not only to regulate the competition, but to set the terms of competition and to assign rewards for work done in accordance with these terms at any given time. It is the canons by which men are judged and work criticized that are the most important intellectual feature of the clique. To my previous point about "the ethos of the technicians" of the bureaucratic social science—their qualities of mind and their influence upon the making of reputations and

hence upon dominant fashions in social science and upon the canons of
critical judgment that prevail—I here need only add that the means by
which the internal tasks of the clique are accomplished include: the giving
of friendly advice to younger men; job offers and recommendations of promotion; the assignment of books to admiring reviewers; the ready acceptance of articles and books for publication; the allocation of research
funds; arranging or politicking for honorific positions within professional
associations and on editorial boards of professional journals. Insofar as
these means constitute assignments of prestige, which is, in turn, very
much a determinant of academic careers, they affect the economic expectations of the individual scholar as well as his professional reputation.

Once upon a time academic reputations were generally expected to be
based upon the productions of books, studies, monographs—in sum, upon
the production of ideas and scholarly works, and upon the judgment of
these works by academic colleagues and intelligent laymen. One reason
why this has been so in social science and the humanities is that a man's
competence or incompetence has been available for inspection, since the
older academic world did not contain privileged positions of competence.
It is rather difficult to know whether the alleged competence of a corporation president, for example, is due to his own personal abilities or to the
powers and facilities available to him by virtue of his position. But there
has been no room for such doubt about scholars working, as old-fashioned professors have worked, as craftsmen.

However, by his prestige, the new academic statesman, like the business
executive and the military chieftain, has acquired means of competence
which must be distinguished from his personal competence—but which
in his reputation are not so distinguished. A permanent professional
secretary, a clerk to run to the library, an electric typewriter, dictating
equipment, and a mimeographing machine, and perhaps a small budget
of three or four thousand dollars a year for purchasing books and period-
icals—even such minor office equipment and staff enormously increase
any scholar's appearance of competence. Any business executive will laugh
at the pettiness of such means; college professors will not—few professors, even productive ones, have such facilities on a secure basis. Yet such
equipment *is* a means of competence and of career—which secure clique
membership makes much more likely than does unattached scholarship.
The clique's prestige increases the chance to get them, and having them
in turn increases the chance to produce a reputation.

This, then, I think, is one kind of situation which helps to explain
how men may acquire considerable reputation without having, in all
truth, produced very much. About one such man, a colleague interested
in posterity recently remarked, in a quite friendly way: "As long as he
lives, he'll be the most eminent man in his field; two weeks after he dies,

no one will remember him." That the statement is so harsh perhaps testifies to the painfulness of the anxieties that must frequently haunt the statesmen in their world of academic cliques.

If there is competition among several cliques in a field of study, the relative positions of the several competitors tend to determine clique strategies. Cliques that are small and considered unimportant can in due course be expected by leading cliques to go out of business. Their members will be ignored or won over or rejected, and in the end die off without having trained the next generation. It must always be kept in mind that one important function of cliques is the shaping of the next generation. To say that a clique is unimportant is to say that it will not have much voice in this shaping. But if there are, for example, two leading schools, each with leaders who are quite powerful and enjoy much prestige, then the relations between the two often tend to become problems of merger, problems of building a larger cartel. And of course if a school is under effective attack by outsiders, or by other cliques, one of the first strategies of defense is the denial that there actually is a clique or even a school; it is on such occasions that the statesmen come into their own.

Tasks of importance to the clique often are confused with tasks of importance to the actual work of a school. Among younger men, this affects the chances of their careers; among older men, there is a clique premium upon administrative and promotional, political and friendship skills. Especially among these older men, reputations may thus become rather ambiguously based. Is this man's high reputation—outsiders may ask— due to the intellectual value of work actually accomplished or is it due to his position in the clique?

When we consider the relations between cliques we immediately encounter those who are not spokesmen for one clique, but for "the field" as a whole. They are not merely executives of one firm, they are industrial spokesmen. One who aspires to play the role of statesman for an entire field must usually in effect deny that real intellectual differences exist between, say, the two leading cliques of the field. In fact, as their joint spokesman, it is his prime intellectual task to show that "they are really working toward the same goal." He comes to be a prestige symbol of that which each clique claims to be its own speciality, and as well a symbol of their "actual" or at least eventual unity. Borrowing prestige from each of the cliques, he bestows prestige upon both of them. He is a kind of broker, dealing in the allocation of prestige for both teams.

Suppose, for example, in some field of study there are two leading schools, one called Theory and one called Research. The successful statesman carries on a busy traffic with both; he is seen as in both and yet as standing between them as well. By his prestige, he seems to promise that Theory and Research are not only compatible but parts of an integrated model of work in social science as a whole. He is a symbol of that promise.

The promise does not rest upon any actual books or studies he has done. What is going on is this: in any work of Research that is to be celebrated, the statesman seeks Theory—and in an altogether optative manner, invariably finds it there. In any duly celebrated work of Theory, the statesman seeks Research—and again, in an altogether optative way, finds it. These "findings" are of the order of extended book reviews, having as much to do with the allocation of prestige to men as with examinations of studies in their own right. The accomplished study, in which Theory and Research are displayed truly as one, is, as I have noted, a promise, a symbol. In the meantime, the prestige of the statesman does not rest upon any such study; in fact, it seldom rests upon any study at all.

There is, I think, a tragic fact inherent in all such statesmanlike roles. Often those who play them have first-rate minds—in fact, mediocrities cannot really play such a role, although many do of course imitate it in a verbal way. The role the statesman has come to play keeps him from actual work. The prestige he has accumulated is so disproportionate to what he has actually accomplished, the promise that he has held out is so grand, that he is often quite inhibited from getting down to "The Study" and when he does have a major part in some study or book, he is reluctant to finish it or to publish it even when others think it is finished. He complains then about the committees and the other statesman-like burdens that he is carrying, but at the same time he accepts—indeed, he often seeks—many more such burdens. His very role as statesman is at once the cause and the excuse for his not getting down to work. He is trapped, as he so frequently says; but also he really must continue to trap himself—else his very role as a statesman will be recognized by others and by himself as a mere excuse.

The world of cliques is not all there is in the academic world. There are also the unattached, who come in many varieties indeed and whose work is also varied. From the standpoint of a leading clique, the unattached may be seen as friendly or at least neutral about the cliques' school; perhaps they are "eclectic" in their work or merely not "socially inclined." To the extent that their work is attracting favorable attention or they are judged to be of merit, use, or worth, members of the clique may seek to attract them, to show them the way, and eventually to recruit them. Celebration that is merely mutual celebration—by, of, and for clique members—that is not enough.

But among the unattached there may also be those who don't play the game, won't cash in the prestige claims. Of these some are merely indifferent and absorbed in their own work, and some are downright hostile. They are critics of the school's work. If it is possible, the clique will ignore both them and their work. But only if the clique enjoys truly great prestige, is this simple strategy suitable and safe. It can be done in a truly lordly way, moreover, only if the clique coincides with virtually the whole field of study, and is monolithically in control of it. This, of course, is not the usual case; usually there are many neutral people and eclectic workmen, and other cliques as well, within the same field. There are also associated fields of study; and beyond that, a variety of nonacademic audiences and publics whose interest or acclaim upsets, at least as yet, monolithic control of prestige, reputation, and career by cliques.

Accordingly, if the critics cannot be ignored, other strategies must be adopted. All means used for the internal management of a school's members are of course also used for dealing with hostile outsiders; I need only briefly to discuss one of them: book reviewing, the most common medium for prestige allocation. Suppose an unattached scholar produces a book to which sufficient attention is paid to make ignoring it inconvenient. The crude ploy is to give it to a leading member of the clique, especially to one known to be in competition with or even directly hostile to the author's views, or at least associated with contrary views. It is more subtle to assign it to a minor yet upcoming member of the clique who has not published much himself and whose views are therefore not widely known. This has many advantages. For the young man it is a payoff for his loyalty and as well an opportunity to win recognition by his criticism of an older and better-known man. By implication it places the book in a position of less importance than if it had been assigned to an eminent scholar. It is also a safe role for the young man to play: the better-known man, out of a certain snobbery, may not wish to "answer" the review; it is not conventional for the author of a book to answer criticisms of it by professorial reviewers; in fact, it is the policy of some learned journals to discourage it, or not to allow it. But even if the review is answered, it does not really matter too much. Everyone who has not only reviewed but also written books knows that one of the easiest of all intellectual tasks is to "debunk" a book—any book—in a two- or three-column review, and that it is virtually impossible to "answer" such a review in the same space. It would not be impossible if the book itself has been read with some care by all readers of the controversy; that this cannot be assumed gives to the reviewer an overwhelming advantage.

If, however, the book in question gains a very great deal of attention inside or outside the field or both, then the only thing to do is to assign it to a leading clique member, preferably a statesman who will duly praise it without too much attention to its content, and also show how it contributes in its way to the dominant and promising trends in the field as a whole. The one thing that any serious and dedicated clique must try to avoid is having the book assigned to another unattached scholar who would, first, state accurately and clearly what the book contains and, second, criticize it in terms altogether independent of schools and cliques and fashions.

III

Among the slogans used by a variety of schools of social science, none is so frequent as, "The purpose of social science is the prediction and control of human behavior." Nowadays, in some circles we also hear much about "human engineering"—an undefined phrase often mistaken for a clear and obvious goal. It is believed to be clear and obvious because it rests upon an unquestioned analogy between "the mastery of nature" and "the mastery of society." Those who habitually use such phrases are very likely to be among those who are most passionately concerned to "make the social studies into real sciences," and conceive of their own work as politically neutral and morally irrelevant. Quite usually, the basic idea is stated as "the lag" of social science behind physical science and the consequent need to close up the gap. These technocratic slogans are a substitute for a political philosophy among many of The Scientists of whom I have just written. They are, they suppose, out to do with society what they suppose physicists have done with nature. Their political philosophy is contained in the simple view that if only The Methods of Science, by which man now has come to control the atom, were employed to "control social behavior," the problems of mankind would soon be solved, and peace and plenty assured for all.

Behind these phrases there are curious notions of power, of reason, of history—all of them unclear and all of them in a deplorable state of confusion. The use of such phrases reveals a rationalistic and empty optimism which rests upon an ignorance of the several possible roles of reason in human affairs, the nature of power and its relations to knowledge, the meaning of moral action and the place of knowledge within it, the nature of history and the fact that men are not only creatures of history but on occasion creators within it and even of it. Before I take up such issues, as they bear upon the political meanings of the social sciences, I want briefly to examine the key slogan of the technocratic philosophers—the one about prediction and control.

To talk so glibly as many do about prediction and control is to assume the perspective of the bureaucrat to whom, as Marx once remarked, the world is an object to be manipulated. To make the point clear, take an extreme example: If a man has an apparatus of control, both subtle and powerful, over an army division on an isolated island with no enemy, he is, you must agree, in a position of control. If he uses his powers fully and has made definite plans, he can predict, within quite narrow margins, what each man will be doing at a certain hour of a certain day in a certain year. He can predict quite well even the feelings of various of these men, for he manipulates them as he would inert objects; he has power to override many of the plans they may have, and occasionally may properly consider himself an all-powerful despot. If he can control, he can predict. He is in command of "regularities."

But we, as social scientists, may not assume that we are dealing with objects that are so highly manipulable, and we may not assume that among men we are enlightened despots. At least, to make either assumption is to take a political stand that for professors seems a rather curious one. No historical society is constructed within a frame as rigid as that enclosing my hypothetical army division. Nor are social scientists—let us be grateful —generals of history. Yet to speak of "prediction and control" in the same breath, as so many do, is usually to assume some kind of one-sided control such as that of my imaginary general, whose powers I have somewhat exaggerated in order to make the point clear.

I want to make it clear in order to reveal the political meaning of the bureaucratic ethos. Its use has mainly been in and for nondemocratic areas of society—a military establishment, a corporation, an advertising agency, an administrative division of government. It is in and for such bureaucratic organizations that many social scientists have been invited to work, and the problems with which they there concern themselves are the kinds of problems that concern the more efficient members of such administrative machines.

I do not see how anyone can reasonably disagree with Professor Robert S. Lynd's comment on *The American Soldier*:

> These volumes depict science being used with great skill to sort out and to control men for purposes not of their own willing. It is a significant measure of the impotence of liberal democracy that it must increasingly use its social sciences not directly on democracy's own problems, but tangentially and indirectly; it must pick up the crumbs from private business research on such problems as how to gauge audience reaction so as to put together synthetic radio programs and movies, or, as in the present case, from Army research on how to turn frightened draftees into tough soldiers who will fight a war whose purposes they do not understand. With socially extraneous purposes controlling the use of social science, each advance in its use tends to make it an instrument of mass control, and thereby a threat to democracy.[2]

The slogans of the human engineers serve to carry the bureaucratic ethos beyond the actual use of this style of thought and method of inquiry. To use these slogans as a statement of "what one is about" is to accept a bureaucratic role even when one is not enacting it. This role, in short, is very often assumed on an *as if* basis. Assuming the technocratic view, and as a social scientist trying to act upon it, is to act *as if* one were indeed a human engineer. It is within such a bureaucratic perspective that the public role of the social scientist is now frequently conceived. To act in this as-if-I-were-a-human-engineer manner might be merely amusing in a society in which human reason were widely and democratically installed, but the United States is not such a society. Whatever else it is, surely this is evident: it is a society in which functionally rational bureaucracies are increasingly used in human affairs and in history-making decisions. Not all periods are alike in the degree to which historical changes within them are independent of willful control, go on behind all men's backs. Ours seems to be a period in which key decisions or their lack by bureaucratically instituted elites are increasingly sources of historical change. Moreover, it is a period and a society in which the enlargement and the centralization of the means of control, of power, now include quite widely the use of social science for whatever ends those in control of these means may assign to it. To talk of "prediction and control" without confronting the questions such developments raise is to abandon such moral and political autonomy as one may have.

Is it possible to speak of "control" in any perspective other than the bureaucratic? Yes, of course it is. Various kinds of "collective self-control" have been conceived. Adequate statement of any such idea includes all the issues of freedom and of rationality, as ideas and as values. It also includes the idea of "democracy"—as a type of social structure and as a set of political expectations. Democracy means the power and the freedom of those controlled by law to change the law, according to agreed-upon rules —and even to change these rules; but more than that, it means some kind of collective self-control over the structural mechanics of history itself. This is a complicated and difficult idea, which I shall later discuss in some detail. Here I want merely to suggest that if social scientists, in a society which contains democratic aspirations, wish to discuss seriously the issues of "prediction and control," they must consider such problems carefully.

Is it possible to speak of "prediction" in any perspective other than the bureaucratic? Yes, of course it is. Predictions may rest upon "unintended regularities" rather than upon prescriptive controls. Without having control, we can predict best about those areas of social life over which no one else has much control either, those in which "voluntary" and nonroutine activities are at a minimum. The usages of language, for example, change and persist "behind men's backs." Perhaps such regularities also occur in connection with the structural mechanics of history. If we can grasp what John Stuart Mill called the "principa media" of a society, if we can grasp its major trends; in brief, if we can understand the structural transformation of our epoch, we might have "a basis for prediction."

Yet we must remember that, within specific milieus, men do often control how they act; the extent to which they can do so are among the objects of our study. There are real generals, we ought to remember, as well as hypothetical ones, and also corporate executives and heads of states. Moreover, as has often been remarked, the fact that men are not inert objects means that they may become aware of predictions made about their activities, and that accordingly they can and often do redirect themselves; they may falsify or fulfill the predictions. Which they will do is not, as yet, subject to very good prediction. In so far as men have some degree of freedom, what they may do will not be readily predictable.

But the point is: To say that "the real and final aim of human engineering" or of "social science" is "to predict" is to substitute a technocratic slogan for what ought to be a reasoned moral choice. That too is to assume the bureaucratic perspective within which—once it is fully adopted—there is much less moral choice available.

The bureaucratization of social study is a quite general trend; perhaps, in due course, it is likely to come about in any society in which bureaucratic routines are becoming paramount. It is naturally accompanied by a rather Jesuitical and high-flown theory, which does not interact as such with administrative research. Particular researches, generally statistical and bound to administrative uses, do not affect the great elaboration of Concepts; this elaboration in turn has nothing to do with the results of particular researches, but rather with the legitimation of the regime and of its changing features. To the bureaucrat, the world is a world of facts to be treated in accordance with firm rules. To the theorist, the world is a world of conceptions to be manipulated, often without any discernible rules. Theory serves, in a variety of ways, as ideological justification of authority. Research for bureaucratic ends serves to make authority more effective and more efficient by providing information of use to authoritative planners.

Abstracted empiricism is used bureaucratically, although it has of course clear ideological meanings, which are sometimes used as such. Grand theory, as I have indicated, has no direct bureaucratic utility; its political meaning is ideological, and such use as it may have lies there. Should these two styles of work—abstracted empiricism and grand theory —come to enjoy an intellectual "duopoly," or even become the predominant styles of work, they would constitute a grievous threat to the intellectual promise of social science and as well to the political promise of the role of reason in human affairs—as that role has been classically conceived in the civilization of the Western societies.

NOTES

1. Paul Lazarsfeld, "What is Sociology?" Universitets Studentkontor, Skrivemaskinstior, Oslo, September, 1948 (mimeo), pp. 19-20. Italics mine.

2. "The Science of Inhuman Relations," *The New Republic*, August 27, 1949.

THE RELEVANCE OF HISTORY
TO THE SOCIOLOGICAL ETHOS

Hans Gerth and Saul Landau

Sociological thought emerged in response to the crisis of a newly dynamic European society, fresh from industrial and political revolution. The aim of this new thought process was to forge intellectual tools which would make the complex web of social relations more transparent. Sociology was born and grew in a rapidly changing world, a world that seemed to be drifting, and in which man was again and again surprised and frightened by experiencing the unforeseen and unintended consequences of his actions. From the Enlightenment, the wars for revolution and independence on the European and American continents, the Napoleonic conquests and defeats, the czarist and Metternichean reaction, and the explosion of British industrial and commercial energies, emerged sociology—the intellectual quest pursued by a new type of scholar.

In 1816, Friedrich Buchholz, in Germany, saw this quest as "the advent of a science of which former centuries could not dream; namely, the science of society in its necessary and fortuitous relations." Buchholz did not have a name for these new scholars, but he described them as special minds whose "entire endeavor aims at bringing science nearer the state of society, as it actually is, and adjusting science to it.[1] Later, Auguste Comte, the disciple of Saint Simon, named the new intellectual approach "sociology," and sloganized its ethos as *"Savoir pour prévoir, prévoir pour pourvoir."* This new science of society, as its originators thought of it was designed to overcome blind drift, fate, or the unforeseen and unintended consequences of man's action. The end of knowledge was to be prediction, the end of prediction, control.

The great founders of sociology were not traditional academicians in any sense. Men like Buchholz, Comte, and Spencer were academic outsiders; Ferdinand Tönnies and, later, Max Weber were at least relative outsiders.[2] Those that were in the academy did not behave like the average college professor, for they would not, and could not, be confined to one academic discipline. Buchholz, a pastor's son from Brandenburg, was a free-lance writer and critic. Karl Marx, the "non-Jewish Jew," [3] was an economist, philosopher, sociologist, historian, and social revolutionary. And not only was he obviously outside traditional academic life, but, as an exile who did not assimilate, he was a cultural outsider as well. Certainly for Tönnies and Simmel, Spencer, Weber, and Durkheim (a Jew in Paris in the days of Dreyfus and Zola), the narrow confines of the traditional professor were intolerable.

This fact is related to the nature of the contribution which these men made; for to probe deeper into the analysis of society, to see society in its transition toward a world market, supported by world-wide industrialization, required a sense of time and reality, and a breadth of vision, that could only be possessed by men outside, or at least partially outside academic walls. Most of the older academicians were involved in a process of division of labor which increasingly tended to confine their scholarship to expertness (the expert has rightly been defined as a man who knows more and more about less and less), and the court historian of old, the biographer of kings and captains, was giving way, in an age of high-pitched nationalism, to the national historian concerned with the heroes and martyrs of his nation. But at the same time, and in opposition to this tendency to contraction, the great minds were developing a sense of world history. Men like Adam Smith, Hegel and Marx, Burckhardt, Ranke, and Mommsen all tried to see the world as a whole.

To the sociologists, seeing the world in totality involved the concrete comprehension of historical causality, not to be explained by reference to "the spirit of the times." For to them, "spirit of the times" seemed a handy phrase that begged the real issues, a slogan substituted for real knowledge. Interestingly, Goethe, who coined the term "world literature," spoke through Faust on the same subject:

> The spirit of the times,
> At bottom merely the spirit of the gentry
> In whom each time reflects itself,
> And at that it often makes one weep
> And at the first glance run away,
> A lumber room and a rubbish heap,
> At best an heroic puppet play
> With excellent pragmatical Buts and Yets
> Such as are suitable to marionettes.[4]

From the inception of sociology as a way of thinking, its practitioners conceived of decision making as a property of all men and women. History was made by all men, albeit some contributed minutely and some grandly. But each individual in his society meant something, and, since he was a maker of history, all parts of his life had to be studied and analyzed. His vocational life and his political life were inseparable; and so, for the sociologist, history and biography merged in the analysis of society.

The case study was born as a steppingstone to the construction or documentation of *types*.[5] It was the use of these types that helped the sociologist to conceptualize society as a whole. Each individual was important, but for the purposes of analysis he had to be seen with reference to a type construct, whether it was "intellectual" or "yeoman farmer," Marx's "bourgeois" or "lumpen proletariat," or Max Weber's heroic Puritan. The heroic individual and unique individual of historical biography was now replaced on the analytical pedestal by the type. The individual could be measured as an approximation of, or deviation from what was typical. Type man enabled the sociologist to broaden the intellectual horizon by making comparative studies of societies and groups of men. Thus, the study of "Caesarism" replaced the study of Caesar, so that Alexander the Great and Napoleon could now be studied comparatively as "Caesarists." The type approach did not deny the importance of great historical personages, but rather, it made for analysis of the great man in a different way, concretely and comparatively. Men like Jay Gould and John D. Rockefeller might be used to study economic supermen, or "robber barons"[6] as they were called by the muckrakers. These Promethean bourgeois, in turn, could be compared with the English merchant capitalist from Sir Walter Raleigh to Smythe and his cohorts on the Muscovy, East India, and Virginia companies.

Thus, whatever the limitations of the great social analysts, it is apparent that they attempted to see things in their interconnections, and on a world scale. They all consciously worked within a dynamic social structure, and each saw his own age as one of crisis and transition. For Marx it was an age of transition from capitalism to socialism; for Spencer it was an age of conflict between peaceful industrial society running according to natural law, and despotic military society which threatened chaos. For Max Weber, the revival of imperialism spelled disaster for Germany, which he feared would be divided, along with the rest of Europe, between the "rule of the Russian official's ukase and Anglo-Saxon conventionality with a dash of Latin *raison* thrown in."[7]

II

The coming of the twentieth century saw America's emergence as a world power. The nineteenth century sociologist's schematization of the past, whether in terms of evolutionism, or progress toward national efficiency and/or "virtuous perfection," seemed to have been outgrown. By 1919, the Kaiser and his armies were no more. The world should now have been safe for democracy, and the War had supposedly ended all wars. The obstacles to the Wilsonian mission—the guilty Germans and the stubborn Bolsheviks—were placed in the diplomatic dog house where they belonged for not cooperating. The prophet of the Western world, President Wilson, sailed to Paris with a proposal for a League that would usher in a new age of mankind. The United States sat on top of the world. Its age in world history had been reached.

Just as United States leaders began to realize their dream of a world economic empire headed by American corporate power, the American sociologist dispensed with world concepts. He dismissed, as metaphysics, all thought and theory that dealt with world or total structures. The world simply was taken for granted. To be sure, there was still work to be done, but it was no more than a scattering of problems that remained to be solved, involving industrial efficiency and the rational adjustment of certain immigrant-alien milieus to the American system. The integration of the world was left to the businessmen and politicians. The sociologist wanted to routinize the functioning of the good society at home, focusing on industrial problems, the family, and the behavior of groups in their natural setting.

To do this, statistical and survey techniques, and small precision group work had to be perfected. Robert Park, in Chicago in the 1920's, contributed more than any other man to the origination of milieu sociology. Park was fascinated by the cultural hybrid, the bilingual immigrant, the marginal man.[8] As a journalist, he offered rich descriptive techniques, in the tradition of Balzac's realism, to help conceptualize the changing milieus in the post-World War I United States. Sociologists became intrigued by this kind of study. Following the old maxim that "nothing human is alien to me," but without the "let's go slumming attitude" of the debutante, sociologists descended upon the slums and studied the sex codes of slum dwellers. They also associated with café society to study the behavior patterns of the night-life set. Humanity was studied in the raw, and in its environment—Chinese peasants in their villages, bandits of the Robin Hood type in forests, gunmen in the old West, and Al Capone and Anastasia types in American gangland. Salesladies at Macy's, schoolteachers, Chicago and New York street gangs, POW's—all were studied in their respective roles in their respective settings.

This analysis of society into segments for separate study, necessarily led to specialization. Comte and Spencer, the nineteenth-century mainstays of United States sociology, gave place to the empirical scholars, who proceeded to tackle problems, small and smaller, of milieu, families, and small groups in general, until a sociologist was no longer just a sociologist, but a specialist in family sociology, public opinion, criminology, statistics, small groups, methodology and methods, race relations, and so on, *ad infinitum*. The "experts" and "specialists" emerged and conquered. Fame went to the innovating specialist, the more so if his new specialty fed material into IBM statistical machines. The kind of material fed into the machines came to matter less and less. The synthesizing minds, both past and present, that possessed what C. Wright Mills calls the "sociological imagination," began to be berated as impractical and unscientific. Karl Mannheim and Pitirim Sorokin were dismissed by many of the new "expert specialists" as out of date. The questions that Marx, Comte, Spencer, Ross, and Weber had wrestled with, and the great theoretical legacy they had bequeathed were cast into limbo. Their works were largely unread: in some academic circles they were unknown; in others they were sanctified as classics, and so did not have to be read. And one result of this intense division of labor was that sociologists failed to predict anything. Meanwhile, the war that had ended all wars generated steam for a second war to end war, while bolshevism, fascism, and nazism made a mockery of the Wilsonian dream.

Certainly, society had to be broken down and studied in its units. Certainly, too, milieu sociology refined and broadened the tools of the trade, developing advanced techniques of inquiry and scientific methods of analysis. The closeup-microcosmic lens was utilized with admirable pictorial results, and observations were made with millimetric exactitude. But all this was achieved at the expense of total structure; that is, by disjoining history and sociology. And such exactitude, even when applied to a society as a whole, cannot be a substitute for the examination of social movements in terms of their roots and far reaching consequences.

The impact of the Bolshevik revolution on the structure of the Western world, to say nothing of the Asian world, cannot be revealed through milieu studies, no matter how thorough. The history of czarist Russia, in the context of world history, must be analyzed in order that the sociologist may see the roots of the upheaval and its future direction. A study of Russian workers or peasants, while valuable, could not reveal much more than some aspects of worker and peasant attitudes. Even if several milieu studies were put together, they would only form an incomplete compilation of some of the clues. Without a view of the total structure, from a historical bridge, only narrow currents can be analyzed, and much of their content will necessarily remain unknown. Similarly, to take a less revolutionary example, the far-reaching results of the long Slavonic migration to Prussian Junker labor barracks, or of immigrants arriving in boatloads from Poland, and heading to the mines, mills, and factories of the New World in Pennsylvania, Chicago, and Milwaukee, cannot be grasped through the close-up camera, or attitude studies of changes in Old World patriarchalism. While such studies by Thomas and Znaniecki[9] and other milieu sociologists greatly enriched the tool kit of the profession, the more basic issues were neglected: the analysis of *structures,* which *cause* milieu changes, was forsaken for more "empirical" investigation.

Thus, compartmentalization and the confinement of precision work to milieu and industrial sociology have threatened to smother the original sociologists' ethos. Interest in sterile verbal systems and faddist professional jargon have often replaced the concern with the substance of society. The fact that "all the facts are not in" has been used as an excuse for the failure to examine important problems, and the failure to examine important problems has, of course, resulted in the failure to predict. It was not until 1940, after the hot war was underway, that the *American Journal of Sociology* decided to publish an article on the Nazi Party.[10] In all, from 1933 to 1947, only two articles on National Socialism appeared in the *Journal*.[11] A fifty-year index of the *Journal* shows exactly three listings under Marx or Marxism, and under Lenin (or Leninism) there are no citations.[12] By and large, the sociologists of today have shut the world crisis out of their vision, focusing their intellectual energy on the crisis of the family, while the Chinese revolution, involving 600,000,000 people —perhaps the greatest mass movement of mankind—is totally neglected.

III

Hot and cold wars have tortured the earth since the beginning of this century. No one has escaped the horrors of the age of imperialism and its wars, or the effects of the rapid bureaucratization of industrial societies and their empires, and of the movement toward centralized control in almost all areas of the world. The effects of all this on the social sciences are hard to measure. Bureaucracy of all sorts has built high walls of "necessary secrecy" (official secrecy classified from confidential to top secret), and has befogged the human mind with the "necessary" vapors of publicity and rival propagandas. Mass media, themselves products of the age of total warfare and bureaucratization, have transformed the journalist of old into an adjunct of a state and/or business bureaucracy (who sees him any more as a crusader and fighter for truth, except in grade B movies?). Likewise, the academician, although one step removed from the market place and the political arena, does not escape, and does not want to escape, his obligation to state and corporate power. "Science in uniform" is the order of the day, and the sociologist, along with his colleagues, has become an auxiliary of the bureaucracies, in an age in which bureaucracies have become almost universal.

But there are hopeful signs. Among the newer sociologists, C. Wright Mills demonstrates in his work a fresh concern with the important questions of modern society. His *White Collar* and *The Power Elite* represent important and challenging attempts to analyze the nature and direction of American society. His work has something relevant to say to an intelligent reading public that is concerned about the future of American society and of the world.

This concern of Mills and others with the drift of social structures and the concatenation of institutional orders and social strata accounts, in part, for the recently greater receptivity on the part of sociologists to the work of Max Weber, who epitomizes the former sociological concern with the totality of man's social life and future. Weber, who practiced what Comte preached as a motto for sociology, wrote comparatively little on the methodology of prediction, but he predicted much, fusing history with sociology. The death of czarism in Russia and the subsequent rise of bolshevism did not surprise Weber, who had devoted twelve hundred pages to the study of Russia since Admiral Togo sank the Czar's Baltic navy in the Tsushima straits and General Nogi's troops killed 90,000 Russian soldiers and took 40,000 prisoners of war in 1906, in the battle of Mukden. And in his study of Confucian China, its village and agrarian problems, he expressed his awareness of what lay ahead by apprehending the attraction that agrarian bolshevism might have for the Chinese peasantry.[13] On the basis of his study of Chinese society, Weber was able to predict the future of China. The same professor, who accompanied the German peace delegation to Versailles, had no Wilsonian illusions. He warned his students about the "polar night of icy darkness" that lay ahead for Germany after World War I.[14]

The notion that the development of mankind can be formulated in terms of a single law of evolution has been almost unanimously rejected. Social scientists have learned to appreciate the relativity of cultural contexts and the diversity of developments in simultaneously existing cultures. Yet, though we no longer refer to "backward nations," we nevertheless recognize the existence of "underdeveloped areas" (that is, pre-industrial areas such as India and a large part of Africa) side by side with the United States and the Soviet Union. But when the most educated of the Indian electorate, the people of the state of Kerala (47 per cent are literate, as against 16 per cent for the whole of India), returned a Communist majority in 1957, in a democratic election, not only Prime Minister Nehru was shocked.

The revolutionary transitions of large parts of the world since World War I make it urgent for sociologists to study the historical backgrounds of value systems and social structures other than those of the United States, and it is in this direction—with the aid of Fulbright grants—that we hope to see a reorientation of American sociology in the postwar generation, in an age in which the maintenance of peace is a more urgent necessity than ever before. Historiography offers a great storehouse of facts and ideas to the sociologist in quest of insight into total social structures, their phases of growth, decline, and destruction. Only in this way, with one eye on history and one on the future, can the sociologist broaden his scope to meet the obligations of the contemporary world.

And the contemporary world certainly imposes obligations. Today, the planning bureaucracy of bolshevism speaks for almost one billion people (a fact which was hardly expressed in U.N. votes); so that it is perhaps time for the sociologist to begin to ponder the success of industrialization processes under the new system of planning. It is in addressing ourselves to this situation that Weber's work may be of invaluable help, for it is permeated with a keen sense of the historicity of social structures and ideas. And just as Weber devoted a great part of his life's work to the study of the rise and spread of capitalism, we must now turn our attention to the spread of bolshevism to Thuringia and China. Only by readdressing ourselves to the big questions, and by analyzing character formation and social structures in historical perspective, may we perhaps, at long last, overcome the blind drift and arrive at the level of development where Comte's *savoir pour prévoir, prévoir pour pouvoir* becomes a fact rather than a pious hope for sociologists.

NOTES

1. Hans Gerth, "Friedrich Buchholz: Auch Ein Anfang der Soziologie," *Zeitschrift für die gesamte Staatswissenschaft* CX (1954), pp. 665-692.

2. Ferdinand Tönnies became a professor more than thirty years after his great work, *Community and Society*, had been published. He received a chair in 1918, but was ousted in 1933 with the advent of National Socialism in Germany. Weber, although technically on the faculty of Heidelburg, did not teach for nineteen years. Prince Max of Badeniea appreciated Weber's essays in the *Frankfurter Zeitung*, and exerted his influence to keep Weber on the faculty.

3. See Isaac Deutcher, "The Wandering Jew as Thinker and Revolutionary," *Universities and Left Review* I (Summer 1958), pp. 9-13.

4. Stephen Spender, ed., *Great Writings of Goethe* (A Mentor Book, 1958), p. 76.

5. For the best single exposition on the use of the type see Max Weber, *The Methodology of the Social Sciences*, Edward A. Shils, ed. (Glencoe, Ill.: Free Press, 1949), pp. 50-112; for a good example of a type study monograph see Frederic M. Thrasher, *The Gang; a Study of 1313 Gangs in Chicago* (Chicago: University of Chicago Press, 1936).

6. Mathew Josephson, *The Robber Barons* (New York: Harcourt, Brace & World, Inc., 1934).

7. Max Weber, *Gesammelte Politische Schriften*, Johannes Winckelman, ed. (Tübingen: J. C. B. Mohr, 1958), p. 164.

8. Robert E. Park, "Human Migration and the Marginal Man," *American Journal of Sociology* XXXIII (1928), pp. 881-893; Everett V. Stonequist, *The Marginal Man: A Study in Personality and Culture Conflict* (New York: Charles Scribner's Sons, 1937).

9. William Isaac Thomas and Florian Znaniecki, *The Polish Peasant in Europe and America* (Chicago: University of Chicago Press, 1918).

10. Hans H. Gerth, "The Nazi Party: Its Leadership and Composition," *American Journal of Sociology*, XLV (1940), pp. 517-541. This article was later incorporated into the *Civil Affairs Handbook* published by the War Department in 1943.

11. *American Journal of Sociology: Index to Volumes I-LII*, 1895-1947, p. 70, p. 83; see Nazism, National Socialism, and Germany.

12. *Ibid.*, p. 78, p. 77.

13. Max Weber, *The Religion of China; Confucianism and Taoism*, Hans H. Gerth, trans. (Glencoe, Ill., Free Press, 1956), p. 76.

14. Max Weber, "Politics as a Vocation," in *From Max Weber*, Hans Gerth and C. Wright Mills, eds. (New York: Oxford University Press, 1958), p. 128.

Part II

VALUE NEUTRALITY
AS DISGUISE AND DEFENSE

———◄◄●►►———

ANTI-MINOTAUR:

THE MYTH

OF A VALUE-FREE SOCIOLOGY

Alvin W. Gouldner

This is an account of a myth created by and about a magnificent minotaur named Max—Max Weber, to be exact; his myth was that social science should and could be value-free. The lair of this minotaur, although
reached only by a labyrinthine logic and visited only by a few who never
return, is still regarded by many sociologists as a holy place. In particular,
as sociologists grow older they seem impelled to make a pilgrimage to it
and to pay their respects to the problem of the relations between values
and social science.

Considering the perils of the visit, their motives are somewhat perplex-
ing. Perhaps their quest is the first sign of professional senility; perhaps
it is the last sigh of youthful yearnings. And perhaps a concern with the
value problem is just a way of trying to take back something that was,
in youthful enthusiasm, given too hastily.

In any event, the myth of a value-free sociology has been a conquering
one. Today, all the powers of sociology, from Parsons to Lundberg, have
entered into a tacit alliance to bind us to the dogma that "Thou shalt not
commit a value judgment," especially as sociologists. Where is the intro-

"Anti-Minotaur: The Myth of a Value-Free Sociology." A Presidential address de-
livered at the annual meeting of the Society for the Study of Social Problems, August
28, 1961. From *Social Problems* (Winter 1962), 9, No. 3, 199-213. Copyright © 1962 by
Social Problems. Reprinted by permission of *Social Problems* and the author.

ductory textbook, where the lecture course on principles, that does not affirm or imply this rule?

In the end, of course, we cannot disprove the existence of minotaurs who, after all, are thought to be sacred precisely because, being half man and half bull, they are so unlikely. The thing to see is that a belief in them is not so much untrue as it is absurd. Like Berkeley's argument for solipsism, Weber's brief for a value-free sociology is a tight one and, some say, logically unassailable. Yet it is also absurd. For both arguments appeal to reason but ignore experience.

I do not here wish to enter into an examination of the *logical* arguments involved, not because I regard them as incontrovertible but because I find them less interesting to me as a sociologist. Instead what I will do is to view the belief in a value-free sociology in the same manner that sociologists examine any element in the ideology of any group. This means that we will look upon the sociologist just as we would any other occupation, be it the taxicab driver, the nurse, the coal miner, or the physician. In short, I will look at the belief in a value-free sociology as part of the ideology of a working group and from the standpoint of the sociology of occupations.

The image of a value-free sociology is more than a neat intellectual theorem demanded as a sacrifice to reason; it is, also, a felt conception of a role and a set of (more or less) shared sentiments as to how sociologists should live. We may be sure that it became this not simply because it is true or logically elegant but, also, because it is somehow useful to those who believe in it. Applauding the dancer for her grace is often the audience's way of concealing its lust.

That we are in the presence of a group myth, rather than a carefully formulated and well-validated belief appropriate to scientists, may be discerned if we ask, just what is it that is believed by those holding sociology to be a value-free discipline? Does the belief in a value-free sociology mean that, in point of fact, sociology is a discipline actually free of values and that it successfully excludes all nonscientific assumptions in selecting, studying, and reporting on a problem? Or does it mean that sociology *should* do so? Clearly, the first is untrue and I know of no one who even holds it possible for sociologists to exclude completely their nonscientific beliefs from their scientific work; and if this is so, on what grounds can this impossible task be held to be morally incumbent on sociologists?

Does the belief in a value-free sociology mean that sociologists cannot, do not, or should not make value judgments concerning things outside their sphere of technical competence? But what has technical competence to do with the making of value judgments? If technical competence does provide a warrant for making value judgments then there is nothing to prohibit sociologists from making them within the area of their *expertise*. If, on the contrary, technical competence provides no warrant for making value judgments then, at least sociologists are as *free* to do so as anyone else; then their value judgments are at least as good as anyone else's, say, a twelve-year-old child's. And, by the way, if technical competence provides no warrant for making value judgments, then what does?

Does the belief in a value-free sociology mean that sociologists are or should be indifferent to the moral implications of their work? Does it mean that sociologists can and should make value judgments so long as they are careful to point out that these are different from "merely" factual statements? Does it mean that sociologists cannot logically deduce values from facts? Does it mean that sociologists do not or should not have or express *feelings* for or against some of the things they study? Does it mean that sociologists may and should inform laymen about techniques useful in realizing their own ends, if they are asked to do so, but that if they are not asked to do so they are to say nothing? Does it mean that sociologists should never take the initiative in asserting that some beliefs that laymen hold, such as the belief in the inherent inferiority of certain races, are false even when known to be contradicted by the facts of their discipline? Does it mean that social scientists should never speak out, or speak out only when invited, about the probable outcomes of a public course of action concerning which they are professionally knowledgeable? Does it mean that social scientists should never express values in their roles as teachers or in their roles as researchers, or in both? Does the belief in a value-free sociology mean that sociologists, either as teachers or researchers, have a right to covertly and unwittingly express their values but have no right to do so overtly and deliberately?

I fear that there are many sociologists today who, in conceiving social science to be value-free, mean widely different things, that many hold these beliefs dogmatically without having examined seriously the grounds upon which they are credible, and that some few affirm a value-free sociology ritualistically without having any clear idea what it might mean. Weber's own views on the relation between values and social science, and some current today are scarcely identical. While Weber saw grave hazards in the sociologist's expression of value judgments, he also held that these might be voiced if caution was exercised to distinguish them from statements of fact. If Weber insisted on the need to maintain scientific objectivity, he also warned that this was altogether different from moral indifference.

Not only was the cautious expression of value judgments deemed permissible by Weber but, he emphasized, these were positively mandatory under certain circumstances. Although Weber inveighed against the professorial "cult of personality," we might also remember that he was not against all value-imbued cults and that he himself worshiped at the shrine of individual responsibility. A familiarity with Weber's work on these points would only be embarrassing to many who today affirm a value-free sociology in his name. And should the disparity between Weber's own views and many now current come to be sensed, then the time is not far off when it will be asked, "Who now reads Max Weber?"

What to Weber was an agonizing expression of a highly personal faith, intensely felt and painstakingly argued, has today become a hollow catechism, a password, and a good excuse for no longer thinking seriously. It has become increasingly the trivial token of professional respectability, the caste mark of the decorous; it has become the gentleman's promise that boats will not be rocked. Rather than showing Weber's work the respect that it deserves, by carefully re-evaluating it in the light of our own generation's experience, we reflexively reiterate it even as we distort it to our own purposes. Ignorance of the gods is no excuse; but it can be convenient. For if the worshiper never visits the altar of his god, then he can never learn whether the first still burns there or whether the priests, grown fat, are simply sifting the ashes.

The needs which the value-free conception of social science serves are both personal and institutional. Briefly, my contention will be that, among the main institutional forces facilitating the survival and spread of the value-free myth, was its usefulness in maintaining both the cohesion and the autonomy of the modern university, in general, and the newer social science disciplines, in particular. There is little difficulty, at any rate, in demonstrating that these were among the motives originally inducing Max Weber to formulate the conception of a value-free sociology.

This issue might be opened at a seemingly peripheral and petty point, namely, when Weber abruptly mentions the problem of competition among professors for students. Weber notes that professors who do express a value stand are more likely to attract students than those who do not and are, therefore, likely to have undue career advantages. In effect, this is a complaint against a kind of unfair competition by professors who pander to student interests. Weber's hope seems to have been that the value-free principle would serve as a kind of "fair trades act" to restrain such competition. (At this point there is a curious rift in the dramatic mood of Weber's work; we had been listening to a full-throated Wagnerian aria when suddenly, the singer begins to hum snatches from Kurt Weill's "Mack the Knife.")

This suggests that one of the latent functions of the value-free doctrine is to bring peace to the academic house, by reducing competition for students and, in turn, it directs us to some of the institutional peculiarities of German universities in Weber's time. Unlike the situation in the American university, career advancement in the German was then felt to depend too largely on the professor's popularity as a teacher; indeed, at the lower ranks, the instructor's income was directly dependent on student enrollment. As a result, the competition for students was particularly keen and it was felt that the system penalized good scholars and researchers in favor of attractive teaching. In contrast, of course, the American system has been commonly accused of overstressing scholarly publication, and here the contrary complaint is typical, namely, that good teaching goes unrewarded and that you must "publish or perish." In the context of the German academic system, Weber was raising no trival point when he intimated that the value-free doctrine would reduce academic competition. He was linking the doctrine to guild problems and anchoring this lofty question to academicians' *earthy* interests.

Another relation of the value-free principle to distinctively German arrangements is also notable when Weber, opposing use of the lecture hall as an arena of value affirmation, argues that it subjects the student to a pressure which he is unable to evaluate or resist adequately. Given the comparatively exalted position of the professor in German society, and given the one-sided communication inherent in the lecture hall, Weber did have a point. His fears were, perhaps, all the more justified if we accept a view of the German "national character" as being authoritarian, that is, in Nietzsche's terms a combination of arrogance and servility. But these considerations do not hold with anything like equal cogency in more democratic cultures such as our own. For here, not only are professors held in, shall I say, more modest esteem, but the specific ideology of education itself often stresses the desirability of student initiative and participation, and there is more of a systematic solicitation of the student's "own" views in small "discussion" sections. There is little student servility to complement and encourage occasional professorial arrogance.

When Weber condemned the lecture hall as a forum for value affirmation he had in mind most particularly the expression of *political* values. The point of Weber's polemic is not directed against all values with equal sharpness. It was not the expression of aesthetic or even religious values that Weber sees as most objectionable in the University, but, primarily, those of politics. His promotion of the value-free doctrine may, then, be seen not so much as an effort to amoralize as to depoliticize the University and to remove it from the political struggle. The political conflicts then echoing in the German university did not entail comparatively trivial differences, such as those now between Democrats and Republicans in the United States. Weber's proposal of the value-free doctrine was, in part, an effort to establish a *modus vivendi* among academicians whose political commitments were often intensely felt and in violent opposition.

Under these historical conditions, the value-free doctrine was a proposal for an academic truce. It said, in effect, if we all keep quiet about our political views then we may all be able to get on with our work. But if the value-free principle was suitable in Weber's Germany because it served to restrain political passions, is it equally useful in America today where, not only is there pitiable little difference in politics but men often have no politics at all. Perhaps the need of the American University today, as of American society more generally, is for more commitment to politics and for more diversity of political views. It would seem that now the national need is to take the lid off, not to screw it on more tightly.

Given the historically unique conditions of nuclear warfare, where the issue would not be decided in a long-drawn-out war requiring the sustained cohesion of mass populations, national consensus is no longer, I believe, as important a condition of national survival as it once was. But if we no longer require the same degree of unanimity to *fight* a war, we do require a greater ferment of ideas and a radiating growth of political seriousness and variety within which alone we may find a way to *prevent* war. Important contributions to this have and may further be made by members of the academic community and, perhaps, especially, by its social science sector. The question arises, however, whether this group's political intelligence can ever be adequately mobilized for these purposes so long as it remains tranquilized by the value-free doctrine.

Throughout his work, Weber's strategy is to safeguard the integrity and freedom of action of both the state, as the instrument of German national policy, and of the university, as the embodiment of a larger Western tradition of rationalism. He feared that the expression of political value judgments in the University would provoke the state into censoring the University and would imperil its autonomy. Indeed, Weber argues that professors are not entitled to freedom from state control in matters of values, since these do not rest on their specialized qualifications.

This view will seem curious only to those regarding Weber as a liberal in the Anglo-American sense, that is, as one who wishes to delimit the state's powers on behalf of the individual's liberties. Actually, however, Weber aimed not at curtailing but at strengthening the powers of the German state, and at making it a more effective instrument of German nationalism. It would seem, however, that an argument contrary to the one he advances is at least as consistent; namely, that professors are, like all others, entitled and perhaps obligated to express their values. In other words, professors have a right to profess. Rather than being made the objects of special suspicion and special control by the state, they are no less (and no more) entitled than others to the trust and protection of the state.

In a *Realpolitik* vein, Weber acknowledges that the most basic national questions cannot ordinarily be discussed with full freedom in government universities. Since the discussion there cannot be completely free and all-sided, he apparently concludes that it is fitting there should be no discussion at all, rather than risk partisanship. But this is too pious by far. Even Socrates never insisted that all views must be at hand before the dialogue could begin. Here again one might as reasonably argue to the contrary, holding that one limitation of freedom is no excuse for another. Granting the reality of efforts to inhibit unpopular views in the University, it seems odd to prescribe self-suppression as a way of avoiding external suppression. Suicide does not seem a reasonable way to avoid being murdered. It appears, however, that Weber was so intent on safeguarding the autonomy of the University and the autonomy of politics, that he was willing to pay almost any price to do so, even if this led the University to detach itself from one of the basic intellectual traditions of the West— the dialectical exploration of the fundamental purposes of human life.

Insofar as the value-free doctrine is a mode of ensuring professional autonomy, note that it does not, as such, entail an interest peculiar to the social sciences. In this regard, as a substantial body of research in the sociology of occupations indicates, social scientists are kin to plumbers, house painters, or librarians. For most if not all occupations seek to elude control by outsiders and manifest a drive to maintain exclusive control over their practitioners.

Without doubt the value-free principle did enhance the autonomy of sociology; it was one way in which our discipline pried itself loose—in some modest measure—from the clutch of its society, in Europe freer from political party influence, in the United States freer of ministerial influence. In both places, the value-free doctrine gave sociology a larger area of autonomy in which it could steadily pursue basic problems rather than journalistically react to passing events, and allowed it more freedom to pursue questions uninteresting either to the respectable or to the rebellious. It made sociology freer—as Comte had wanted it to be—to pursue all its own theoretical implications. In other words, the value-free principle did, I think, contribute to the intellectual growth and emancipation of our enterprise.

There was another kind of freedom which the value-free doctrine also allowed; it enhanced a freedom from moral compulsiveness; it permitted a partial escape from the parochial prescriptions of the sociologist's local or native culture. Above all, effective internalization of the value-free principle has always encouraged at least a temporary suspension of the moralizing reflexes built into the sociologist by his own society. From one perspective, this of course has its dangers—a disorienting normlessness and moral indifference. From another standpoint, however, the value-free principle might also have provided a *moral* as well as an intellectual *opportunity*. For insofar as moral reactions are only suspended and not aborted, and insofar as this is done in the service of knowledge and intellectual discipline, then, in effect, the value-free principle strengthened Reason (or Ego) against the compulsive demands of a merely traditional morality. To this degree, the value-free discipline provided a foundation for the development of more reliable knowledge about men and, also established a breathing space within which moral reactions could be less mechanical and in which morality could be reinvigorated.

The value-free doctrine thus had a paradoxical potentiality: it might enable men to make *better* value judgments rather than *none*. It could

encourage a habit of mind that might help men in discriminating between their punitive drives and their ethical sentiments. Moralistic reflexes suspended, it was now more possible to sift conscience with the rod
of reason and to cultivate moral judgments that expressed a man's total
character as an adult person; he need not now live quite so much by his
past parental programing but in terms of his more mature present.

The value-free doctrine could have meant an opportunity for a more
authentic morality. It could and sometimes did aid men in transcending
the morality of their "tribe," to open themselves to the diverse moralities
of unfamiliar groups, and to see themselves and others from the standpoint of a wider range of significant cultures. But the value-free doctrine
also had other, less fortunate, results as well.

Doubtless there were some who did use the opportunity thus presented;
but there were, also, many who used the value-free postulate as an excuse
for pursuing their private impulses to the neglect of their public responsibilities and who, far from becoming more morally sensitive, became
morally jaded. Insofar as the value-free doctrine failed to realize its potentialities it did so because its deepest impulses were—as we shall note
later—dualistic; it invited men to stress the separation and not the mutual connectedness of facts and values: it had the vice of its virtues. In
short, the conception of a value-free sociology has had *diverse* consequences, not all of them useful or flattering to the social sciences.

On the negative side, it may be noted that the value-free doctrine is
useful both to those who want to escape *from* the world and to those who
want to escape *into* it. It is useful to those young, or not so young men,
who live off sociology rather than for it, and who think of sociology as a
way of getting ahead in the world by providing them with neutral techniques that may be sold on the open market to any buyer. The belief that
it is not the business of a sociologist to make value judgments is taken, by
some, to mean that the market on which they can vend their skills is unlimited. From such a standpoint, there is no reason why one cannot sell
his knowledge to spread a disease just as freely as he can to fight it. Indeed, some sociologists have had no hesitation about doing market
research designed to sell more cigarettes, although well aware of the implications of recent cancer research. In brief, the value-free doctrine of
social science was sometimes used to justify the sale of one's talents to
the highest bidder and is, far from new, a contemporary version of the
most ancient sophistry.

In still other cases, the image of a value-free sociology is the armor of
the alienated sociologist's self. Although C. Wright Mills may be right
in saying this is the Age of Sociology, not a few sociologists, and Mills included, feel estranged and isolated from their society. They feel impotent
to contribute usefully to the solution of its deepening problems and, even
when they can, they fear that the terms of such an involvement require

them to submit to a commercial debasement or a narrow partisanship, rather than contributing to a truly public interest.

Many sociologists feel themselves cut off from the larger community of liberal intellectuals in whose pithy satire they see themselves as ridiculous caricatures. Estranged from the larger world, they cannot escape except in fantasies of posthumous medals and by living huddled behind self-barricaded intellectual ghettos. Self-doubt finds its anodyne in the image of a value-free sociology because this transforms their alienation into an intellectual principle; it evokes the soothing illusion, among some sociologists, that their exclusion from the larger society is a self-imposed duty rather than an externally imposed constraint.

Once committed to the premise of a value-free sociology, such sociologists are bound to a policy which can only alienate them further from the surrounding world. Social science can never be fully accepted in a society, or by a part of it, without paying its way; this means it must manifest both its relevance and concern for the contemporary human predicament. Unless the value relevances of sociological inquiry are made plainly evident, unless there are at least some bridges between it and larger human hopes and purposes, it must inevitably be scorned by laymen as pretentious word-mongering. But the manner in which some sociologists conceive the value-free doctrine disposes them to ignore current human problems and to huddle together like old men seeking mutual warmth. "This is not our job," they say, "and if it were we would not know enough to do it. Go away, come back when we're grown up," say these old men. The issue, however, is not whether we know enough; the real questions are whether we have the courage to say and use what we do know and whether anyone knows more.

There is one way in which those who desert the world and those who sell out to it have something in common. Neither group can adopt an openly critical stance toward society. Those who sell out are accomplices; they may feel no critical impulses. Those who run out, while they do feel such impulses, are either lacking in any talent for aggression, or have often turned it inward into noisy but essentially safe university politics or into professional polemics. In adopting a conception of themselves as "value-free" scientists, their critical impulses may no longer find a target in society. Since they no longer feel free to criticize society, which always requires a measure of courage, they now turn to the cannibalistic criticism of sociology itself and begin to eat themselves up with "methodological" criticisms.

One latent meaning, then, of the image of a value-free sociology is this: "Thou shalt not commit a critical or negative value judgment—especially of one's own society." Like a neurotic symptom this aspect of the value-free image is rooted in a conflict; it grows out of an effort to compromise between conflicting drives: On the one side, it reflects a conflict between the desire to criticize social institutions, which since Socrates has been the legacy of intellectuals, and the fear of reprisals if one does criticize—which is also a very old and human concern. On the other side, this aspect of the value-free image reflects a conflict between the fear of being critical and the fear of being regarded as unmanly or lacking in integrity, if uncritical.

The doctrine of a value-free sociology resolves these conflicts by making it seem that those who refrain from social criticism are acting solely on behalf of a higher professional good rather than their private interests. In refraining from social criticism, both the timorous and the venal may now claim the protection of a high professional principle and, in so doing, can continue to hold themselves in decent regard. Persuade all that no one must bell the cat, then none of the mice need feel like a rat.

Should social scientists affirm or critically explore values they would of necessity come up against powerful institutions who deem the statement or protection of public values as part of their special business. Should social scientists seem to compete in this business, they can run afoul of powerful forces and can, realistically, anticipate efforts at external curbs and controls. In saying this, however, we have to be careful lest we needlessly exacerbate academic timorousness. Actually, my own firsthand impressions of many situations where sociologists serve as consultants indicate that, once their clients come to know them, they are often quite prepared to have sociologists suggest (not dictate) policy and to have them express their own values. Nor does this always derive from the expectation that sociologists will see things their way and share their values. Indeed, it is precisely the expected difference in perspectives that is occasionally desired in seeking consultation. I find it difficult not to sympathize with businessmen who jeer at sociologists when they suddenly become more devoted to business values than the businessmen themselves.

Clearly all this does not mean that people will tolerate disagreement on basic values with social scientists more equably than they will with anyone else. Surely there is no reason why the principles governing social interaction should be miraculously suspended just because one of the parties to a social relation is a social scientist. The dangers of public resentment are real but they are only normal. They are not inconsistent with the possibility that laymen may be perfectly ready to allow social scientists as much (or as little) freedom of value expression as they would anyone else. And what more could any social scientist want?

The value-free image of social science is not consciously held for expedience' sake; it is not contrived deliberately as a hedge against public displeasure. It could not function as a face-saving device if it were. What seems more likely is that it entails something in the nature of a tacit bargain: in return for a measure of autonomy and social support, many social scientists have surrendered their critical impulses. This was not usually a callous "sell-out" but a slow process of mutual accommodation;

both parties suddenly found themselves betrothed without a formal ceremony.

Nor am I saying that the critical posture is dead in American sociology; it is just badly sagging. Anyone who has followed the work of Seymour Lipset, Dennis Wrong, Leo Lowenthal, Bennett Berger, Bernard Rosenberg, Lewis Coser, Maurice Stein, C. Wright Mills, Arthur Vidich, Philip Rieff, Anselm Strauss, David Riesman, Alfred McClung Lee, Van den Haag, and of others, would know better. These men still regard themselves as "intellectuals" no less than sociologists: their work is deeply linked to this larger tradition from which sociology itself has evolved. By no means have all sociologists rejected the legacy of the intellectual, namely, the right to be critical of tradition. This ancient heritage still remains embedded in the underground culture of sociology; and it comprises the enshadowed part of the occupational selves of many sociologists even if not publicly acknowledged.

In contrast with and partly in polemic against this older tradition, however, the dominant drift of American sociology today is compulsively bent upon transforming it into a "profession." (Strangely enough, many of these same sociologists see nothing contradictory in insisting that their discipline is still young and immature.) This clash between the older heritage of the critical intellectual and the modern claims of the value-free professional finds many expressions. One of these occurred at the sociologist's national meetings in Chicago in 1958. At this time, the convention in a session of the whole was considering Talcott Parsons' paper on "Sociology as a Profession." After long and involved discussion, which prompted many members suddenly to remember overdue appointments elsewhere, Chicago's E. C. Hughes rose from the floor and brought a warm response by insisting that we were not a professional but, rather, a learned society. It was at this same meeting that the American Sociological Society rechristened itself as the American Sociological Association, lest its former initials evoke public reactions discrepant with the dignity of a profession.

Another indication of the continuing clash between the critical intellectual and the value-free professional is to be found in the Phoenix-like emergence of Young Turk movements, such as SPSSI, the Society for the Psychological Study of Social Issues, which arose in response to the depression of 1929. When it was felt by Alfred McClung Lee and others that these Turks were no longer so young, they founded the SSSP, the Society for the Study of Social Problems. Both these organizations remain ongoing concerns, each characteristically interested in value-related work, and each something of a stitch in the side of its respective parent group, the American Psychological Association and the American Sociological Association.

The tension between the older conception of sociologists as intellectuals and the newer drive to professionalization is also expressed by the differences between the current Columbia or Harvard outlook and the so-called "Chicago tradition" which, with the change in that Department's character, is now either centered in Berkeley or is homelessly hovering. The difference between these two perspectives is most evident when they both embark on studies of the same institution.

A case in point can be found in the recent studies of medicine conducted by Columbia or Harvard and Chicago trained men. It is difficult to escape the feeling that the former are more respectful of the medical establishment than the Chicagoans, that they more readily regard it in terms of its own claims, and are more prone to view it as a noble profession. Chicagoans, however, tend to be uneasy about the very idea of a "profession" as a tool for study, believing instead that the notion of an "occupation" provides more basic guidelines for study, and arguing that occupations as diverse as the nun and the prostitute, or the plumber and the physician, reveal instructive sociological similarities. Chicagoans seem more likely to take a secular view of medicine, seeing it as an occupation much like any other and are somewhat more inclined toward debunking forays into the seamier side of medical practice. Epitomizing this difference are the very differences in the book titles that the two groups have chosen for their medical studies. Harvard and Columbia have soberly called two of their most important works, "The Student-Physician," and "Experiment Perilous," while the Chicagoans have irreverently labeled their own recent study of medical students, the "Boys in White."

One of the most interesting expressions of resistance to the newer, value-free style of "professional" sociology is the fascination with the *demi-monde* of a talented group of these ex-Chicagoans. For them orientation to the underworld has become the equivalent of the proletarian identifications felt by some intellectuals during the 1930's. For not only do they study it, but in a way they speak on its behalf, affirming the authenticity of its style of life. Two of the leading exponents of this style are Howard S. Becker and Erving Goffman; the latter may become the William Blake of sociology.

As a case in point, Goffman's subtle study, "Cooling the Mark Out," takes its point of departure from an examination of the strategy of the confidence rackets. In the con game, Goffman points out, after the mark's loot has been taken, one of the con men remains behind "to cool the mark out," seeking to persuade him to accept his loss of face rather than squeal to the police. Goffman then uses this stratagem as a model to explode a great variety of legitimate groups and roles—the restaurant hostess who cools out the impatient customer, the psychoanalyst who cools out those who have lost in love. The point is insinuated that the whole world may be seen as one of marks and operators and that, in the final analysis, we are all marks to be cooled out by the clergy, the operator left behind for the job. This, it would seem, is a metaphysics of the underworld, in which conventional society is seen from the standpoint of a group outside of its own respectable social structures.

This group of Chicagoans finds itself at home in the world of hip, Norman Mailer, drug addicts, jazz musicians, cab drivers, prostitutes, night people, drifters, grifters, and skidders, the cool cats and their kicks. To be fully appreciated this stream of work cannot be seen solely in terms of the categories conventionally employed in sociological analysis. It has also to be seen from the viewpoint of the literary critic as a style or *genre* and in particular as a species of naturalistic romanticism, a term which I do not in the least intend opprobriously. That is, it prefers the offbeat to the familiar, the vivid ethnographic detail to the dull taxonomy, the sensuously expressive to dry analysis, naturalistic observation to formal questionnaires, the standpoint of the hip outsider to the square insider.

It may of course be asked, "Is it any the less sentimentally romantic to regard medical research on incurable patients as an 'Experiment Perilous'?" Possibly not. But it is at least much more *decorous* than seeing it as a process of "cooling the mark out." That, I suspect, is nearer the bone. The one thing that "classicists," whether sociological or literary, can never abide is a lack of decorum, even if the performance is in other respects brilliant. In sociology, objections to a lack of decorum as such are not made and, instead, often take the form of criticizing methodological deficiencies or moralistic proclivities. And, in truth, this Chicago group does betray persistent moral concerns, as evidenced, for example, by their readiness to focus on the degrading impact of the mental hospital on its inmates, or on the legal straitjacket in which the drug addict is confined.

The pathology characteristic of the *classicist* is too well known to require much comment: theirs is the danger of ritualism, in which conformity to the formal canons of the craft is pursued compulsively to the point where it warps work, emptying it of insight, significant truth, and intellectually viable substance. Of the classicist degenerating into neo-classicism we might say, with Roy Campbell, "They use the snaffle and the curb, all right, but where's the bloody horse?"

For its part, romantic social criticism is vulnerable from two directions. The usual occupational hazard of the romantic is, of course, excess, of the emotions or of the imagination. It may be guessed, however, that such excess stems not only from the personalities indigenous to those whom Romanticism attracts but, just as much, from the bitter attack upon them by the neo-classicist and from their resultant polemic. Again, and perhaps more importantly, this Romantic standpoint is vulnerable to the crasser temptations of its own talent-earned success. Indeed, they have now learned to mute their jive to the point where they can communicate profitably with their stockbrokers. Perhaps the time will come when they will no longer have to pretend to be respectable and when they will, instead, have to work at seeming cool. But that time is not yet. Whatever the outcome, they have shown us still another facet of the resistance to the emergence of a value-free professionalism in sociology, and they have given us still another evidence of the intellectual vitality of a critical stance.

Despite the vigor of this and other groups, however, I believe that they are primarily secondary currents whose very visibility is heightened because they are moving across the main ebb. The dominant drift in American sociology is toward professionalization, the growth of technical specialists, toward the diffusion of the value-free outlook to the point where it becomes less of an intellectual doctrine and more of a blanketing mood. American sociology is in the process of accommodating itself.

In its main outlines, such efforts at accommodation are far from new. For the doctrine of a value-free sociology is a modern extension of the medieval conflict between faith and reason. It grows out of, and still dwells in, the tendency prevalent since the thirteenth century to erect compartments between the two as a way of keeping the peace between them. One of the culminations of this tendency in the Middle Ages is to be found in the work of the Arabian philosopher Ibn Rochd, better known as Averroës. Averroës had believed that absolute truth was to be found not in revelation but in philosophy, which for him meant Aristotle. He felt that revelation, faith, and the work of the theologians was a kind of footman's philosophy, necessary for those devoid of intellectual discipline and useful as a way of civilizing them.

Seeing theology as containing a measure of truth, albeit one inferior to that of philosophy and, being a prudent man, Averroës recommended that philosophers and theologians ought each to mind his own business and, in particular, that the philosophers, being intellectually superior, should show *noblesse oblige* to the theologians. He suggested that philosophers should keep their truth to themselves and write technical books which did not disturb or confuse simpler minds.

His disciples, the Latin or Christian Averroists, particularly at the University of Paris, accentuated this prudential side of their master's work; their strategy of safety was to define themselves as specialists, as technical philosophers. Their only job, said they, was to teach philosophy and to show the conclusions that flowed from it. These conclusions were "necessary" but, when at variance with the truths of revelation, it was not their job to reconcile them, said the philosophers. From this developed the so-called Doctrine of the Twofold Truth—the truths of philosophy which were logically necessary and the divine truths of revelation. If there were contradictions between the two, the philosophers merely reaffirmed their belief in revelation, and let it go at that. This sometimes took a cynical form as, for example, in John of Jaudan's comment, "I do believe that is true; but I cannot prove it. Good luck to those who can!" They thus built a watertight compartment between philosophy and faith, a separation which Saint Thomas continued and yet sought to transcend. To Saint Thomas, knowing and believing are distinct processes, each having its own separate and legitimate function and therefore not to be invaded by the other. In this view, there were two main classes of truths, both of which, however, derived from Divine Revelation. There were truths obtainable by natural reason alone, and there were truths of revelation, genuine articles of faith which elude the grasp of reason and which were susceptible neither to proof nor disproof by reason.

With the development of modern science varying efforts to accommodate it to religion continued, often taking the form of some kind of separatist doctrine in which each is assigned a different function and each is chastened to acknowledge the authority of the other in its own sphere. Weber's doctrine of a value-free sociology, which creates a gulf between science and values, is in this tradition; it may be regarded as a Protestant version of the Thomistic effort at harmonizing their relations.

The core of Weber's outlook rested on a dualism between, on the one hand, reason or rationality, especially as embodied in bureaucracy and science, and, on the other hand, more elemental emotional forces, partly encompassed in his notion of Charisma. He regards each of these forces as inimical to the other. He himself is ambivalent to each of them, viewing each as both dangerous and necessary.

On the one side, Weber is deeply concerned to protect the citadel of modern reason, the University, and fiercely opposes the professorial "cult of personality" which was the academic expression of the charismatic claim. This in turn disposes him to project an image of the University which is essentially bureaucratic, as a faceless group of specialists, each sovereign in his own cell and all sworn to forsake their individuality. Nonetheless he also hates bureaucracy precisely because it submerges individuality and dehumanizes men and is thus led to deny that he intended to bureaucratize the University in pleading for the doctrine of a value-free social science. (Yet while this was doubtless not his *intention,* his two-pronged polemic against the cult of academic personality and in favor of the value-free doctrine does seem to drive him toward such a bureaucratic conception of the University.)

If Weber is concerned to protect even the bureaucratic dwelling places of rationality, he also seeks to confine bureaucracy and to circumscribe the area of its influence. In particular, he wishes to protect the highest reaches of statecraft from degenerating into a lifeless routine; he seeks to preserve politics as a realm in which there can be an expression of personal will, of serious moral commitment, a realm where greatness was possible to those who dared, persevered and suffered, a realm so powerful that it could overturn the institutional order or preserve it. He wants to safeguard high politics as an arena of human autonomy, of pure value choices, at its finest.

Yet Weber also fears for the safety of rationality in the modern world.

He knows that there are powerful forces abroad which continue to threaten rationality, that there are still untamed things in men which he, more than most, had had to face. Not unlike Freud, Weber was both afraid of and drawn to these unbridled forces, the passionate Dionysian part of men. While he believed that they were being slowly subdued by an onmarching rationalization, he continued to fear that they could yet erupt and cleave modern institutional life. Although fearing these irrational forces, he also felt their disappearance from the modern world to be a "disenchantment," for he believed that they contained springs of vitality and power indispensable to human existence.

Weber is a man caught between two electrodes and torn by the current passing between them; he fears both but is unable to let go of either. He attempts to solve this dilemma by a strategy of segregation, seeking the exclusion of charismatic irrationality from certain modern *institutions,* such as the University, but admitting it into and, indeed, exalting its manifestations in the inward personal life of individuals. He wanted certain of the role structures of modern society to be rational; but he also wanted the role-players to be passionate and willful. He wanted the play to be written by a classicist and to be acted by romanticists. Unusual man, he wanted the best of both worlds. Yet whatever the judgment of his intellect, his sentiments are not poised midway between them, but tend toward one of the two sides.

This becomes clear when we ask, if science cannot be the basis of value judgments, what then, according to Weber, was to be their basis? To answer this, we must go beyond his formal doctrine of a value-free sociology, to Weber's own personal profession of belief. Weber certainly did not hold that personal values should derive from the existent culture, or from ancient traditions, nor again from formal ethical systems which he felt to be empty and lifeless. Unless men were to become inhuman robots, life, he insisted, must be guided by consciously made decisions. If men are to have dignity, they must choose their own fate.

To Weber as a man, only those values are authentic which stem from conscious decision, from a consultation of the inner conscience and a willful commitment to its dictates. From his *personal* standpoint, it is not really true that all values are equally worthy. Those consciously held by men are more worthy than those which are merely traditional and unthinkingly repeated. Those values that men feel deeply about and passionately long to realize are better than those which are merely intellectually appealing and do not engage their entire being.

In short, Weber, too, was seeking a solution to the competing claims of reason and faith. His solution takes the form of attempting to guard the autonomy of both spheres but, most especially I believe, the domain of conscience and faith. He wants a way in which reason and faith can cohabit platonically but not as full partners. The two orders are separate but unequal. For in Weber, reason only consults conscience and perhaps even cross-examines it. But conscience has the last word, and passion and will the last deed. Here Weber stands as half-Lutheran, half-Nietzschean.

If Weber thrusts powerfully at traditionalism, nonetheless his main campaign here is waged against science and reason and is aimed at confining their influence. To Weber, even reason must submit when conscience declares, Here I stand; I can do no other! Weber saw as authentic only those values that rest on the charismatic core of the self and on its claims to intuitive certainty. Weber, too, was a seeker after certainty, the certainty that is more apt to come from the arrogance of individual conscience. For while much may be truly said of the arrogance of reason, reason always seeks reasons and is ready to sit down and talk about them.

To Weber as a Protestant, the individual's conscience is akin to the voice of revelation. He would have been dismayed at the implications of considering it as the echo of parental remonstrations. To him, individual conscience was transcendental, while reason and science were only instrumental. Science is the servant of values and of personal conscience, which, like the heart, has reasons of its own. From Weber's standpoint, science and reason could only supply the means; the ends were to be dictated by values which, even if inscrutable, were to have the final voice.

I have therefore come to believe that the value-free doctrine is, from Weber's standpoint, basically an effort to compromise two of the deepest traditions of Western thought, reason and faith, but that his arbitration seeks above all to safeguard the romantic residue in modern man. I have personal reservations not because I doubt the worth of safeguarding this romantic component, but, rather, because I disagree with the strategy of segregation which Weber advances. *I believe that, in the end, this segregation warps reason by tinging it with sadism and leaves feeling smugly sure only of itself and bereft of a sense of common humanity.*

The problem of a value-free sociology has its most poignant implications for the social scientist in his role as educator. If sociologists ought not express their personal values in the academic setting, how then are students to be safeguarded against the unwitting influence of these values which shape the sociologist's selection of problems, his preferences for certain hypotheses or conceptual schemes, and his neglect of others. For these are unavoidable and, in this sense, there is and can be no value-free sociology. The only choice is between an expression of one's values, as open and honest as it can be, this side of the psychoanalytical couch, and a vain ritual of moral neutrality which, because it invites men to ignore the vulnerability of reason to bias, leaves it at the mercy of irrationality.

If truth is the vital thing, as Weber is reputed to have said on his deathbed, then it must be all the truth we have to give, as best we know it, being painfully aware and making our students aware, that even as we offer it we may be engaged in unwitting concealment rather than revelation. If we would teach students how science is made, really made rather than as publicly reported, we cannot fail to expose them to the whole scientist by whom it is made, with all his gifts and blindnesses, with all his methods and his *values* as well. To do otherwise is to usher in an era of spiritless technicians who will be no less lacking in understanding than they are in passion, and who will be useful only because they can be used.

In the end, even these dull tools will through patient persistence and cumulation build a technology of social science strong enough to cripple us. Far as we are from a sociological atomic bomb, we already live in a world of the systematic brainwashing of prisoners of war and of housewives with their advertising-exacerbated compulsions; and the social science technology of tomorrow can hardly fail to be more powerful than today's.

It would seem that social science's affinity for modeling itself after physical science might lead to instruction in matters other than research alone. Before Hiroshima, physicists also talked of a value-free science; they, too, vowed to make no value judgments. Today many of them are not so sure. If we today concern ourselves exclusively with the technical proficiency of our students and reject all responsibility for their moral sense, or lack of it, then we may someday be compelled to accept responsibility for having trained a generation willing to serve in a future Auschwitz. Granted that science always has inherent in it both constructive and destructive potentialities. It does not follow from this that we should encourage our students to be oblivious to the difference. Nor does this in any degree detract from the indispensable norms of scientific objectivity; it merely insists that these differ radically from moral indifference.

I have suggested that, at its deepest roots, the myth of a value-free sociology was Weber's way of trying to adjudicate the tensions between two vital Western traditions: between reason and faith, between knowledge and feeling, between classicism and romanticism, between the head and the heart. Like Freud, Weber never really believed in an enduring peace or in a final resolution of this conflict. What he did was to seek a truce through the segregation of the contenders, by allowing each to dominate in different spheres of life. Although Weber's efforts at a personal synthesis brings him nearer to St. Thomas, many of his would-be followers today tend to be nearer to the Latin Averroists with their doctrine of the twofold truth, with their conception of themselves as narrow technicians who reject responsibility for the cultural and moral consequences of their work. It is precisely because of the deeply dualistic implications of the current doctrine of a value-free sociology that I felt its most appropriate symbol to be the man-beast, the cleft creature, the Minotaur.

SOCIAL SCIENCE?

SOME PROBATIVE PROBLEMS

John R. Seeley

My private object in the original presentation of this paper corre-
sponded rather happily with my public duty. I wanted to raise with my
colleagues, rather than settle, some difficulties that have, for me, been
hardy perennials in my own attempt to see myself as a social scientist,
to locate myself in social, moral, scientific, or epistemological space. I
assumed that many of them were problems also for others, perhaps in
different states of resolution or irresolution. There is, of course, considerable bias in the selection of the problems themselves: there may well be,
within the social scientific enterprise as a whole, sub-enterprises to which
these perplexities have little or no relevance. It would be an important
advance if we could clarify what these sub-enterprises are. What constitutes the *principle* on which one set to which the questions *are* highly
relevant can be separated from the other? How does the conjuncture of
the two sub-sets in an enterprise that receives *one* single social definition
affect the whole—and the parts? In what follows, I shall neglect that part
of social science, if any, to which my critique is irrelevant; but for brevity
and simplicity's sake, I shall talk of "social science" when I mean that
part of it to which the critique *is* germane—leaving due qualification for
others, otherwise preoccupied.

I am also simply going to assume a social scientist who talks, tells, or
publishes, a social scientist who does not keep all his observations, reflections, and findings to himself. I assume also a literate society that reads
or listens, and hence, at least eventually, knows what he said. The problem of time may be treated initially as not of great importance, so that
we may regard as "virtual instantaneity" the period from observation to
writing, to publication, to restatement in, say, Life, to republication in the

"Social Science? Some Probative Problems." From a paper presented at a Department
of Psychology and Sociology Colloquium at Brandeis University on November 14, 1962.
Printed by permission of John R. Seeley.

Reader's Digest, to summary in the editorial page or advice-to-the-love-lorn column in the community throwaway newspaper. Indeed, at first, borrowing from physics the right to postulate a perfect friction-free machine, I ought perhaps to postulate a sizable cadre of social scientists who "tell all"—and who are heard telling all, instantaneously, by all. Some of the problems presented fit that model; some have to do with departures.

Let me start with what I might call the *uniqueness theorem.* All institutions, except perhaps at one time the Church, have in effect a mandate to serve the society by discharging their part-functions *within* the widest agreed social definitions. The Church furnishes a nice ambiguous case: in its heyday, before the advent of social science, it did in form and fact appeal to an order held to lie beyond and above society, or indeed humanity. In relation to that order, it could not only criticize society—no holds barred, no values excepted—but even depose princes and unmake kings. By a self-definition, widely conceded socially, it lay in a sense (as it saw itself and was seen) *outside* the mere society of men, even humankind. Today, insofar as, by the action of social scientists the church is seen and sees itself as merely a social institution, it does not differ in this respect from other social institutions such as the school or the underworld: it is within the society—contained by, rather than containing. (Artists similarly lay claim to some extrasocietal *Standpunkt,* but their claim is barely audible and hardly allowed.) The social scientist, in contrast with all other role-players must—*conceptually* must—be conceded the right and given the duty of bringing the whole society under review (from some standpoint yet to be defined). The very notion of being a social scientist, a scientist of society, cannot be divorced from the notion of the right and duty to study the whole society (all society, all societies), if only because a mandate to study a part might very well be nugatory except in the light of knowledge regarding the whole. No other socially defined body of men must proceed so. Only the social scientist has as his mandate the study of the society that gave him his mandate (as well as other societies). The task is unique—and it gives rise to some peculiar problems so far barely recognized. As long as a supernatural order and a process of revelation taking place in essentially a different medium, the spiritual, is considered a datum, it is easy to see how, in principle, one *could* study, and bring under criticism or judgment, the society of men as a human, mere human, society. But what is the analogical ground on which the social scientist is to stand—something above or beyond or outside the social—while he performs his function? Science itself is surely not, or not sufficiently, trans-social, as any student of the psychology or sociology of science (let alone the politics or sociology of sociology) will tell us. *Wo ist das Land . . . ?*

Among the possible attempts to avoid this perhaps insuperable difficulty, probably as famous a "solution" as any, is that embodied and self-consciously discussed in Gunnar Myrdal's *American Dilemma*. His argument is by now familiar but worth summary: the strategy in terms of which he elects to conduct his analysis of the negro-white problem begins with the identification in American life, but particularly as it bears on the "problem," of at least two mutually incompatible value commitments, so that further action to serve the one implicitly disserves the other. On the basis of this identification he seems to require no special position of his own: he takes it from the society he is studying. This *seems* very good. It is, incidentally, the principal strategy some of us use with counselees, patients, even on ourselves and with our friends. But note how little it really "solves" the problem posed. What Myrdal does is to take a pose or posture that, on second glance, is quite peculiar: he *pretends* to take at face value what (some) Americans *say* in their perhaps better moments—"The American dream"—and then confronts them with what they say and do in their worse. This is really not far short of making psychological warfare on Americans—certainly awarding cruel and unusual punishment: cruel because so subtle and difficult to resist and helpful-seeming; unusual because there are few capable of forcing so devastating a self-realization on so many. How does the social scientist console himself in this situation, where it should be clear at least that he is both taking for granted (and, in a sense, promoting and imposing) a value for consistency of behavior that few people would really hold, and a disvalue on ignorance that most people, if they understood themselves at all well, would put great stock in? He consoles himself—he must do so—either by recognizing his frank partisanship with the underdog (presently, generally, the Negro) or by appealing from the general social investment in inconsistency and ignorance (both of which allow the pleasures of impulsive behavior) to something he believes to be intrinsically better or higher. But that "better" or "higher" must then represent either the personal or professional commitment of the social scientist *as over against* the society generally. For if it were the commitment of the society generally, there would be no need for *him* to appeal to it: it would be operative. And if not, if like the American dream itself, it is either a commitment for all but some of the time, or for some and all of the time, then he is again intervening in its behalf in the name of something still higher in *his* view: for example, a conviction that a society "ought to" pay more attention to its highest values. Clearly enough, on any such construction, Dr. Myrdal appears as a preacher or parent or therapist (which is a subtype of both); and despite the excellence of his sociological study, it must be recognized, nevertheless, as a tract.

Most other attempts to find a foundation founder the same way, I believe, if we are not willing to concede that the social scientist must either find for his mandated role a "trans-social" position, yet undefined, or adopt merely his own personal value and perception position which would, I think, necessitate redefining his function. The commonest attempts smuggle in pretenses that men *do* generally desire to be consistent, rational, good, mature, scholarly, philosophical—which patently they do not, else the occasion for the exercise would seem to be wanting. Let me leave it at this: that the social scientist does and must criticize the society from a viewpoint that he cannot justify by an appeal to the society as it is —apart from his *mandate* which *he* defines as he goes.

Let me turn now to a difficulty closely connected with the foregoing, which I might call the *social science is social action theorem*. Certainly in some, probably in most, very likely in all of his activities *as a social scientist*, the social scientist by what he does inevitably intervenes in, interferes with, meddles in the social process.

An illustration I have used before may serve here. What people do with their new potencies of atomic fission is not, whatever else it is, a problem *in* atomic physics. But what they do with Mr. Warner's reports of class in America *is* a problem in sociology (in part, even, a further problem in "class in America"); and what they do, each of them, with Mr. Freud's allegations regarding psychopathology in everyday life, is a psychological problem (and, indeed, a further problem in the psychopathology of everyday life). It is certainly a further problem for the science in terms of accounting for the behavior. I think it is a problem also for the planning or social engineering or political action—which is usually thought to be separable from the scientific problem itself, though I cannot help seeing the distinction as obscure, if not untenable.

The view taken, moreover, leads me toward an *inexhaustibility theorem*: the subject matter of something cannot in principle be exhausted if the first description both alters and, in any case, increases the subject matter to be described. One version of the inexhaustibility theorem would go, "You cannot describe a culture when every description is, by definition, as soon as it is made, *in* the culture."

The inexhaustibility theorem appears to me to open toward a *freedom theorem*—an antidote to radical determinism, on the only intelligible basis I have been able to give it. If every theory regarding human behavior enters into human behavior—or if most or some theories do—as a "new factor," then there is no sense in which the behavior can be said to be determined in any definite (finite) sense. Empirically, it seems to me that an assertion, even if initially fully justified by inference from all previous cases (such as a statement that boys feel unlimited rivalry with their fathers in reference to their mothers) may and frequently does enter in a very short interval into the behavior of all the parties, in such a way as to make necessary its own qualification. The view or belief consequent upon the statement may, for instance, so affect pride, or anger or felt potency, or anything else as to change *in and of itself*, the *ceteris paribus* on which the validity of the statement originally depended. It is a little like telling a student, "You are a failure." God knows—or at least, I don't—what the consequences for his success-failure outcome may be. The contention obviously goes well beyond Merton's theory of the self-confirming prophecy, to a generalized theory of *inevitable intervention*.

Let me develop this theorem just a little further.

It seems to me that sociologists—and psychologists and other social scientists, analogically—broadly do three things. They state or *define* or recognize *problems*. They write what I shall call, analogically with elementary geography, *sociography*. They do *sociology*. By sociography I mean an enterprise of description, perhaps an idiographic enterprise; by sociology I mean an attempt at a causal analysis, a nomothetic enterprise. In all three cases, however, the social scientist makes, to my mind, a decisive intervention, one attended by very difficult intellectual problems of self-location, and ethical problems of warrantability.

I shall deal lightly with the first case, though it is no light matter. The very "recognition" of something as a scientific problem, instead of some other kind of problem, marks a shift, an implicit act of legislation so profound as to deserve the title revolutionary. Nothing, I should think, except the commonness in our day of these acts of scientific territory-seizing, could obscure the radical change involved, a change that by itself threatens to shake the foundations of the present society and to erect a new one of unforeseeable characteristics—perhaps an iatrocratic one—in its place.

Numerous illustrations will readily come to mind. A recent one is alcoholism: the minute alcoholism is *defined* as a problem for science, even before any causal connections are established, let alone controls or remedies found, *in virtue of the definition* what alcoholism is held to be, and therewith attitudes to, practices upon and even custody of, care and responsibility for the alcoholic are immediately implicitly, and later explicitly, altered. *The social relation is altered by the definition per se;* society is reconstituted out of the simple fiat (if effective) that alcoholism is a problem for science. With "mental disease" and "neurosis" as forerunners, with "sexual deviation" trembling on the border of redefinition, with delinquency half in, half out, but coming in, with no bar in principle to the admission under the rubric of any desired or undesired condition—"authoritarianism," for instance—is it not visible, almost patent, that more and more is being defined out of the old and nonscientific society and into the new one taking gigantic shape in its womb? I see no bars in principle. If the causes of authoritarianism can be scientifically determined, why cannot the causes of democratism?—and why cannot the one be countered while the other is nurtured?—except, of course, that an induced or caused democratism is not what we really wanted to begin with. (The last point has to do with what someone recently called the problem of the "morality pill.") All I want to establish for now is the *science-as-legislation theorem*: that "recognition" of a problem as scientific at all, as clearly legislates a revolutionary difference into human affairs as any nineteenth-century Act of Annexation did in affairs political.

I now want to deal with what looks like the most innocent, innocuous, or least interventive aspect of our trade: mere sociography or psychography: description of what is—map-making, if you will, or data assembling and ordering.

Description of a vital human activity in and of and by itself constitutes, in my opinion, an attack upon that activity, both from the viewpoint of the participants and from the viewpoint of the disinterested (neither participant, nor social scientist) observer. To the degree that it is a successful description, ethically neutral, deadpan, it tears apart for the participants the veil of unreality that is the foundation of the activity. A scientific description—of a social gathering, for instance—might well yield the participants something, even something of considerable worth, but could not leave something that was also valuable to them unaffected for the worse. Everyone purports to value light, but too much light is pitiless glare, and what goes on in and after the glare is impossibly what went on in the welcome and familiar twilight. How could a love relationship survive, for instance, an extended equitable enumeration of the characteristics of the beloved? How does other-directed behavior survive its categorization (stigmatization) as such? What becomes of the organization man, once he is identified by self and others as such? I am almost tempted to analogize: the light of social science is ultraviolet; the bacteria cannot survive the light; life cannot live without bacteria; social science sterilizes; the sterility kills.

We have long confronted this problem as the problem of "unmasking." I think nearly every description, again in and of itself, of any vital social or psychological matter, involves or risks such unmasking. In both sciences we have comforted ourselves (I think, falsely) by protecting the identity of the unit we are describing (the patient, person, community, or factory). I suggest it is false comfort, if only because it is insufficient: it avoids the inequity of fining a particular speeding motorist, as it were, by fining them as a group. When, finally, our initial operation results in a new "descriptive" image of parents, doctors, academics, teachers, professional men generally, businessmen, executives, unwed mothers, suburbs, churches, parishes, community chests, neurotics, alcoholics, pedophiles, hoboes, slums, gold coasts, Americans, Japanese, Indians, Protestants, Catholics, Jews, fundamentalists, or mystics, the living conditions for definable classes of people are altered—generally, I think, in the direction of a more complex, strenuous set of demands on them accompanied by a diminished armanentarium of available defenses.

It may or may not be significant that a long standing point of friction between Americans and Russians in Geneva has been the issue of *inspection*. As Kenneth Boulding has repeatedly pointed out, we have little or

nothing of a sociology or psychology of inspection. Social and psychological descriptions are not merely inspection but *reported inspection*, and,
in the long run, continuous inspection. It is not even clear which way,
ethically and psychologically, the categorical, nonpersonal form of the
reporting works; for the true professional, perhaps a description, a potential exposure, of the *enterprise* with which he is associated—the
Church, the teaching profession, his type of community—is infinitely
worse than an exposure of *himself,* as a mere actual repository of an ideal
embodied in the naïve social definition.

Again, we cannot, I think, console ourselves in any easy way. We cannot, as indicated above, get off the hook by shifting the focus from individuals to groups or categories. Nor, which may be less obvious, by
shifting from persons or institutions to types of behavior—say, antagonistic cooperation, or sibling rivalry or gamesmanship—without again
encountering the probability that we merely make life harder for everyone; or, more commonly, harder for some who share preferentially in the
behavior and easier for those who do not. Nor may we comfort ourselves,
I think, by believing that in time we will get around to everyone in all
respects, so that at least we will hold the balance of disadvantage even.
There is an infinity of possible categorizations to be viewed in an infinity
of possible perspectives; and there will not be an infinity of infinities of
monographs written or read. So we exert a *judicial* function in deciding
what to describe. Description is like taxation; the right to describe absolutely is the right to destroy absolutely.

What we do, in practice, is, I think, to intervene (by description) against
some "bad guys" in favor of some "good guys"—but by unacknowledged
canons and on no ordered, let alone explicit and shared, principle.

If sociography and psychography are implicit interventions, what is to
be said of the bulk of psychology and sociology, if by these we mean the
sciences that trace supposed cause and effect relations in their fields?

A fortiori, these represent, as I have said elsewhere, not mere findings,
but findings *for* and *against*, judgments as well as verdicts and, in their
redefinitional effects, acts of legislation as well.

Let me assert first that there is a fatal peculiarity about the normal
notion of cause when an attempt is made to apply it in the social sciences.
I take it for granted that, in society as in nature, everything is related to
everything else and hence in some ultimate, metaphysical sense everything is the cause of any one thing. But by "*the* cause" or "a cause" we
mean in science, as in practical everyday life, that particular thing which
it would be most "convenient," economical or efficient to change in order
to secure a desired change in what we are pleased to call an effect. Thus
mosquitoes, if we do not mind exterminating them, are "the cause" of
malaria in men; though apart from this canon of convenience we might
equally have said that blood was the cause of malaria if we could do without it, or men, if we were prepared to exterminate them.

The differences on this score between the natural and social sciences is that, in the former but not in the latter, there exist two plain, open and public canons of causal selection: there is, first, a basic judgment for man *against* the rest of the animate, and, *a fortiori*, the inanimate universe; and second, in general, in reference to things there is an economics mediated by a single fungible medium, money, that permits or appears to permit comparative measures of convenience and inconvenience in terms of relative costs. (A whole set of social conventions does underlie this procedure, but the natural scientist is not bound to examine them.)

But the minute we try to apply this mode of reasoning in the social sciences we are faced with two problems: one perhaps only technically difficult (interconvertibility of costs or disutilities), and the other, I think, insuperable. For when we say "convenient" in the social sciences, we must ask further *"Convenient to whom?"* And unless we can either identify a general interest—which we have so far failed to do—or a supervenient criterion (such as pleasingness to God) we cannot fail, in effect, in attributing causality at all, simply to award costs to X out of the social, psychological, or material pocket of Y. For by the very act of picking out of the infinity of actual causal connections some one or ones as designated and hence recognized causes, we are altering definitions, redistributing tasks and responsibilities, increasing and decreasing prestige or repute, changing balances of psychic and social incomes, assets and liabilities.

Take the problem of accounting for "delinquency" as an instance. Admittedly, this is selected from the field of "social problems," where the procedure is most evident, but an attempt to account for apathy or anxiety, or administration or bureaucracy would serve nearly as well. As I have said elsewhere, the cause of delinquency, "other things being equal," is any one or more of the following: poor street lighting, alleys, immigration, paternal infidelity, differential association, neurotic acting out, broken homes, the American income distribution, lack of alternate meaningful activities, advertising and display, failure to nail down prized objects, the slum, the ecological organization of the American city, materialism, its opposite; preoccupation with one's worth as a person, the law itself, the absurdity of society or the human condition; the want of religion, the nuclear family, the political system which needs crime which needs as a training ground prisons and reformatories; schools that engage few or no loyalties, the perversity of the individual delinquent, or his parents, or theirs; psychological ignorance, the unconscious wishes of those who deplore the activity or condemn the actors. "Choose your pick," as they say. There can hardly be a question that all are involved, and an infinity—literally—of other candidates for causal ascription besides. And each of these "causal factors" is also connected for the purposes of science with an infinity of other causes. The selection for reporting and hence attention of any one cause—say, the ghettoization of Negroes in the Black Belt, leading to rent extortion, leading to overcrowding, leading to heightened necessities for certain types of experiences and escapes—is as clear an act of judgment (in the legal sense) as if when a bridge collapsed a judge were to select a particular passenger over it as the cause of its downfall from the combined excessive weight of all of them on it at the time.

The selection of any one of these for study *is* a political act, an expression of a political position—a power-redistributing value-function that the social scientist knowingly or unknowingly holds. Let me leave this here for now as the *cause-tax or etiology-fine theorem.*

I would like to turn next to the problem involved in the *ceteris paribus,* or context-taken-for-granted problem. Let me suppose a sociologist or psychologist interested in the rehabilitation of the imprisoned delinquent. He might be asked and he might assent to the study of any of the following, roughly ordered, problems. How, after we have thoroughly strapped a defiant child, can we mitigate his feelings, so that he is not led by the feelings into a vicious cycle of further defiance and increased punishment (surely a humane desire, within its context)? Or, how can we find a substitute punishment for strapping that would have the same effect—the breaking of resistance—without the too patent sado-masochistic risks (surely also humane enough in its context)? Or, how can administration be smooth and overwhelming without resort to patent punishment, defined as such? (I think this is the commonest type of problem our clients bring us.) Or, given morally meaningless confinement, how can we minimize coercion? Or, given the need for order and the absurd rules of the society, what alternatives can we find for confinement (e.g., free marijuana)? Or, what alternatives are there to the absurd rules, given the present sociopolitical structure? Or, what alternatives are there to that structure, given the need for national stability in the face of the cold war? Or, what alternatives to cold war, given no radical reconstruction in the minds and hearts of men? . . .

With every shift in context, it is obvious that the whole scientific problem shifts. With every success at an early level in the list, the likelihood that a subsequent item might be successfully examined is reduced. If a really successful outcome for strapping could be assured with the aid of science (as perhaps it could), the view that we might need to re-examine larger problems would be most unlikely to find research funds—or listeners. So the decision as to where to cut in to a social problem, what other things to take as being equal or to be taken for granted, is in effect an act of intervention tending to ensure that they remain not only equal but unchanged. One way to reduce theft from department stores, for instance, would be to institute a pay-what-you-like system (including no payment), with losses turned into profits by tax subsidies. Why not? But the problem is not usually posed so. Which means that the problem, as set, is within a complex net of assumptions and goals, the *ceteris paribus,* that in effect constitutes an invitation to join the conservative party.

Hence, the way to deal with alcoholism is likelier to be found by science to be the setting up of more clinics where the socially hurt can be reconciled to their fate and persuaded to find substitute comforts, than it is to be the elimination of the sources of anxiety, aggression, self-denial, and self-castration that appear to underlie all or most self-defeating self-indulgence. Even when we shift away from the study of *problems*, defined as such, to the study of persons or small groups—again "all other things being equal" being the very precondition for the study—we flee, I believe, in motive as well as effect, from the larger questions, just as we divert resources, and, worse, attention from these much more far-reaching matters. American sociology and psychology go that way, I believe, not on the mere ground of scientific safety, or ease of management of the problem, but from covert alliances with the going order, in its major aspects, already in the heart of the scientist.

I am sure it does not need emphasis that, just as the best is sometimes the enemy of the better, so most often the better is the enemy of the best. A sure-fire psychotherapy might well put off for three thousand years any attempt to cope with the institutional ways that ensure the breakdowns that the therapy deals with. I will leave this as the *accepted context equals alliance theorem*. The Communists used to use the phrase "blunting the edge of revolution" for the effect of minor (or perhaps particularly major) reforms; and while we may not wish to espouse the politics, the perplexity remains; whether we are electing to deal with a narrow-context social problem or a sociological problem: one is more likely to stand in the way of more radical action, the other in the way of more significant knowledge.

Let me drive home the point of the context once more, but in a different way: a social scientist studying, say, the psychology of resignation in the context of Belsen is doing something far different from someone studying the same problem in the context of midtown Manhattan, or for that matter, Lhasa, Tibet. No less, I believe, with the development of learning theories that explore the analogies of human learning with the behavior of machines, pigeons, or students of Zen.

Nor can we comfort ourselves, I think, with the consolation that we all act freely on manifold interests, and that these individual impulses can be ordered by the market, intellectual or commercial. Our "interests" are themselves potential matters of scientific investigation, and would, I doubt not, turn out to be closely connected with a personal politics that gains no advantage from being inexplicit, if not denied. The actual and practical upshot seems to me even short of Louis Wirth's attribution to the whole, to sociology as such, of the term "an omnium gatherum"; it fails the completeness of the first term and the orderliness of the second. Indeed, its first-order social consequence—and it may not be unintended, it may be the very condition under which we are socially allowed to practise—looks very like the scattering and frittering away of most of the best minds of any given generation over the whole field of the variously trivial. Perhaps not; perhaps there is more order or sense than I see; but my first impression is that the result would well justify the opening stanzas of Allen Ginsberg's *Howl*.

Another insufficiently explored set of problems in the social sciences flows, I believe, out of the interpenetrations of knowledge and commitment. I have sufficiently, I hope, indicated my view as to how such knowledge in general flows only out of commitments (or implies them) whether one is more or less witting as to the nature of, or basis for, the commitments in question. It goes without saying that the commitment may well be and quite generally is made over in the light of the knowledge gained on the basis of it.

I want to drive the point home somewhat further by beginning with psychoanalysis—of any school, as far as I know—as a model, and I want to ask: What kind of social scientific knowledge is not analogical *in the process necessary* to reach it? I do not wish to enter here into any discussion of any particular psychoanalytic tenet. But the formal status of the knowledge gained in analysis is, *ex hypothesi,* that it cannot be embraced (or tested) until certain kinds of experiences have been had which alter, probably irrevocably, the intelligence that proposes to assess them. It is open to those who have not made the commitment and had the experience to say either that the deliverances are false or not demonstrable. But this will no more—and properly so—shake the devotees, than the like arguments against the existence of God shake the religious. Indeed, the arguments are formally similar in that a first act of faith brings into vision—and to the participant it appears a vision that is at least as uncontestable as everyday or "scientific" vision—an object or class of objects, that justifies a further venture of faith, that brings into sight more objects or more of the same object . . . and so indefinitely.

Now I do not believe that this form of discovery, if you are willing to admit the word, is limited to psychoanalysis. Nothing short of a mature mind is capable, I believe, of defining (or even recognizing more than perfunctorily) what a mature mind might be. But such a definition in effect moves ahead of, rather than behind, the maturing mind: the insight contributes to the maturity, and thereby brings new visions, and the necessity of redefinition into sight.

We attempt commonly, in sociology at least to pay tribute to something of what is involved by speaking of the process of "participant-observation." Sometimes we speak as though we could occupy a position anywhere on a scale from total observation without participation to total participation without observation. And for limited purposes such talk may serve us well enough. But it seems to me there is a major class of matters in which nothing but total, unreserved participation will bring the object to be observed into sight in anything except a fatally distorting light. The model might be the mystical experience: I doubt if it can be had on the basis of a trial or a limited or divided commitment; neither perhaps can a love experience, although obviously celibate sociologists could write some things learnedly about love and marriage. But the central social facts—love, hate, friendship, enmity—are constituted by faith, and entered upon, for any purpose except most trivial comprehension, only in ways that set up the process of building knowledge on faith and faith on knowledge in a succession of steps that simultaneously opens one to some observations while blinding one to others. The most obvious statement might be that we can understand nothing until our modes of perception have been ineradicably set in many ways by some culture; but once this process is well begun, we can understand some things and not others. The knowledge has thus essentially in its very structure the nature of an historic or ontological process, in which successive steps in the activity produce irreversible changes in the actor so that the convention that approximates reality in the natural sciences—the contrary of Heraclitus' assertion that you cannot step into the same river twice—has no counterpart in the social sciences, or finds only a minor echo there. Insofar as this view is adopted in any large part, I should think it ought to give a quite different perspective upon a career in social science, and the training appropriate for it, and the meaning of contrasting deliverances by different social scientists. Commonly, these are viewed as erroneous judgments on one part by the other, or explained away in terms of a sociology of knowledge. But the possibility that they may be equi-valid as consequences of different commitment-knowledge sequences, while invoked as a criticism in terms of ideology, is rarely allowed as legitimate and desirable as well as, perhaps, unavoidable.

There are a number of other intriguing problems connected with the practice of our trade which I have touched on at other times and places, and which are closely connected with some of the foregoing.

There is a problem concerning even manner and place of publication, for insofar as knowledge is useful or even comforting, the manner of publication involves the problem of redistributing power (or gratification) in certainly unplanned and perhaps undesired ways. The present laissez-faire effect is, I believe, at best to secure and maintain a Pareto-curve for the distribution of vital knowledge of self and others; at worst, the effect of present publication practices is to heighten inequalities in access to important inside dope, and hence further to favor the managerial society.

There is a problem connected with the activity itself in its bearing on social stability: social change is already quite directly tied to technological change, in turn directly tied to quasi-autonomous natural science research. We are just entering the period where the society will be ever more rapidly changed (and I believe, shaken) by the much more far-reaching products of social scientific research. But again, this problem is not the natural scientists' concern, whereas it must be ours. In Lenin's words, "What is to be done?" Are we to take no "scientific" or ethical interest in the results of our own social intervention? Whose "field of study" is this, if not ours?

There is a problem connected with the ambiguities of the notion of "mastery" in relation to social affairs. With the aid of social science, what is to be mastered by whom, for whom, and with what conceivable results? There is also the opposite problem; the impotency-perception problem, as thinking in terms of causes and effects—the essential vocabulary of science—gradually replaces thinking in terms of agency, the essential vocabulary of action and drama, the former gradually leading man to view and feel himself as product rather than producer of himself and his "world."

There are so many such fundamental questions, so far-reaching in terms of the consequences that different answers to them would imply, that I am often left with the feeling that the house of social science is still largely founded on sand. Whether that is so or not, it seems evident that men do increasingly turn to social science, directly or indirectly, to structure perception and guide conduct, individual and collective, in more and more of their affairs. Before we have to take the strain that must ensue as our style of perception and explanation becomes the dominant style, as they shortly may, I should like to know more surely that we know, at least in large outline, what we are about.

Part III

THE SUPPRESSION OF
HISTORICAL CONCERNS

———◄◄❖►►———

STRATEGY IN SOCIAL SCIENCE
Barrington Moore

> The main evidence that a methodology
> is worn out comes when progress within
> it no longer deals with main issues.
>
> Whitehead

To some persons the very notion of scientific strategy seems contradictory. How can one conceive of a strategy for discovering the unknown? Does not the discovery of new knowledge always imply doing what one did not know how to do before? Such persons stress the accidental nature of past scientific discoveries. They are reluctant to criticize any form of research, even that which at the moment seems most futile and trivial, on the grounds that anything turned up by human curiosity may some day contribute to one of the great insights that mark a forward leap in human knowledge.

There is some merit in this contention. Since we cannot know in advance the fundamental discoveries of the future we cannot decide with complete certainty whether any particular investigation is worthwhile or not. Nevertheless, the intellectual and physical resources of both natural and social science are limited at any one point in time. Cultural and social factors also limit the direction of inquiry, emphasizing some problems and pushing others into the background. In other words, scientific strategy does differ from one society to another and from one historical epoch to another. Whether we want to or not, we must have scientific strategies and must continually choose among them. A completely liberal policy of encouraging all sorts of inquiry on the grounds that a few may eventually succeed is therefore an utopian impossibility. In science, as in war, we are compelled to make estimates about promising and unpromising lines of attack. We can reduce the element of uncertainty in scientific strategies, but we can never eliminate it completely.

Aware, then, that the problem is unavoidable and the solution necessarily uncertain, let us begin with a backward glance at the strategy of social science in nineteenth-century society. Historians tell us that the society we designate loosely by the term nineteenth century existed mainly in Western Europe and the United States between Napoleon's defeat and the outbreak of World War I. For our purpose we do not have to be precise about either the chronological or the geographical boundaries. We can start easily enough with de Tocqueville and end with Freud. Any selection is bound to be somewhat personal and arbitrary. The other men will therefore be mainly sociologists, though we may be allowed glimpses at other fields. No one would put Marx, Durkheim, Weber, and Mosca on exactly the same plane of intellectual attainment. Nevertheless, nearly everyone would agree that they had important things to say about human society. Even the casual reader will sense at once, I believe, a qualitative difference between these nineteenth-century thinkers and men widely regarded as leaders in the field of sociology today: Parsons, Merton, Stouffer, and Lazarsfeld. Without going very far into details, and therefore perhaps with some injustice to all concerned, let us try to put our finger on the nature of this difference.

It is legitimate, I think, to regard our nineteenth-century writers as participants in a single debate about the possibility of putting into practice the principles proclaimed earlier by the French Revolution. To be more precise, they were arguing about the feasibility of creating a rational society under the conditions of industrial advance and with the human materials available at that time. For them "rational" had a definite social content and implied, even if loosely, the kind of society that would enable man to make the most of his creative capacities. None of them, not even Marx, were naïve utopians. All of them saw in their own way that mankind had destructive capacities as well as creative ones. But they also cast about in terms of their own discoveries and insights to find ways of taming, limiting, or eliminating these destructive forces.

There was a strong historical current in the thinking of all these men. Through different lenses and from widely differing political standpoints all of them saw as their scientific problems those which the course of human history had put on the agenda as the significant ones of their epoch. Since these problems are still very much with us, it may be helpful in assessing our own strategies to recall very briefly some of the ways in which these nineteenth-century figures viewed them.

Leaning slightly toward the conservative viewpoint, Alexis de Tocqueville set out to discover what happened when a society transplanted from Europe and freed from some of the incubus of European conditions and traditions tried to realize the ideals of the French Revolution. Though he found much to admire in America, he was disturbed by a certain uniformity of tone in American life that derived, he thought, from the absence of social contrasts, and especially the absence of any class that was the carrier of an aristocratic tradition. He was apparently the first to perceive clearly the possible dangers of a system of mass democracy, a theme that became more and more prominent in nineteenth-century social thought.

Mosca also, to continue the conservative argument, found his original intellectual stimulus in the French Revolution. Influenced by Taine's critique, he set out to criticize some of the humanitarian ideals that had accompanied the Revolution and were an important part of his intellectual climate as well as ours. Though Mosca's theories shade over at times toward fascism, his thinking still remained within the framework of liberal thought. His ideal society was English parliamentary democracy of the nineteenth century, which he recognized as actually an oligarchy with benevolent traits. Though he set out to demonstrate, in opposition to Aristotle, that all governments are in practice oligarchies, he recognized important differences among them. To my mind his most important contribution was to put social and historical content into older legalist ideas about the division of powers in the state. Like de Tocqueville he recognized that liberty under law required, if it were to mean anything in practice, a situation of conflicting and competing interest groups in society such that no one class or group could completely dominate the state. For the same reason he distrusted social doctrines that pretended to have all the answers. "When power rests," he said, "on a system of ideas and beliefs outside of which it is felt there can be neither truth nor justice, it is almost impossible that its acts should be debated and moderated in practice." [1] Writing long before the advent of modern totalitarian regimes, he was one of those who foresaw this possibility as a consequence of the decline of a property-owning middle class and the rise of secular schemes of salvation.

Among the radicals, Marx, the "bad conscience of the bourgeoisie," is, of course, the main figure. Today we try to quiet this bad conscience by saying that Marx was more a moralist than a scientist. Insofar as he was a scientist, so the argument against him continues, he may have called attention to some of the uglier features of nineteenth-century capitalism (though he has been accused of overdoing these as well),[2] which modern capitalism has subsequently overcome. His basic notion, the opponents claim further, that one could discover "laws of motion" from history and the study of contemporary society, represents an illegitimate transfer of antiquated notions from physical science into the study of human affairs. From these considerations the conclusion emerges that enlightened modern intellectuals can afford to treat Marx as an antiquarian curiosity.

To discuss these issues would take a book in itself. We must confine ourselves to one or two sketchy remarks. Few serious thinkers today would deny that Marx is antiquated in important respects. Even those sympathetic to Marx are likely to concede, for example, that there is little factual basis now for the hope that the proletariat will revolt and destroy the repressive features of modern capitalism. After these and other concessions have been made to Marx's opponents, what remains is, to my way of thinking, still very impressive. The conception of social class as arising out of an historically specific set of economic relationships and of the class struggle as the basic stuff of politics, constitute some of the most important ideas that students of history and political behavior carry around in their heads, whether they are Marxists or not. As for the characteristics of capitalism, certainly the modern American version is something very different from that envisaged by Marx. Nevertheless, I doubt very much that one can either understand the nature of this transition or analyze the present situation without drawing very heavily on Marxist ideas. The trend toward monopoly is, after all, an inherent part of the Marxist analytical scheme. As for the present situation, there can be no doubt that for a whole generation now the stimulus of war industry has played a vital part in maintaining American capitalism as a going concern. To put the point squarely, we have not had for some time the kind of capitalism that cured its own "faults," either through intelligent public policy, or through some automatic economic mechanism—if indeed such an animal ever existed. Whether we have learned enough to do this now, and whether the future will give us the opportunity to put this knowledge into practice, are questions to which we can have no certain answer.

One crucial aspect of Marx's strategy as a social scientist remains to be mentioned. More than any of the other writers considered here, he started from the conviction that the social institutions of his day were evil. With his somewhat optimistic historical view, he believed that this evil was both transitory and unnecessary. At the same time he thought of himself as a scientist—a savage one to be sure, constantly using hard facts to strip away the veil of hypocrisy and unconscious self-deception that concealed the ugly realities underneath. For Marx there was no conflict between his position as a moralist and a scientist. The whole enterprise of science made sense for him only in terms of moral convictions. On this score Marx differs entirely from the dominant spirit in contemporary social science. Furthermore, Marx took it for granted that in any society there was a sharp divergence between the values and aspirations expressed in a society and the way the society actually worked. He would have been the last one to deduce social institutions from values, a line of thought

that is prominent today. Perhaps he went too far in the opposite direction. Nevertheless, puzzled surprise at the gap between ideals and reality,
as expressed in this professional review of a book on class in American
society, is foreign to Marx's thought:

> The facts, so far as they are known, about stratification in the United States
> are well introduced by Kahl's book. It remains to be found out why the dom-
> inant American ideologies tend to deny them. In spite of vast differences in
> economic privilege, the dominant creed holds this to be a classless society. In
> spite of the vast differences in power between the citizens and between their
> organizations, this is visualized as a democratic society in which everybody
> shares equal powers. . . . It is indeed baffling that statements about society
> in the major ideologies of the time and the land bear such little relation to the
> factual structure of society.[3]

The main conservative themes in serious nineteenth-century thinking
about society occur in de Tocqueville and Mosca, the main radical ones
in Marx. Are there, then, neutrals among the men mentioned above? If
we designate as neutral any theory that has no significant political implications, it becomes very difficult to pin this label on any of these writers as
long as we look at their work as a whole. Freud, as everyone knows,
fought a long uphill struggle against social taboos that prevented men
and women from acknowledging even the existence of the facts he discovered about humanity. In this respect his discoveries are revolutionary
and critical. On the other hand, his work to some extent justified the re-
straints laid by Western civilization on instinct and impulse. One could
call Freud a neutral only by saying that these two trends in his thinking
cancel each other out, a dubious and not very illuminating statement.
As a man who was extremely skeptical about the possibilities of a rational society—a skepticism he expressed very clearly in *Civilization and
Its Discontents*—we might best be justified by placing him in the conservative tradition. Where we place him is vastly less important than
realizing both the conservative and revolutionary implications of his
work.

Weber and Durkheim are the two that modern thinkers would be most
inclined to classify as neutrals, at least at first glance. There are certain
trends in the thought of these men that lead toward the superficially
neutral stance of modern social science, as well as some of its other traits
that strike me as very dubious. We shall come to these points shortly.
But there is good evidence against labeling them neutrals.

To be sure, Max Weber said some very pungent and worthwhile things
against using the academic lecture platform to inoculate students with
the teacher's personal philosophy. These remarks may reflect his fundamental decency and political courage. To my knowledge he never implied
either in word or deed that social science should withdraw from burning

political issues, though he did feel that there were limits to what science, strictly conceived, could contribute to their solution.[4] From time to time he was savagely critical of reactionary forces in German society,[5] and also of what he regarded as pseudo-democratic wishful thinking about modern industrial society.

Toward the close of a long essay on the possibilities of middle-class democracy in Russia, published shortly after the 1905 revolution in that country, Weber expressed very pessimistic and critical views that make interesting and disturbing reading a half century later.

> It is highly ridiculous to ascribe to advanced capitalism, as it is now being imported into Russia and as it exists in America—this "inevitable stage" of our economic growth—any real affinity for democracy or even with freedom (in *any* sense whatever of the word). Rather, the only real way to put the question is: How are any of these things possible at all in the long run under its rule? . . .
>
> We individualists and partisans of democratic institutions are against the stream of material events. He who wants to be the standard bearer of a "developmental tendency" should abandon these old-fashioned ideals as soon as possible. . . . It is in the large continental areas, of North America on the one hand and of Russia on the other, whose monotonous plains favor schematization, that the center of gravity . . . of Western culture is moving forward unceasingly, as it once did in late classical times. . . .
>
> "Correct" Social Democracy drills the masses in the mental goose-step and directs them toward a Paradise in this world instead of toward an otherworldly one (which in Puritanism certainly had respectable achievements to show in the interest of freedom in this world). In this way it makes a sort of vaccine that serves the interests of the existing social order.[6]

Similar ideas continue to find expression along the maverick fringe of social science today. But generally times have changed. Naturally Weber was no man to parade the pageant of a bleeding heart before the public. At the same time he had no fear of the sacred cows in his society. Can one really imagine today a president of the American Sociological Society as the author of a biting history of General Motors, or a penetrating attack on the political philosophy of the CIO?

Durkheim may come a little closer to deserving the title of neutral, though on balance he seems to me to belong with the critical conservatives. Yet at least two of his major works, *Suicide* and the *Division of Labor,* may legitimately be read as muted indictments of the modern world. The concept of anomie is part of a long tradition with overtones of romanticism that stresses the heartless mechanical nature of modern society. The same theme runs through the *Division of Labor.* His standpoint also, be it noted, remains historical. He uses the facts of suicide to illuminate modern society as a whole against a broad historical canvas, doing his best to connect forms of suicide with the stages and epochs of human history. The reason we might call Durkheim a conservative is that very little that society at any point requires of the individual can from his standpoint be a proper subject of rational criticism.

The last observation leads us toward the trends in the thought of these two men that culminate in some of the less fortunate assumptions of contemporary social science. There are virtues in these defects. In Durkheim and Weber the virtues perhaps still outweigh the defects.

One trait, particularly noticeable in Durkheim, is the positivist desire to base theory on facts and on facts alone. This strategy at times implies choosing smaller problems for the sake of firmer results, as Durkheim did in *Suicide*. Despite the loose edges of uncertainty that do remain, a modern reader is likely to feel real intellectual pleasure at watching Durkheim demolish one fuzzy hypothesis after another with an array of carefully chosen facts, to emerge with a theory of his own that fits the facts available to him. Here at last, one begins to feel, sociology is getting its feet firmly on the ground.

On further reading and reflection some of this sense of satisfaction may disappear. The positivist commitment begins to produce some odd results as early as Durkheim. Respect for the facts tends to become an inhibition on criticizing the facts, though Durkheim's historical perspective saves him from a complete acceptance of whatever exists.

His difficulties become apparent as he tries to develop an empirical method of making value judgments by taking over from medicine the distinction between the normal and the pathological. As he develops his case, he first concludes that whatever social facts are common are normal and that the unusual ones are the pathological ones. *"Nous appelerons normaux les faits qui présentent les formes les plus générales et nous donnerons aux autres le nom de morbides ou de pathologiques."* [7] This view would, of course, commit one to an acceptance of the status quo as "normal." A few pages further on he modifies this criterion very seriously, pointing out that social facts may be an adaptation to circumstances that are historically obsolete. Then he goes on to note that a social fact may be very widespread and still have no more than the appearance of normality.[8] As the historical perspective declines in later sociological thinking, so too does the capacity to analyze critically the existing social order. Sociology runs the risk of being left with only the first half of Durkheim's formula.

The decline of the historical perspective is already visible in the later works of Max Weber, particularly in *Wirtschaft und Gesellschaft,* the first part of which is available in English under the title of *The Theory of Social and Economic Organization*.[9] Here Weber was trying to conceptualize the enormous mass of historical material at his command. Though the classification remains illuminating where it brings out actual connections between real facts, as in the discussion of types of political systems and their relation to forms of economic life, a large part of the work is an arid desert of definitions. Here begins the tradition of abstract formalism in sociology. After Weber, Simmel carries it further, trying to abstract from social life the elementary and invariant forms, such as domination, subordination, and many others. The tradition would seem to have developed about as far as it could in the work of Leopold von Wiese.[10] After that, however, the tradition passed to the United States, where Talcott Parsons has elaborated it further. Now it constitutes the main body of sociological doctrine in this country. Since we have already discussed some of the main features of the formalist tradition in the preceding essay, there is no need to examine them further at this point.

Instead we are ready to attempt an answer to the earlier question: what is the main difference between the older strategy in social science and the prevailing one? When we set the dominant body of current thinking against important figures in the nineteenth century, the following differences emerge. First of all, the critical spirit has all but disappeared. Second, modern sociology, and perhaps to a lesser extent also modern political science, economics, and psychology, are ahistorical. Third, modern social science tends to be abstract and formal. In research, social science today displays considerable technical virtuosity. But this virtuosity has been gained at the expense of content. Modern sociology has less to say about society than it did fifty years ago.

The difference "jumps in your eyes," as the French say, if we compare the opening sentences of important statements on a significant problem, the nature of social classes, in a few of the authors mentioned: Marx, Weber, and Parsons. The contrast in what authors choose to put first in their discussions can scarcely be accidental. Anyone who knows the three authors reasonably well would agree, I think, that these three passages do not misrepresent the character of their thought.

Let us begin with the famous discussion of the class struggle as it opens in the *Communist Manifesto*:

> The history of all hitherto existing society is the history of class struggles. Freeman and slave, patrician and plebeian, lord and serf, guild-master and journeyman, in a word oppressor and oppressed, stood in constant opposition to one another, carried on uninterrupted, now hidden, now open fight, a fight that each time ended either in a revolutionary reconstitution of society at large, or in the common ruin of the contending classes.[11]

This sweeping generalization can be read mainly as a factual assertion, though an evaluative element enters in through the use of the words "oppressor" and "oppressed." But to Marx, at any rate, the facts would, as we have seen, make no sense without this evaluative element. He certainly was willing here and on other occasions to talk about the "facts" of oppression, struggle among social classes, and historical change. Indeed, Marx puts them first of all in this discussion.

They have not disappeared in Weber though he begins more formally with a definition:

> The term "class status" will be applied to the typical probability that a given state of (a) provision with goods, (b) external conditions of life, and (c) subjective satisfaction or frustration will be possessed by an individual or a group. These probabilities define class status in so far as they are dependent on the kind and extent of control or lack of it which the individual has over goods or services and existing possibilities of their exploitation for the attainment of income or receipts within a given economic order.[12]

The unequal character of class still appears in Weber's first sentence, which is obviously saying something about concrete societies. On the other hand, it is static and ahistorical in comparison with Marx. Compare Talcott Parsons:

> It has come to be widely recognized in the sociological field that social stratification is a generalized aspect of the structure of all social systems, and that the system of stratification is intimately linked to the level and type of integration of the system as a system.
> The major point of reference both for the judgment of the generality of the importance of stratification, and for its analysis as a phenonenon, is to be found in the nature of the frame of reference in terms of which we analyze social action.[13]

From these sentences the process of abstraction, to be discussed in the next section, has eliminated all reference to political struggles, oppression, and historical change.

They have retreated into the background of most academic thinking about society.

II

Let us now examine the ideal that social science sets up for itself. What do its leading practitioners think it ought to be? What are the characteristics of the intellectual structure they are trying to create? Here again I shall speak mainly of sociology, with an occasional glance at other social sciences.

As physical science moved away from the mechanical determinism of the nineteenth century, social science tended to abandon the corresponding grand syntheses of historical determinism to the point where the latter are now generally in very bad repute. In their place there has grown up a body of deductive theory, widely referred to as structural-functionalism. The key idea in this body of theory, the reader may recall, is the view that for every society there exists a certain limited number of necessary activities or "functions," such as obtaining food, training the next generation, etc., and an equally limited number of "structures," or ways in which society can be organized to perform these functions. Essentially, structural-functional theory searches for the basic elements of human society, abstracted from time and place, together with rules for combining these elements. It gives the impression of looking for something in human society to correspond to the periodic table of elements in chemistry.[14]

The ultimate objective in this line of thinking is the establishment of abstract quasi-mathematical formulae about human society from which it should be possible to derive the particulars of human behavior in any specified situation. Or to put the point in another fashion, the proponents of this view hope to subsume more and more individual facts that now appear as isolated observations about society in a single logically coherent structure. This viewpoint corresponds very closely with the natural science ideal of being able to reduce all phenomena to a series of related propositions.[15] The fundamental statements in this structure are expected to be universal propositions or scientific law. Let us see to what extent social science has succeeded in this goal of imitating natural science.

Natural scientists seek in the main two kinds of universal propositions. One takes the form of a static correlation, asserting that when A occurs B also occurs, as when we say that water freezes at 32 degrees Fahrenheit. Ordinarily natural scientists try to go beyond a mere static correlation to explain why the relationship holds. The other kind of proposition takes the form of a mathematical function,[16] asserting that X varies as Y does, as in the relation between pressure and volume in a gas. Again some kind of an explanation is given. While scientific explanations are tied together as firmly as possible, ultimately they take the form of descriptive propositions.

When we compare this model with the actual performance of social science, the contrast is striking. As even those most enthusiastically committed to the model will admit in candid moments,[17] social science, after some two hundred years, has not yet discovered any universal propositions comparable in scope or intellectual significance to those in the natural sciences. The situation does vary, of course, from one discipline to another. Sociology, as one of my colleagues is fond of remarking, constitutes from this standpoint the science with the hollow frontier, since it lacks any core of established theory, or any framework of general propositions strong enough to convince a substantial part of the profession.[18] Psychology is perhaps somewhat better off. Pavlov and those who have followed in his footsteps have established through laboratory methods a fairly large body of propositions. However, their significance in explaining more than a tiny segment of human behavior remains very doubtful. Though the explanatory power of Freudian theory is much greater—perhaps even too great—its scientific status is less secure. Classical economics managed to erect at one time a comprehensive and elegant theory to organize its subject matter in a scientific manner. Somehow the facts have changed since the formulation of the theory. It may be significant that one of the leading figures in the tradition of classical economics, Professor Frank H. Knight, is also one of the most sharp-tongued opponents of a literal-minded transfer of natural science methods into the study of human affairs.[19] Whatever the variety among the different disciplines, it is safe to assert that the generalizations of social science nowhere approach the range and cogency of those in physics or chemistry.

The fact that we do not yet have any laws in social science comparable to those in the natural sciences does not by itself prove that such laws will never be discovered. Nevertheless it justifies raising once more the question whether social science is on the right track in making the search for such laws its chief *raison d'être*. The differences between natural science and social science may concern more than the relative crudity of social science. The logical structure of the kinds of knowledge we seek in social science may not be identical with that in the advanced natural sciences. It may be profitable to consider this possibility through examining the relationship between abstraction and additions to knowledge.

Natural science and social science both make use of abstraction from the raw data of experience in order to frame concepts and theories. Nevertheless, the procedures of abstraction vary from one field of knowledge to another in accord with the nature of the materials studied and the purpose of the inquiry. In many fields, perhaps all of them, there is a certain tension between the desire to do justice to all the facts and the need to frame a logically coherent and esthetically satisfying theory. There is, in other words, a tension, perhaps an irreducible one, between particulars and universals.

Abstraction is not an end in itself. Indeed, the end or purpose for which the scientist makes abstractions and seeks propositions lies, to some extent, outside the realm of empirical science. Even strict positivists now recognize this point. Philipp Frank has recently asserted that the validation of scientific theories "cannot be separated neatly from the values which the scientist accepts." [20] Therefore any system of abstraction that omits facts which the investigator wants to understand is automatically inadequate. There are then strong grounds for suspecting that we have so few universal propositions in the social sciences because such propositions frequently do not give us the kind of knowledge we really seek.

In human affairs the mere fact of uniformity or regularity, expressible in the form of a scientific law, may often be quite trivial. To know that Americans drive on the right hand side of the street is to know something that permits predictions about American behavior and meets all the formal requirements of a generalizing science. Such knowledge does not, however, meet the criterion of significance. The same comment applies to many generalizations that social scientists seek with a technical apparatus and logical rigor that contrasts ludicrously with the results. Here is a recent example. From a study of "Male Sex Aggression on a University Campus" we learn that:

> Of the 291 responding girls 55.7 per cent reported themselves offended at least once during the academic year at some level of erotic intimacy. The experiences of being offended were not altogether associated with trivial situations as shown by the fact that 20.9 per cent were offended by forceful attempts at intercourse and 6.2 per cent by "aggressively forceful attempts at sex intercourse in the course of which menacing threats or coercive infliction of physical pain were employed." . . . A 3×3 table yielding a Chi square significant at the .05 level suggests that episodes of lesser offensiveness are concentrated in the fall and more offensive episodes in the spring.[21]

The professional journals are full of similar articles where careful methodology is used on trivial problems. Unfortunately most of them are not as amusing as this one. If the demonstration of uniformities like these were all that social science had to offer, it would constitute no more than an enormous diversion from more important problems.

Uniformities in social behavior become significant for us only when they concern important problems, such as freedom and compulsion. What is important is not a matter of subjective whim, but is the consequence of a specific historical situation. The important regularities in human behavior, as well as some of the trivial ones, are found within the context of historical change. For example, one can observe recurring patterns in the behavior of a slave-holder and still other patterns in those of a feudal lord. There may even be some common features in all the major historical forms of domination. To find them would be a worthwhile task, and in an earlier essay I have suggested possible common features in the "natural history" of systems of domination. But we certainly cannot stop there, even if we arrive at such a point. Accurate knowledge requires that we understand each social type, slave-holder, feudal lord, capitalist entrepreneur, and socialist bureaucrat, within its proper historical context, that is, in relation to previous forms and possible subsequent ones.

Above all we must not make the mistake of thinking that some universal necessity inheres in social relationships that are limited to a particular historical epoch, such as capitalism or, for that matter, socialism. To abstract from all historical situations in the hope of discovering some panhuman or universal kind of social necessity does not seem to me a very promising procedure. Can we really make any worthwhile generalizations that apply equally well to the Stone Age and to twentieth-century America?[22] Perhaps one cannot answer this question with a flat negative in advance, though I remain most skeptical. One certainly has the right to object vehemently to any science that eliminates from its vision all change that has taken place between the Stone Age and the twentieth century merely for the sake of formulating universal propositions like those in the natural sciences.

Let us look more closely at some of the procedures modern social science theorists use when they try to arrive at universal propositions. As noted earlier, these scholars often tend to abstract from the reality of historical trends in order to concentrate on resemblances and differences in the hope of formulating scientific laws. For them, history, if it is used at all, becomes merely a storehouse of samples. Using historical data, one can supposedly discover the social correlates of democracy, tyranny, class struggle or class peace,[23] and the like. The existing body of theory should, from this standpoint, indicate the likelihood or unlikelihood of finding a particular combination of traits. Historical and social facts are then drawn upon as if they were colored balls from an urn, and the results subjected to tests for statistical significance in order to disprove the hypothesis or derive additional support for it.

The trouble with this procedure is that it starts with the assumption that the facts of history are separate and discrete units. This assumption is basic to statistical analysis. "The fundamental notion in statistical theory," says an advanced theoretical text, "is that of the group or aggregate, a concept for which statisticians use a special word—population. This term will be generally employed to denote any collection of objects under consideration, whether animate or inanimate. The notion common to all these things is that of aggregation."[24] The modern social scientist searches for invariant laws that govern the relationship among these atomized observations reflected in statistics. Such laws are implicitly or explicitly thought to apply to masses of single facts of equal importance, which are expected to display at least the statistical regularity that molecules do in a gas under specified conditions.

It is in this conception, I think, that the modern social scientist goes astray. Though I too would reject any thorough historical determinism, I do not believe that the significant facts of history are mere mechanical aggregates. Instead, they are connected with one another over time.

The point may be clearer if we refer to a concrete problem. Franz Neumann has pointed out how dictatorship has at certain times in history served to prepare the ground for democracy by breaking the resistance of privileged social classes.[25] This is a crucial point that helps us to understand dictatorship, class struggles, and democracy in a context of continuing historical growth. Now, such a point would necessarily be hidden from an investigator who proceeded by some widely used procedures in deductive social science. Dictatorship and democracy would be separated into airtight compartments with carefully worked out definitions of each. Then other facts would be sorted into neat piles labeled "dictatorship" and "democracy." The whole process by which one social structure passes into the other would become invisible. Such a procedure might, to be sure, uncover some important and unsuspected connections. One cannot reject it as totally useless. But the most significant problem would remain hidden.

I doubt very much that the logic of sampling is at all appropriate to historical problems of the type just mentioned, where the investigator is studying the change from one type of social structure to another. In sampling techniques, as shown by the familiar image of drawing balls from an urn, the researcher examines the numerical distribution of traits in the sample to make inferences about the universe from which they are drawn. His main problem is whether or not the sample is representative of the whole. The historian too looks at some of the facts in order to make inferences about the rest of the facts. He also, in other words, has to make a connection between the parts and the whole. But the historian's connection has a different form. The notion that he works with frequently is that of stages of historical development. Now, any given stage of historical development is to some extent the product of a preceding stage and the source of subsequent stages. Even the most antideterminist historian uses such a notion. This kind of concentration is missing, as I see it, in the logic of sampling. In an atomized universe the numerical character of the sample does not "cause" the universe to have a corresponding numerical character, nor does it by itself affect the character of subsequent samples drawn from the same universe.

From a strictly logical standpoint one could avoid the preceding difficulties by including the concept of time as a specific variable, and working with some form of mathematical function. Historical writings often do have the logical form of a mathematical function, as when they assert that political changes have accompanied economic advance or economic decline. Perhaps even some of the Hegelian insights into revolutionary upheavals as the final result of slow cumulative structural change can be expressed in the form of discontinuous functions. Mathematics does not limit itself to the study of quantity, and cannot be excluded from any field of knowledge merely because the latter seeks knowledge that goes beyond quantitative relationships.[26]

Whether one can leap from such observations to the claim that mathematics can weave a web around *any* body of facts is a question I am not competent to answer. This claim does seem to imply potential omniscience in the manner of a Laplace, and therefore strict determinism, a position from which natural science has been retreating rather rapidly for some years. This question does not seem to be a very fruitful one to ask just now. We can easily afford to wait until a mathematical genius encompasses all history with his mathematical net, and decide then if it improves our understanding. In the meantime there is work to be done.

The real question then concerns the gains and losses involved in mathematical abstraction. Here again we cannot give a firm answer because we cannot know what discoveries in mathematics may come along that might some day constitute a powerful analytical tool. But we do know in a general way that we do not want our gains in logical rigor and ease of manipulation to be at the expense of too much historical content.

Nor can mathematical sophistication do much to help us out where our data are inadequate for other reasons. There is no use drawing intriguing curves and computing intricate functions on the basis of badly collected statistics. Such devices merely conceal the real problem. Good judgment on all these questions requires training on problems that lie outside mathematics as such. We can use the mathematical notion of function, but it will not do everything for us. Current overuse and misuse of statistics and abstract mathematical models in social science stem in my opinion partly from the failure to present fledgling students with other adequate criteria for distinguishing important truth from accurate triviality. For this reason it is not a problem that can be solved merely through the improvement of mathematical techniques.

Certain virtues in the mathematical way of thinking deserve explicit recognition here. The use of mathematics compels the investigator to state his propositions in an unambiguous manner that automatically permits a tight chain of deductions leading to a firm result. If the original premises are correct, and the chain of deductions made without error, the truth of the conclusion is guaranteed. The difficulty, on the other hand, is that at present the act of putting statements about society in the form of mathematical premises requires such simplification that the essential elements in the facts are likely to be lost or seriously distorted. The lack of ambiguity in the original propositions may therefore be spurious. The trouble here may lie as much in mathematics as in social science proper. So far, at any rate, the results have not been striking. As one of the most enthusiastic advocates of mathematical methods in the social sciences has observed recently, "Even the most ardent optimist would not claim that mathematics has yet led to important discoveries in the behavioral sciences." [27]

The decline of the historical perspective and the rise of a formalist deductive tradition in search of laws has been accompanied by an increasing static bias in much contemporary social science. For this there are several reasons. The search for categories that apply without reference to time or place easily introduces a static bias unless we are extremely careful to notice the historical limits of our generalizations. The very notion of a scientific law implies a relationship that holds whenever and wherever it occurs. Naturally if one could really demonstrate that any given law really held for human affairs, it would be nonsense to assert that formulating such a law and writing it down introduced a static bias into thinking about society. What often happens, however, is something else. The investigator discovers, or thinks he has discovered, a relationship that actually holds for a limited period of history, and extends it unjustifiably into the future. Most scholars are too cautious to make flat statements like this in print, and a clear example from recent writings does not come to mind readily. The bias is in the air more than in print. Not long ago social scientists used to say to one another in informal conversations that Soviet experience "proved" the need for inequalities of income, prestige, and authority in any form of industrial society.[28] Actually Soviet experience merely tends to demonstrate the necessity for such inequalities at a particular stage of industrial and technological growth. The Stalinist era also shows that totalitarian methods are effective for catching up rapidly with advanced industrial countries. Future technological progress, such as more advanced automation, may make possible very gross changes in the structure of authority, prestige, and inequality. If we looked at this problem with nothing but dubious laws in our heads about the "functional imperatives of industrial society," we could easily go astray. Though the notion of functional imperative has its uses and can lead to valuable insights, we must be careful to realize its limitations.

Closely related to the preceding difficulties are those derived from the importation of equilibrium theory into social science, which may also produce a static bias. In equilibrium theory the key assumption is that any social system tends toward a state of rest in which the conflicts and strains among its component parts are reduced to a minimum. Most people are aware that in real life this movement toward a state of rest may not actually take place. Some try to get around the difficulty by asserting that the equilibrium assumption is not one about empirical facts, but a purely theoretical assumption that serves to order the factual material into a consistent whole.[29] No one would object if this were the case, but it is difficult to see how the equilibrium viewpoint can account for certain fairly well established facts. For example, in the judgment of some historians, the attempts made by later Roman emperors to strengthen the empire contributed to the growth of feudalism, or, in other words, to the replacement of one social system by a quite different one. In technical language, meeting the "functional imperatives" of the system had destroyed one social system and led to its replacement by another. Again, in modern times the New Deal may be plausibly regarded as an attempt to shore up American capitalism. But the effort to do this led in turn to marked modifications of American society. Perhaps structural-functional theory could somehow account for these changes by saying that these efforts to restore equilibrium led to unanticipated and dysfunctional consequences. We may leave aside the question of what gain to real knowledge such statements bring. To my mind they amount to throwing the equilibrium assumption overboard by saying that tendencies toward equilibrium are unexpectedly producing change.

The Hegelian dialectic with its conception of developing contradictions that lead to intermittent abrupt changes provides, one may argue, a better heuristic guide to the explanation of many important processes of historical growth. In any case it would appear that the decision whether equilibrium theory applies or not is basically an empirical one, to be decided after careful study of the facts.

We come then to the conclusion that a static bias and a tendency toward triviality pervades much contemporary social science quite largely, though not entirely, because of the model that it sets for itself in copying the successful procedures of the natural sciences. Other social factors play a part in this. They may even be the more important ones, though I have purposely left them aside to concentrate on the smaller problem of the way in which social science may limit itself through its own ideals. In closing this part of the discussion it may be worthwhile to mention briefly some of the social factors which favor the present direction of social science.

One factor may be that the United States, where the kind of social science just discussed flourishes best of all, is at the present juncture a prosperous country at a high point in its power. American society has some of the qualities of an *ancien régime,* though it is worthwhile remembering that the Soviet Union has a good many of these too. The critical spirit may not flourish just now because our social and economic problems are mild relative to those of other times and other places. Furthermore, the historical point of view is likely to remind us of the transitory nature of social institutions, generally an uncomfortable thought in an *ancien régime.*

At a more detailed level of analysis one may note that many modern social science research projects are very expensive affairs. They require the collaboration of a large number of persons with a variety of skills and training. Often their cost exceeds several hundred thousand dollars. It may be unfair to remark that the results are not always in proportion to the costs. But it is true that the present situation in social science is the exact reverse of what prevailed during the great theoretical discoveries in physics in the nineteenth and early twentieth centuries. Revolutionary advances were made with limited funds and, by modern standards, crude laboratory equipment. Today, in social science at any rate, the effect of large grants is to give to those in control of the allocation of research funds a highly strategic position for determining which problems will be investigated and which ones will not. It is also true, of course, that older systems of economic support for intellectuals, such as patronage and direct dependence on the market, exercised some influence over the ideas developed by professional intellectuals. The varying impact of all these factors is certainly not understood in any detail. But it is clear that in older times patronage and the market did not succeed in shutting off thought critical of the existing social order. Under the present situation, the need to be a cooperative member of a research team may do more to stultify original and critical thinking than direct economic pressure. At the same time, it is difficult to conceive of the foundation director who will readily allocate several hundred thousand dollars for a research project that is likely to come up with conclusions that reflect very seriously on important interest groups in the United States. The result is that creative thinking has to take place, if it can take place at all, mostly in the interstices between Big Theory and Big Research.

III

The importance of historical relationships has come up repeatedly in the discussion so far. It is to the historian, therefore, that we may turn in search for a different approach to the problems of human society. The historian's approach too has its severe limitations. But first let us look at the way he pursues his craft.

The most fruitful historical research generally begins with an awareness of some problem that is felt to be significant. This importance may stem either from some major contemporary issue, a starting point that in my view arouses unnecessarily the suspicions of many professional historians, or some unresolved problem in explaining the sequence of human institutions. In the most successful cases the collection and interpretation of the facts is a one-man operation. Though historians emphasize, I believe correctly, the individual nature of creative thought, it would be unfair to overlook the services that are provided for them by large-scale bureaucratic organizations. I have yet to hear the most individualist scholar object to the advantages offered by a large and well-run library.

Though some famous historians have been men who have pursued an *idée fixe,* this type of work sooner or later runs into some of the disadvantages of overemphasis on logical deduction discussed in the preceding section. The best results emerge from the confrontation of the evidence with a wide variety of ideas, often contradictory ones, acquired in the course of broad reading and some experience of men and affairs. Sometimes the most important discoveries may occur as a consequence of the temporary block produced by an inconvenient fact which forces the investigator to abandon previously accepted explanations. Darwin too says somewhere that one can always learn most from facts that are exceptions to our theories.

The preceding methods the historian shares more or less with other students of society. There remains a very important difference between the way historians and modern quantitative social scientists treat their facts.

The quantitative social scientist, as we have seen, abstracts from his materials only those features that can readily be arranged in a numerical order. After running these features through a statistical sieve, he draws conclusions from the size of the different piles before him. The historian, on the other hand, usually examines each piece of potentially useful data carefully, turning it over and over in his hands in its raw state, as it were, to see what light it may shed on his problem. In this way the historian brings to bear on each new piece of information all the knowledge that he has acquired up to that point. The historian's knowledge grows while he is examining the individual facts. That of the quantitative social scientist comes only after a large number of facts have been sorted.

The famous Swiss historian Jacob Burckhardt describes the historian's approach succinctly in the introduction to his magnificent *History of Greek Culture*. Though the procedure lacks method in the superficial and mechanical sense of the word, the logical justification rests on the way it produces cumulative insight and knowledge. I quote directly from Burckhardt's German, since it has a personal flavor impossible to reproduce in translation:

> Woher weiss [der Forscher] was konstant und charakteristisch, was eine Kraft gewesen ist und was nicht? Erst eine lange und vielseitige Lektüre kann es ihm kund tun, *einstweilen* wird er lange Zeit manches übersehen, was von durchgehender Wichtigkeit war, und einzelnes wieder für bedeutend und charakteristisch halten, was nur zufällig war. Bei der Lektüre ferner wird ihm, je nach Zeit und Stimmung, Frische und Ermüdung, und besonders je nach dem Reifepunkt, auf welchem sich seine Forschung gerade befindet, alles, was ihm gerade in die Hände fällt, unbedeutend und inhaltlos oder bezeichnend und interessant in jedem Worte erscheinen. Dies gleicht sich nur bei fortgesetztem Lesen in den verschiedenen Gattungen und Gegenden der griechischen Literatur aus; gerade mit heftiger Anstrengung ist hier das Resultat am wenigsten zu erzwingen: ein leises Aufhorchen bei gleichmässigem Fleiss führt weiter. . . .
>   Wir sind "unwissenschaftlich" und haben gar keine Methode, wenigstens nicht die der andern.[30]

The chief advantages of the historian's procedure are its flexibility and cumulative insight. Since the historian is also primarily interested in change, his image of social reality stresses growth, transformation, and decay. On these counts we may conclude that the historian is superior to the modern social scientist.

Nevertheless, when the historian faces the problem of making his knowledge capable of explaining more than particular historical facts, he often fails miserably. He is generally unwilling or unable to transfer the knowledge gained from understanding one set of social relationships, say the history of modern Germany, to another set, say modern France. The professional equipment and predilections of the historian make him unfit for such a task. (We shall try in a moment to answer the question whether this is a reasonable task to impose on a historian or, for that matter, on anybody.) When the historian is pressed to make his information useful in a practical way, such as by presenting an estimate of future trends in some part of the world with which he is familiar, he frequently responds in one of the following ways. First of all, he may simply refuse, saying rather smugly, "History must not be confused with prophecy." If pressed still further, he may make a guess on the basis of a single crude parallel, predicting, for example, the future of Russia on the basis of events following the French Revolution. Most frequently of all he will retreat from such pressures into literary snobbishness and pseudo-cultivation. This takes the form of airy generalizations about the way history provides "wisdom" or "real understanding." Phrases to this effect often occur toward the end of historians' reviews of other historians' books in media for the general public, like *The New York Times.* Anyone who wants to know how this wisdom can be effectively used, amplified, and corrected will find that his questions usually elicit no more than irritation.

Thus the historian, as a rule, is unwilling to proceed beyond intuitive hints to a form of knowledge that approaches science in becoming a set of explicit propositions that can be tested and corrected. What is the reason for this situation? Social scientists today generally make the following diagnosis of their own difficulties, and include the historian merely as an extreme case. The principal difficulty, they assert, in obtaining transferable knowledge or valid generalization lies in the inadequacy of our contemporary conceptual schemes. Here, therefore, is the front on which the main attack should be directed. Natural science, according to this view, had the same difficulty in its early stages. Scientists overcame it by learning new ways of thinking about their subject matter.[31]

The social scientists are mistaken, I believe, in making the difficulty only a subjective one of getting the right ideas into our heads. Actually the problem is a rather subtle one involving both the character of the materials we study and the things we want to learn about them. If knowledge in any field of inquiry is to be transferable, the material itself must display certain uniformities and regularities. We cannot force this regularity on the material through sheer intellectual agility. These uniformities may not only be absent; they may also be, in terms of important human values, the less significant aspects of the subject matter we study. Where such uniformities are either absent or constitute for us the less significant aspects of the material, we gain nothing by trying to force the subject matter into a framework of scientific generalizations.

The latter situation prevails rather widely in the study of human society. As H. Rickert, the main proponent of this thesis, points out, we are not interested in the qualities Goethe shared with other human beings, such as the fact that he had two eyes, two arms, and two legs. Goethe is not a lump of coal, whose only interest to us is the qualities it shares with other lumps of coal and whose properties can be expressed in the form of scientific generalizations. What we want to know and understand about Goethe is his unique contribution to human civilization. To some extent we can acquire this understanding only by uncovering a unique pattern of connections between unique events.[32] The usual argument against Rickert's thesis holds that we only understand the unique to the extent that we can analyze it into elements that are not unique. Certainly this is one way in which the advance of knowledge proceeds. But it is not, to my mind, the only way. We can readily perceive the connection between a series of historical events, even though what is important to us in these events cannot be placed in a category with other events. This argument holds even for studying large-scale historical units, encompassing more than one society, such as royal absolutism, parliamentary democracy, totalitarianism.

Essentially Rickert's argument comes down to saying that it is unfair to ask the historian for knowledge that is generalizable, while it is nevertheless possible for the historian to give us, in principle at least, rigorous and unambiguous factual answers to important questions. Some significant questions do not require and indeed do not permit answers in the form of a scientific generalization.

Though this is not the whole story, it is worthwhile pursuing this line of thought further and examining its consequences. Two antithetical positions can emerge and have emerged from this radical historicism. One is a nihilistic and self-defeating pedantry that wishes to study history for its own sake. Its one redeeming virtue is that it seeks to eliminate from our view of the past the distortion that arises from an excessive effort to perceive our own difficulties in earlier stages of civilization, such as the mechanical projection of contemporary problems onto the waning Roman Empire. Though I do not think that the sole function of scholarship is utilitarian, yet why should we put our best energies into studying the past, or for that matter the present, if the results cannot serve somehow as a guide amid our own perplexities and anxieties?

The other position is an exaggerated form of voluntaristic optimism, which denies that the past exerts any determining force on the present. Karl Popper, the philosopher, seems to me to represent an extreme version of this doctrine. If history is not subject to any laws of development, the implication follows that man is free to control his own destiny. To my way of thinking this optimism too is demonstrably shallow. Throughout human history nearly all human beings have been confronted with the overwhelming weight of a society they as individuals did nothing to create. They have lived out their lives within a very narrow range of alternatives. Only a few gifted persons have had the opportunity and the ability to break through the barriers of their time and place.

The historical approach to human affairs, it appears, finally runs out into absurdities and trivialities as it is pushed without reflection toward its logical conclusion. So too, I have tried to argue, does social science in the image of mathematics and natural science. At this point we seeem to have reached a dead end. If one rejects both the major positions discussed in this paper, what is left? Now it is one of the conventions of current discussion that a writer must end his paper with constructive and positive suggestions. It is tempting to break with this convention and write: *Finis*.

IV

However, man's struggle to understand himself and his world continues, and has no small successes to its credit. In what follows I can do no more than outline in a sketchy manner what seems to me a promising strategy for the future.

First of all, there is no blinking the fact that in the study of human affairs we are often confronted with the need to comprehend the unique. At the same time there is no reason to be especially agitated about this situation. In many other areas of life men orient themselves to reality by learning its unique features. The navigator, for instance, depends on charts that show the location of individual reefs and shoals. The same virtue inheres in first-rate descriptions of current social institutions, especially where they are sufficiently grounded in history to permit rough estimates of the dynamics of the situation. Here we simply have to reconcile ourselves to the probability that much research will never be cumulative in the sense that research is cumulative in the physical sciences. Social facts do not display the same degree of repetitive uniformity as do those of inorganic nature. To concentrate on what repetitive uniformities there are in social facts is to lose sight of their most important characteristic, growth and change over time.

As we look more closely at chains of historical causation and the way they are treated by reflective historians, we may realize that there is still another way of resolving, at least partially, the tension between the particular and the general. Those who have come either directly or indirectly under the influence of Hegel see the general as manifested *in* the particular or the unique. Thus, Marx saw the general features of mid-nineteenth-century capitalism, as it had developed out of earlier social forms, in the single case of nineteenth-century England. England was at that time the most advanced form of a capitalist economy. On the basis of an understanding of the inherent dynamic characteristics of competitive capitalism, he tried to predict the form it might take in the future. He made mistakes, as any man can do with any method. This does not prove that the method itself is unsound any more than mistakes in arithmetic count against the science of mathematics. Many other historians perceive, or think they perceive, the general culmination of an historical trend in a particular event. Thus a historian studying the decline of the Roman Republic may easily say in effect, "By this time the situation had developed to the point where Caesar took the decisive step and crossed the Rubicon."

In using this procedure the historian tries to perceive the general in the atypical or even the unique, resolving in this fashion the tension be-

tween universals and particulars. Perhaps this way of putting the point
gives it too much of a deductive and scholastic air. What actually happens, at least in many cases, is that a unique fact or event enables the
historian to choose between two or more interpretations that have been
building up in his mind on the basis of materials he has been examining up to then. It is clear that this procedure is not limited to the historian's craft or the analysis of past events. We use it on those that are
happening currently. For example, whenever a significant new piece of
information becomes available about the Soviet Union some hypotheses
are proved wrong and others proved correct. To pursue this example
further, when a major figure is dropped from the Soviet leadership, some
hypotheses about the nature of significant political processes in that
country (not merely intrigues at the top) can often be confirmed or dis-
proved. As the Marxist philosopher Karl Korsch pointed out some twenty
years ago, this procedure is similar to that of the crucial experiment in
natural science.[33]

There are important differences, however. In the natural sciences, researchers are able to repeat their experiments, an advantage that social
science lacks for its most important problems. Furthermore, within limits,
the actions people take in important historical crises can alter the nature
of the situation. Before General Zhukov was removed from the Party
Presidium in 1957, the hypothesis that the army was gaining power might
have been just as correct as the hypothesis that the Party had control of
the situation. (Actually, of course, we don't know.) His removal resolved
the ambiguity, at least for the time being. Thus a particular historical
event can do more than confirm or disprove a hypothesis. It can change
the situation so that one hypothesis or another *becomes* correct. There
would seem to be an irreducible element of indeterminancy here, roughly
similar to that in modern physics.

Nevertheless it is very difficult to believe seriously that the sequence of
historical events is purely random, or that anything can happen at any
time. The range of possible variation would seem to be markedly reduced
when we consider the sequence of major institutional structures, such as
the transition from the Roman Republic to the Empire. There is in human affairs an area of freedom, but it is limited. What the limits are at
any one point of time, including the present, has to be determined in
large measure through empirical investigation. Social scientists sometimes
feel themselves to be second-class citizens in the scientific community because they cannot make as firm predictions as their colleagues. There is
no need for this if they define their task as making accurate assessments
of the limits and possibilities of effective human behavior. Such assessments make sense of course only in terms of some prior set of values.
There is no reason for the social scientist to cut himself off from reasoned
discourse on such questions when in fact he ought to have some of the
most important things to say.

It is worthwhile drawing attention to further characteristics of this procedure and the way it differs from those used rather widely in the social sciences today. Seeing the general in the historically unique is a method of abstraction different from that of omitting more and more of the characteristics of what we are studying until the residue is something approaching pure form without content. The latter procedure is the one that the formalist tradition now follows in sociology. Furthermore, this way of seeking generality through history also differs from trying to understand a society by observing the social practices that are most common in it and that thereby supposedly "typify" the society. Instead, the historical approach teaches us to try to "see the grass growing beneath the ground" or to find in atypical practices and beliefs the seeds of possible future developments. To be sure one often has to discover, often by statistical counting, what is typical before one knows what is atypical. But to do this is merely the first step in the analysis.

Social science, we may conclude, is therefore not precluded from finding principles of change that apply to more than a single series of events. It is here I believe that the great theoretical achievements of the future will some day come. They will, no doubt, come slowly and develop out of existing traditions, from Hegel to the evolutionary doctrines of the late nineteenth century. Some contributions from the formalist school and structural analysis may also find their proper place in a larger synthesis. Let us see if we can discern, even if very dimly, what some of these ideas might be.

When we say that something changes, we usually mean that there is also some constant feature, which enables us to see that we still have before us the original object. What constant element can we legitimately point to in the study of human society? The concept of social evolution, though under a cloud today, provides an answer to this question. Social evolution is a process that remains essentially the same while continually producing new results.

When the concept of social evolution came to the fore in nineteenth-century sociology, mainly through the influence of Herbert Spencer, it became entangled with a number of other notions that served to discredit it. These notions do not, however, constitute essential elements in the concept and can be discarded without damage to the valid core.

One of these entanglements was the notion of unilinear development. Sooner or later, according to this view, all societies pass through the same stages of social development.[34] Clearly this theory will not stand up and has been effectively disposed of by Boas and others. It is more accurate to think of evolution as a series of related processes leading to very different consequences.

Even though no society passes through *all* the stages, the concept of stages in social evolution is still a valuable one. It can be applied to specific aspects of society and culture, such as economic structure and technology. From this standpoint one could construct a chronological series of major types of economic institutions from primitive hunting down to the large-scale modern bureaucratic firm.

Certain societies, it would then appear, have been the major vehicles or concrete manifestations of each stage. Furthermore, as Hegel and Marx recognized in their different ways, each society that constituted a specific stage of social development carried the process of growth in a particular direction about as far as it could. Then the society fell victim to limitations produced by its own success, as the level of adjustment, crystallized into social institutions, prevented further advance. Human societies often come to resemble middle-aged tennis players who continue to rely on a second-rate serve learned long ago. After the process of growth has ceased, owing to vested interests and other causes in one society, another previously backward society may carry it forward again.

I am not altogether convinced by the Marxist argument that changes in the way men produce and exchange material goods constitute the main propelling force in this process of change. New ideas may also play an equally important role. Perhaps the two are inseparable. Was not the steam engine originally an idea? This point I do not propose to discuss further. There is nevertheless a strong tendency, which Marx recognized, for the various institutions and beliefs in any society to hang together in at least a roughly coherent fashion. Modern structural-functional theory has caught sight of the same fact and elaborated it, while attempting to rip it out of the evolutionary and historical context. Along with this tendency for social institutions to adjust to one another, at a particular stage of social development—what Sumner called the strain toward consistency —we must recognize the continual disruption that occurs in particular societies through the skipping of historical stages. The modern Orient, where the most advanced technology jostles ancient social institutions, such as caste, constitutes a familiar example of stage-skipping.

Another cardinal point in nineteenth-century evolutionary doctrine concerns survivals. Here we enter territory where it is more difficult to separate the wheat from the chaff. At first, anthropologists thought they saw societies which they called primitive "living fossils" of early stages of social history. These "living fossils" they then tried to arrange in an evolutionary series. This attempt largely failed. Anthropologists soon realized that their "primitives" or "living fossils" were actually our contemporaries and had behind them just as long a history as we do ourselves. Furthermore, in some respects, especially kinship, these societies were extremely complex, while modern society had become very simple. For these reasons anthropologists rejected the notion that these societies could serve as evidence about our social ancestry and shied away from the concept of social evolution. Such societies were simply to be regarded as different and equally valid forms of civilization, to be judged in their own terms. The word primitive disappeared from the anthropologists' vocabulary, not only on account of its evolutionary connotations but also because of its derogatory overtones. Even the term nonliterate replaced preliterate for similar reasons.

This relativist attitude, now on the wane, performed useful services in combatting some of the cruder ethnocentric prejudices in Western scholarship. Furthermore, the attempt to reconstruct an evolutionary series for nonliterate societies undoubtedly contained many dubious propositions. Nevertheless, there are grounds for holding that this wholesale rejection was mistaken. If it is true that any society sooner or later falls victim to the limitations of its own success, cases of arrested development should be the rule rather than the exception. In areas of the world remote from the main centers of cultural innovation, societies might remain at roughly the same stage of advance for centuries. Nor does the presence of elaborate and complex kinship systems in many nonliterate societies contradict the principles of social evolution. Rather we should expect to see that in some parts of the world certain forms of social organization had been tried out, elaborated as far as possible, and then abandoned in the course of subsequent development. It is perfectly possible for kinship to reach a high degree of complexity while technology and economic and political institutions remain rudimentary. In biological evolution, too, the elaboration of one organ, while the rest of the organism remains simple, occurs very often. In man it is only the brain that is highly developed. No one, I suppose, would be inclined to classify a lobster as a more advanced form of life than *Homo sapiens* because it can swim backward faster than an Olympic backstroke champion.

Anthropologists now show some signs of modifying their anti-evolutionary position. Particularly in works addressed to the layman one may observe a stress on the historical growth of human society and culture. This stress marks a return to important evolutionary positions.[35]

If these comments serve at least to reduce the suspicions of those who remain hostile to the conceptions of social evolution, we may proceed to a few remarks about the process itself. In a work almost completely ignored by modern social science, A. G. Keller formulated the main principles in a fashion perhaps crude but basically correct and capable of refinement in the light of additional evidence. To reproduce the main points makes his views sound bald and abstract, a distortion that is nevertheless unavoidable. There are three: (1) Variations occur over time in the way a particular society solves the problem of adapting to its environment. (There are also, of course, variations among different societies in the way they solve their adaptive problems.) (2) Selection takes place which favors the more successful adaptations. (3) The more successful adaptations are transmitted by social mechanisms to the next generation. Variation, selection, transmission—these are the heart of the continuing process by which mankind reaches ever new results.[36]

Several subprocesses, to which other writers have drawn attention, may be grouped conveniently under these main headings. Since this is scarcely the place to write a system of sociology, I shall do no more than draw attention to a few that strike me as especially important. First is the fact, already discussed, that a society's capacity for variation may and often does become limited after a spurt of innovating adjustment.[37] Second is the phenomenon of drift, to which Sapir called attention in his study of language.[38] Generalized out of its linguistic context, drift is the tendency of a society to change continuously over time in a particular direction on account of its structure.[39] There is obviously a fascinating field for research here, to which structural analysis, when freed of its present static limitations, may make important contributions. At the same time we must not overlook the point, also made by Hegel, that changes in society, as in nature, often take the form of qualitative leaps from one kind of structure to a totally different kind.[40] In other words, we must not be blinded by the mistaken dictum of Leibniz, *natura non facit saltus*. This leads us to the third point. Some processes of evolutionary change, such as the growth of scientific knowledge, are clearly cumulative. Others are much less so, or perhaps not cumulative at all. Cumulative growth is possible, it has been suggested, only where the nature of the social task permits specialization and cooperation through the division of labor.[41] In those areas of society and culture where change is less cumulative or even not cumulative at all, we may often discern, against a background of broader historical change, recurring patterns, as essentially the same institutional forms arise and decay in response to basically the same problems.[42]

The theory of social evolution, as is apparent from this discussion, cannot serve as a premise from which the social scientist might deduce the future with unfailing exactness. Such prediction on any really important scale probably is not feasible in the study of human society. The reason for this situation appears to be a matter of principle rather than a question of inadequate knowledge. Increases in knowledge about human society have contradictory results, similar to those expressed by the indeterminacy principle in physics. As we learn more about a political and economic situation in the attempt to forecast its outcome, the additions to our knowledge thereby change the situation and increase the number of possible ways in which it can turn out. Since Keynes's writings have become part of the common stock of economic wisdom, it is rather unlikely, even if other factors were alike, that a depression could run the course described in older economic texts. There may be some theoretical upper limit where the knowledge about the relevant factors in a situation catches up with the knowledge that changes the relevance of these factors. That happy day when social science bites its own tail is far enough away for us to ignore it now.

NOTES

1. G. Mosca, *The Ruling Class*, translated by H. D. Kahn (New York, 1939), p. 139.

2. See F. A. Hayek, editor, *Capitalism and the Historians* (Chicago, 1954).

3. Hans L. Zetterberg, review of Joseph A. Kahl, *The American Class Structure* (New York, 1957) in *American Sociological Review*, vol. XXII, No. 6 (December 1957), 768.

4. See his *The Methodology of the Social Sciences*, translated and edited by E. A. Shils and H. A. Finch (New York: Free Press of Glencoe, Inc., 1949), chap. I. The essay cited was originally published in 1904.

5. See particularly his "Entwickelungstendenzen in der Lage der ostelbischen Landarbeiter," originally published in 1894 and reprinted in *Gesammelte Aufsätze zur Sozial- und Wirtschaftsgeschichte* (Tübingen, 1924), pp. 470-507.

6. "Zur Lage der bürgerlichen Demokratie in Russland," *Archiv für Sozialwissenschaft und Sozialpolitik*, XXII (1906), 347-349. German allows very frequent use of quotation marks to indicate skeptical doubt about the meaning of words. In accordance with English usage I have removed all but those which seemed to me most important.

7. *Les Règles de la Méthode Sociologique* (Paris, 1947), p. 56. The work was originally published in 1895.

8. *Ibid.*, p. 60.

9. Translated by A. M. Henderson and Talcott Parsons (New York: Oxford University Press, 1947).

10. See his *Systematic Sociology*, adapted and amplified by Howard Becker on the basis of the *Beziehungslehre und Gebildelehre*. . . . (New York, 1932).

11. *Capital, The Communist Manifesto, and Other Writings by Karl Marx*, edited by Max Eastman (New York: Modern Library, Inc., 1932), p. 321.

12. *The Theory of Social and Economic Organization*, p. 424.

13. "A Revised Analytical Approach to the Theory of Social Stratification," R. Bendix and S. M. Lipset, editors, in *Class, Status, and Power* (New York: Free Press of Glencoe, Inc., 1953), p. 93.

14. Talcott Parsons, *The Social System* (New York: Free Press of Glencoe, Inc., 1951), is the leading statement of this point of view, though the above characterization is, of course, my own.

15. "A process is any way or mode in which a given state of a system or of a part of a system changes into another state. If its study is an object of science any process is assumed to be subject to laws, which will be stated in terms of determinate interrelations of interdependence between the values of the relevant variables." Talcott Parsons, *The Social System*, p. 201.

16. It should perhaps be pointed out that the mathematical concept of function is not identical with the sociological one.

17. In conversation with the writer more than ten years ago, Professor George Lundberg, the leading advocate of a strict natural science model for sociology, confessed that he was at a loss for a good example of a scientific generalization and was unhappy that the only one he could point to was a rather limited one about migration. See his *Can Science Save Us?* (New York, 1947), p. 41. His remark, as far as I can recollect, was one of the earliest impressions leading me to doubt that the search for scientific laws should constitute the primary task of sociology.

18. Compare George C. Homans, *The Human Group* (New York, 1950), chap. 1.

19. See for example his "The Limitations of Scientific Method in Economics," in *The Ethics of Competition and Other Essays* (London, 1935), pp. 105-147.

20. See the introduction by Philipp Frank, editor, in *The Validation of Scientific Theories* (Boston, 1957), p. viii.

21. C. Kirkpatrick and E. Kanin, "Male Sex Aggression on a University Campus," *American Sociological Review*, vol. XXII, No. 1 (February 1957), 53.

22. Here the Oedipus complex comes to mind, but there are grave doubts as to its universality. See B. Malinowski, *The Sexual Life of Savages* (New York, 1929).

23. Rather than cite other writers, I will point to one of my own works that displays all the faults criticized here. See my article, "A Comparative Analysis of the Class Struggle," *American Sociological Review*, vol. 10, No. 1 (February 1945), 31-37.

24. M. G. Kendall, *The Advanced Theory of Statistics* (5th ed.; New York: Hafner Publishing Co., Inc., 1952), I, 1. Emphases added.

25. Franz Neumann, *The Democratic and the Authoritarian State* (New York: Free Press of Glencoe, Inc., 1957), chap. ix.

26. On this ground I disagree with the Hegelian strictures against mathematics presented in Herbert Marcuse, *Reason and Revolution* (London, 1941), p. 144.

27. Paul F. Lazarsfeld in his "Introduction" to *Mathematical Thinking in the Social Sciences* (New York: Free Press of Glencoe, Inc., 1954), p. 3.

28. My own writings came close to taking this position. *See Soviet Politics: The Dilemma of Power* (Cambridge, Mass.: Harvard University Press, 1950).

29. Compare Talcott Parsons, *The Social System*, p. 481.

30. "How does the scholar come to know what is constant and characteristic, what has been a force and what has not? Only prolonged and wide reading can reveal this to him. *Meanwhile,* for a long time he will overlook many things that were of general importance, and regard details that were merely incidental as significant and characteristic. In the course of further reading, everything that he comes across will strike him as either unimportant and meaningless or characteristic and interesting, in every word —according to the hour of day and his mood, his freshness or weariness, and especially according to the stage of maturity which his research has actually reached at that moment. All this evens itself out only through continued reading in the various genres and areas of Greek literature; least of all can one force the result through violent effort: a gentle and attentive listening, with the effort evenly applied, carries one further ahead. . . . We are 'unscientific' and have no method at all, at least not that of the others." Jacob Burckhardt, *Griechische Kulturgeschichte* (Stuttgart: Kröners Taschenausgabe, 1948), I, 7-8. Italics in original.

31. Ironically enough, one of the more cogent presentations of this view comes from a historian. See H. Butterfield, *The Origins of Modern Science* (London, 1949), esp. chaps. i-iv. The idea is implicit in the works of sociological formalists from Simmel to Parsons.

32. H. Rickert, *Die Grenzen der Naturwissenschaftlichen Begriffsbildung* (3rd ed.; Tübingen, 1921), p. 246.

33. See his *Karl Marx* (London, 1938), pp. 73-81, esp. p. 79.

34. Franz Müller-Lyer was the most pronounced advocate of this version of evolutionary theory. See his *Phasen der Kultur und Richtungslinien des Fortschritts* (München, 1908).

35. See Ralph Linton, *The Tree of Culture* (New York, 1955), Carleton S. Coon, *The Story of Man* (New York, 1954), and William Howells, *Back of History* (New York, 1954). All three books, directed toward the general public, express a belief in human progress to date that recalls the tone of Victorian anthropology.

36. See Albert Galloway Keller, *Societal Evolution* (rev. ed.; New York, 1931), and William Graham Sumner and Albert Galloway Keller, *The Science of Society* (New Haven, 1927).

37. Further insight into this process, from a biological standpoint, but with important sociological implications, has been shed by R. W. Gerard, Clyde Kluckhohn, and Anatol Rapoport, "Biological and Cultural Evolution," *Behavioral Science*, I, No. 1 (January, 1957), 14-15. Too technical to summarize adequately here, the point concerns variations in adaptive capacities as related to the environment.

38. E. Sapir, "Language," *Encyclopaedia of the Social Sciences* (New York, 1937), IX, 163.

39. See also Gerard, Kluckhohn, and Rapoport, "Biological and Cultural Evolution," 21, for further implications.

40. G. W. F. Hegel, *Wissenschaft der Logik* (Leipzig, 1948), I, 379-384.

41. Harvey C. Moore, "Cumulation and Cultural Processes," *American Anthropologist*, LVI, No. 3 (June, 1954), 347-357.

42. See also on this problem the recurrence of certain aspects of class relationships discussed by Franz Neumann, *Democratic and Authoritarian State*, especially pp. 250-251.

THE WORLD VIEW OF TALCOTT PARSONS

Daniel Foss

It is only recently that Talcott Parsons has begun to give major attention to some of the central social issues and problems of our times: those which have to do with economic growth, planning, large-scale social and political change, radical nationalism, political democracy and the threats to it, and bureaucracy and its consequences. These are the problems and concerns of a world in violent flux, of furious conflicts, revolutions, colonial revolts; of totalitarian despotisms rising in China and Cuba; of power exerted at its nakedest complete with mass murders, planned famines, and Ulbricht's Wall; and of a wholesale cultural crisis and collapse of traditions, engineered overtly in other societies by despotic modernizing governments, and covertly or involuntarily in the United States by those who serve, and partially create, the mass markets. It is to be expected that the intellectual apprehension and conceptualization of such a world would offer a supreme challenge to an equilibrium theorist, and we indeed find that on these matters Parsons is a good deal less "systematic" than in the rest of his work.

It is the problem of this paper to summarize Parsons' positions (in so far as he has clearly delineated his positions) on several major issues of contemporary life: the goals and objectives of an industrial society; the industrialization of the underdeveloped world, with respect to both the problems and the means of transformation; and the structure of power in industrial and industrializing societies, with respect to both political organization and change. Since these issues merge one into another, it will be important to understand how Parsons' ideas "hang together" (or how they are "functionally related"), on both the overt and covert levels (that is to say, it is important to understand what Parsons consistently leaves out as well as what he consistently says). I will also attempt to isolate certain points on which Parsons' views may be concretely refuted,

"The World View of Talcott Parsons." An original essay prepared especially for this volume. The author wishes to thank Drs. Lewis Coser, Maurice Stein, Kurt Wolff, and Arthur Vidich for critical comments and helpful editorial suggestions.

although it is beyond the scope of this paper to do any conclusive refut-
ing: many of Parsons' assertions are exceedingly broad and require vast
amounts of research for either proof or disproof.

First we must understand Parsons' conception of what industrial society
is all about. Now, Parsons' theory is built on the fundamental concept
of "action" or behavior oriented to goals. In other words, we would
expect Parsons to look for the central identifying features of an industrial
society in the kind of goals which it manifests. This is, in fact, exactly
what he does. However, he must go some distance up into the conceptual
clouds in order to determine what those goals are.

The industrial society *par excellence* is of course the United States.
Our society, says Parsons, possesses a value system characterized by "instrumental activism." This delectable term represents Parsons' ways of
summing us all up in the most general way he possibly can. For values
are not merely goals; they are broad commitments of individuals to
support certain general *directions* which the entire collectivity or society
may take, and by extension, to accept the consequences for themselves in
terms of the social roles they play in the collectivity or society. And,

> values are, for sociological purposes, deliberately defined at a level of gen-
> erality higher than that of goals—they are *directions* of action rather than
> specific objectives. . . . Still values and goals may be formulated at many
> different levels of generality. What level is appropriate will depend on what
> system is taken as the point of reference for the analysis in question. For
> purposes of this paper, it will be the total society, so the level of generality
> will be very high.
> (Authority, Legitimation, and Political Action." (SAPTMS, p. 172.)

The beauty of this is that Parsons here protects himself against the
possibility of the gross implausibility of his characterization of our society, as well as against the possibility of marked class-specificity of his
so-called societal value, so long as he can demonstrate some applicability
of "instrumental activism" as a designation for the system as a whole.
Meanwhile, "instrumental activism"

> involves an attitude of active mastery toward the empirical situation external
> to the society—both the physical and psychological nature, and other societies
> —an attitude which favors increasing the level of adaptive flexibility primarily
> through increase of knowledge and economic production. (*Ibid.*, SAPTMS,
> p. 172.)

Note carefully the place given to "economic production" in the definition of this value.

The quotes above are taken from an essay written in 1958. In 1959,
Parsons wrote an essay entitled, " 'Voting' and the Equilibrium of the
American Political System," which is found in the volume edited by

Burdick and Brodbeck, *American Voting Behavior*. This article—ostensibly built upon the 1948 study of Lazarsfeld of Elmira (Voting)—is actually almost simon-pure Parsons. Here we return to "instrumental activism" as the central pivot of the American value system. Parsons is at this point attempting to define the "paramount goal" of American society so that he can theoretically determine the functional requisites of the American political system (and possibly also in order to add his two cents to the obsession with "national goals" then sweeping a large part of the intellectual community). At any rate, he refines his earlier definition. "Instrumental activism" is

> oriented to control the action situation in the interest of range and quality of adaptation, but with more economic than political emphasis. In goal definition it is highly indefinite and pluralistic, being committed to a rather general direction of progress or improvement, without any clearly defined terminal goal. Economic production is highly valued as the most immediate focus of adaptive capacity. Beyond that, we value particularly technology and science as means to productivity, and the maximization of opportunity for individuals and subcollectivities. . . . (*American Voting Behavior*, p. 82.)

On this basis, Parsons feels able to state the "over-all goal of American society" (which "must be conceived on a very high level of abstraction") as

> the *facilitation* of effective adaptive development of the society and of the societal conditions associated with it. It centers on economic development, but definitely includes the integrative conditions which are relevant. (*Ibid.,* p. 82.)

More specifically, our society stresses, among other things, "the more immediate facilitation of production and the development of productivity."

Although Parsons double-qualifies everything by the use of the word "tentatively," and although he finds room for other goals such as the facilitation of the "adjustment of personalities," there can be no doubt as to where he puts the emphasis: it is squarely upon economic development and the increase of productivity and production. All other goals seem strictly subordinate and appear to figure in Parsons' chief goal of economic advance in so far as they contribute directly to its attainment, or their attainment facilitates in some way the attainment of the principal goal. Parsons' concentration—or perhaps even fixation—on this particular value-goal arrangement ("value-orientation") which he has called "instrumental activism" as characteristic of industrial societies such as the United States leads him into emphases (or, perhaps, "ideological distortions") which are, as we shall see, disturbing, if not actually horrifying.

But let us now return to the assessment of "instrumental activism."

There is of course no question but that American society is characterized by constant economic growth and development. On the other hand, this fact alone cannot be construed as rendering economic growth and development such a defining characteristic of the total system that it constitutes the basic orientation for our societal goals and values. We recognize, as would most economists, that a certain amount of economic growth is inherent in the structure of the economy and that the pace of development of science and technology becomes ever more rapid. But there are many signs that our society as a whole is sufficiently unconcerned about economic development as to be heading into serious structural economic problems. We have just emerged from a recession in an exceedingly limping and half-hearted fashion; far from growing rapidly, we have barely exceeded our heights of two or three years before. Our average annual growth rate—3 to 4 per cent in good times—barely keeps pace with population growth. We are content to permit the accumulation of a huge pool of youthful unemployed, which James B. Conant has described as "social dynamite," largely because their labor power is unneeded under present conditions of economic growth. Considerable portions of our heavy industry, including the steel industry among the more egregious examples, operate at levels considerably short of full capacity precisely because the managers of the corporations which engage in heavy industry are much more interested in short-run high profits than in the long-term economic growth of the economy as a whole or even of their own industries (and they do this, mind you, while clinging steadfastly to the ideology of "free enterprise"). There are, in fact, plentiful indications to the effect that the major institutionalized nongovernmental interest groups of our society—business, labor, farmers, and so on—are perfectly willing to exert their power to protect their own interests, even at the price of sabotaging the general economic growth at every turn. So long as its own ox is not being gored, a group's apathy over economic growth may be almost infinite.

Thus, although economic growth and development are taking place in a society's economy—even perhaps at high rates—because of structural factors and processes inherent to that economy, it cannot be presumed that economic growth objectives constitute the organizing principles of such a society's value system. As a further illustration of this point, we might imagine Parsons being parachuted into Ming China (about the fifteenth century). He would observe an economic change that had the appearance of a commercial capitalist revolution in trade (which did not, however, last very long). This change resulted from structural factors such as an increase in maritime exploration which led to increased commercial contacts with Southeast Asia. Now, impressive as these economic changes and developments may have appeared, Parsons obviously could never attribute anything like "instrumental activism" to the Chinese value system of that time.

It is certain that the United States has been considerably more pre-occupied with economic development at times in the past than it is now. Parsons would have been much more nearly right about our value system if he were referring to the period 1870-1914, or even to the 1920's. As it is, we cannot but call into grave question Parsons' attributing to our contemporary value system of a dominant characteristic on the order of "instrumental activism."

We might note parenthetically at this point that Robin M. Williams, Jr., an interpreter of Parsons, takes a much more sensible view of the American value system. Instead of the monolithic Parsonian organizing principle of "instrumental activism," Williams isolates the following American "value-orientations": "Achievement" and "Success"; "Activity" and "Work"; "Moral Orientation"; "Humanitarian Mores"; Efficiency and Practicality; "Progress"; Material Comfort; Equality; Freedom; External Conformity; Science and Secular Rationality; Nationalism-Patriotism; Democracy; Individual Personality; and Racism and Related Group-superiority Themes.[1] It is easy to see how Parsons might have generalized from a list more or less similar to this, or from parallel insight, to arrive at the notion of "instrumental activism" with its peculiar economic-development twist. But Williams, although he remarks on the relationships between several of the "value-orientations" on his list to economic development, implicitly denies the existence of any single overriding organizing principle such as that formulated by Parsons:

> It must always be kept in mind that these themes, values, and systems of belief do not operate as single separate units but are in continually shifting and recombining configurations marked by very complex interpenetration, conflict, and reformulation. (*American Society,* p. 468.)

Thus Williams presents a more complex, diversified, and shifting conception of the value system of an advanced industrial society such as the United States than does Parsons. Williams supplies another welcome correction of emphasis in that he regards the values centering around the individual as somewhat independent of, and even in conflict with, those centering around the collectivity. For,

> a very important part of the conflict of value systems in the United States can be economically summarized in terms of tension between values centering around the individual personality versus values organized around categorical organic conceptions. (*American Society,* p. 468.)

Williams thus presents a view refreshingly different from that of Parsons, who is observing from the standpoint of the "needs" of the "total system," and thus gives slighting theoretical consideration to individual values as being other than mere mechanisms to serve the requirements of the totality. In Williams' version of the theory, the individual at least has a chance.

If there has been any lingering fragment of a doubt that by "instrumental activism" Parsons means the Protestant Ethic (our good old friend), it has surely been dispelled by Parsons' paper, "Religious Organization in the United States," written in 1958. In this paper, Parsons seems to have attempted to cloak "instrumental activism" in an overlay of sanctity which is, in my opinion, entirely spurious. But here, for whatever they are worth, are his very words:

> I should like to suggest that in American society there has, in its main outline, evolved the conception of an institutionalized Christianity which is in line with the great tradition of the Christian Society. . . . First, in order of evidence in favor of this view, is the fact that the values of contemporary American society have fundamental religious roots, above all, in the traditions which Max Weber, in *The Protestant Ethic and the Spirit of Capitalism*, called those of "ascetic Protestantism," and that these values have not been fundamentally changed in the course of our national history. The enormous changes which have occurred constitute fundamental changes not of values but of the structure of the society in which those values are maintained and implemented. Essentially by this system of values I mean the continued commitment to values of "instrumental activism," the subordination of the personal needs of the individual to an objective "task" to which he is expected to devote his full energies, and the subjection of the actions of all to universalistic standards of judgment. Associated with this is the importance of universalizing the essential conditions of effective performance through equalization of civil rights and of access to education and health. (SAPMS, p. 311.)

Parsons then goes on to say that the shift of this value system from transcendental to secular reference took place "as Weber so strongly emphasizes, within the highly active religious tradition of ascetic Protestantism." He says further that the contemporary conception of the "good society" (which he does not delineate) is the direct intellectual descendant of the Calvinist Kingdom of God on Earth.

All this is of course highly strained. We recognize the Protestant Ethic of the seventeenth and eighteenth centuries to have been a transitional form which linked a religious world to a commercial one. Whatever their origins, our contemporary values must be, to use Gordon Allport's term, "functionally antonomous." However there is a monumental difference in outlook between the craftsman of yore who worked fanatically at his trade to obey a Divine Call, and was furthermore his "own man" economically as well as spiritually, and the contemporary white collar worker who performs his rather mechanical job according to minute and detailed prescription as set down by the organization, which has endlessly subdivided the routinized process of which the clerk's job is a part.

The latter has little or no passionate interest in his job, and is motivated chiefly by anticipation of the paycheck and fear of the Boss. The craftsman chose to restrict himself to serve God; the clerk has no choice but to permit himself to be restricted in order to serve the System.

Perhaps it is going too far to say that the System is actually Parsons' "functional equivalent" of God, but in his writings it certainly does take on too many divine attributes for comfort. This is illustrated once more by the passage quoted above. For we find that "equalization of civil rights and of access to education and health" proceeds from "the importance of universalizing the conditions of effective performance." We realize, of course, that aside from whatever incidental benefits may accrue from this to individuals, the problems afflicting organizational management and commercial contractual transactions are lessened, and also the channeling of the labor market is made more efficient. Also, the valuational quality of "effective performance" is changed if the individual does it for an organization (unless he is at least moderately high up) rather than for himself.

Since "instrumental activism" is now established as the Protestant Ethic, we might consider the segments of the population which exemplify it. Clearly, the great bulk of the urban lower and working classes must be excluded from the sphere of influence of the Protestant Ethic. As for the urban lower middle classes, they are supposedly a hotbed of "other-direction," the "Social Ethic," and other American diseases. This leaves us with the managerial (upper middle) class and certain groups off the mainstream, such as fundamentalist rural communities (especially in the Midwest and South), and New England agricultural communities. The Protestant Ethic does not represent the character, nor does "instrumental activism" represent the "value orientation," of the bulk of the American population. Parsons thus presents as characteristic of the value system of the entire society, a "value-orientation" which can be located rather specifically in the managerial, or Establishment, classes. But we will return to this matter in connection with Parsons' views on power in industrial society.

To sum up thus far, we may say that in Parsons' view, the central preoccupation of an industrial society such as the United States is continual economic growth and development. This is understood as the presence of "instrumental activism" [as defined above] as the dominant organizing principle of the "value-orientation" of the total society. "Instrumental activism" is presented as hallowed by having emerged from the "ascetic Protestant" tradition, and thus is tinged by more than the barest trace of transcendent spirituality. Furthermore, the group with which "instrumental activism" is most closely associated seems to be the most privileged and powerful of the large social strata in our society. (But even here we must be careful to distinguish "instrumental activism" from the success ethic. The quest for success, status, and prestige does not always carry with it the desire for "active mastery." There is clearly a type of bureaucrat who steadily rises in status through accommodation and opportunism, while shying away from anything resembling "active mastery.") Finally, "instrumental activism" submerges the needs and interests of the individual to the over-all attainment of system goals and objectives in the spheres of economic growth and development.

I have thus far paid so much attention to values because Parsons himself gives values a role of such crucial importance. ("Values define . . . a broad direction of action.") The question of values will recur frequently. But at any rate, we now have Parsons committed to the centrality of the goal of economic growth in an industrial society such as our own. But to reach this goal, says Parsons, you need power. He apparently arrived at his theory of power through his attempt to conceptualize the study of formal organizations (in the essays, "A Sociological Approach to the Theory of Organizations" and "A General Theory of Formal Organization," SAPMS, pp. 17-96). Such organizations, as he sees them, are social systems or societies in miniature.

Everything begins, he says, with "value-orientations." But this is only part of the story, since without power, nothing will move: "The value system *legitimizes* the organization's goal, but it is only through power that its achievement can be made effective" (SAPMS, p. 41). But he is led from this to one of the strangest conceptualizations of all times; power is defined rather circularly, and principally in terms of only one of its consequences: "Power is the generalized capacity to mobilize resources in the interest of the attainment of a system goal." (*Ibid.*, p. 41.) Its generation and utilization is one of the "fundamental functional imperatives of a social system." In order to survive, the system must produce power in order to achieve its goals. That which is produced in order to achieve what Parsons considers the system's goals-to-be is power. And, by extension, nothing else is power. Thus Parsons prepares a tautological trap into which he permits himself to fall with alarming complacency: in an ongoing system, power is being used to achieve system goals. Where power is obviously being exercised, there must be goals of the ongoing system which it is achieving.

Parsons recognizes four "fundamental conditions" for the generation of power by a system. First and foremost, there must be an institutionalized value system which "legitimizes both the goal of the organization and the means by which it functions in the attainment of that goal." (SAPMS, p. 42.) This legitimization is crucial, for all action is ultimately "grounded" in it. It is the "appraisal of action in terms of shared or common values in the context of the involvement of the action in the social system." (SAPMS, p. 175.) And this appraisal is carried out at a very high level of generality. Values, in their institutionalized form, are thus the vital emotional underpinning of the entire organizational structure. Authority is one form of legitimation which is applied to leadership.

The second "fundamental condition" for the generation of power is "the regulation of the organization's procurement and decision-making processes through adherence to universalistic rules and to such institutions as authority and contract." (SAPMS, p. 43.) By this means the organization secures loyalty and cooperation from its own personnel and from "outside" persons with whom it deals. We immediately recognize this second condition as proceeding from the first. For the self-regulation through which loyalty is procured is carried on with direct reference, in the Parsonian view of things, to the "value-orientations" underlying authority and to the noncontractual element in contract. From this, Parsons slides easily over to the third condition, "the command of the more detailed and day-to-day support of the persons whose cooperation is needed." (SAPMS, p. 43.) This would seem, at first glance, to proceed immediately from the second condition, and indeed, the kinship of the two in Parsons' mind is clear. But we can nevertheless discern situations such as slave-labor camps, in which the labor force is held entirely by coercion, and the discontinuity of values between staff and inmates is total. Yet the staff does achieve a fair degree of control over the day-to-day activities of the inmates, and employs terror to compensate for the absence of a common consensus of values. Parsons does not consider the problem of coercion here; he hardly ever considers it anywhere. The fourth condition is "the command of necessary facilities, of which the primary category in our society is financial." (SAPMS, p. 43.) There is of course no quarrel with this last one; it is in fact the only one with which a Marxist might wholeheartedly agree.

In his definition and analysis of power, Parsons slides sketchily and embarrassedly over the questions of opposition, resistance, coercion, and domination. In "Authority, Legitimation, and Political Action" he explicitly rejects the "zero-sum" conception of power, whereby the power possessed by rulers and ruled total up to an absolute quantity of zero. The zero-sum situation, he says, is a mere special case of his own concept, since he is talking about the ability to achieve the goals of the collectivity, and this by definition includes the capacity to overcome opposition. We detect in this faint traces of the image of the all-wise, all-seeing, and benevolent ruler who divines the needs of his people so perfectly that any opposition to him must be *ipso facto* evil. But in "Voting and the Equilibration of the American Party System," written a year later, Parsons does even worse. He first defines power as "the capacity of modern society to mobilize its resources in the interest of goals, defined as positively rather than permissively sanctioned by the system as a whole—goals that are 'affected with a public interest (*American Voting Behavior*, p. 81).' " When it is stated this way, it would seem that opposition to the holders of power is at the very least subversive, and perhaps even anarchistic. But Parsons goes on to write a sentence that deserves to live forever in sociological infamy: "whether there is opposition or not is an empirically very important but theoretically secondary matter." (*Ibid.*) Is Parsons actually saying that the sociological theorist need not concern himself with a fact of political experience which is of direct concern and a point of reference for rulers and ruled alike? It is true that scientific reality is often sharply discontinuous with the world of the senses; but political opposition is something for which you may be shot, and I feel that this alone entitles it to consideration as something more than a "theoretically very secondary matter."

It is clear that in this matter Parsons' primary concern is with emotional support; and also that he here carries on the great tradition set forth in his essay on war propaganda in *Essays in Sociological Theory*. In that essay, Parsons defended the right of the government to lie in its wartime propaganda because of the need for greater integration of all American society in time of national peril. False war propaganda was excused by Parsons as a sort of therapy for socially harmful dissent. But in the *American Voting Behavior* article he becomes disturbingly explicit. Catch the tone of this passage:

> The amount of its power is an attribute of the total system and is a function of several variables. These, as I conceive them, are the *support* that can be mobilized by those exercising power, the *facilities* they have access to (notably the control of the productivity of the economy), the *legitimation* that can be accorded to the positions of the holders of power, and the relatively *unconditional loyalties* of the population to the society in its politically organized aspects. It is above all the factor of support which will be the center of concern here. . . . (*American Voting Behavior*, p. 81.)

We of course recognize here Parsons' four "fundamental conditions," now transformed into components of the power variable. An interesting feature of this passage is that Parsons here neutralizes, through theoretical legerdemain, the potentially hostility-provoking aspects of the fact of concentration in minority hands of the control of the dominant economic institutions. The holders of corporate power, it is implied, are merely doing a job on behalf of the "total system," and would never dream of using their positions solely to advance their own interests. Also, one cannot help but be annoyed by the italicized phrase, "unconditional loyalties," which recalls Dostoevsky's Grand Inquisitor.

In the light of all this, it is not surprising to discover what Parsons has to say about the electoral process (the major subject of the *American Voting Behavior* article). He finds that elections are useful and valuable for reasons almost diametrically opposed to their ostensible purpose:

> From the point of view of bringing about the main shift of political allegiances, the campaign seems relatively "functionless"; it is a "ritual." But from

another point of view, if I interpret this evidence correctly, it seems to serve a very important function. This is, essentially, *to reinforce the generalization of support* . . . an essential condition of the functioning of a two-party democratic system. (*American Voting Behavior,* p. 106.)

By this, Parsons means that election campaigns achieve the temporary loyalty of the population to two political parties which cut across the religious and ethnic groupings into which the population might otherwise divide. Another feature of the system is the right-left balance achieved by dividing the electorate into those favoring conservation and those favoring change, with each group tending to fall into one of the two parties. This then produces a "symmetrical" political situation which tends to equilibrate around a zero point. But social change is of course taking place, and this, disturbingly enough, "introduces a factor of *asymmetry* into the party structure." But fortunately for Parsonian aesthetics, the system of party division imparts a "structured relation" to the otherwise inconvenient change by feeding issues very slowly into the political system, thus gradually shifting the point of equilibrium toward the positions once occupied by those advocating change. Thus, with a theoretical flourish, Parsons categorically attacks the traditional notion of the electoral process as an arena of political conflict. Admittedly, as any political scientist will tell you, the traditional view certainly does contain a very large component of mythology. But the belief has still been maintained, however faintly, that an individual's vote represents his personal participation, however minute, in the societal decision-making process. But looking on from the standpoint of the "total system," Parsons sees something entirely different. The electoral process here is an elaborate ritual whereby support and loyalty are mobilized, in the form of the voting of millions of individuals, on behalf of the holders of power. We observe immediately that the electoral process in the United States is, in the Parsonian view, not in the least analytically different from the analogous process in the Soviet Union, where 99 per cent plus majorities are obtained on behalf of the single slate of candidates. Parsons is supposed to have made this comparison explicit at a recent sociological convention.

It is possible to argue that Parsons has misunderstood the lessons of the chapter in *Voting* where the authors analyze the remarkable late-campaign shift to Truman: the voters return to old class loyalties, and many voters support him along strict class lines despite their original strong distaste for his personality. But there is no getting away from it: whatever his theoretical absurdities on other matters, Parsons' assertion here certainly possesses a considerable, perhaps alarming, degree of truth; it is as true as the old orthodox model, at least when applied to the United States. Every national election in this country seems to return to power the same broad coalition of established interests. The election results may make greater or lesser detailed changes in the composition of the Establishment, but rarely are any major or crucial changes made in the general outline.

Nevertheless we can definitely take issue with Parsons on one aspect of this matter: he is blithely unconcerned with the adverse consequences for individuals of the situation he describes. This is to say that a great part of the identification with the political community held by a member of an industrial society derives from his knowledge of his own participation in it. If the electoral process is, to a large degree, a ritual and a sham performed at regular intervals to secure the semblance of ratification for a relatively unchanging and unchangeable establishment, we must expect bitterness, disillusionment, frustration, cynicism, and wanton political destructiveness on the part of those individuals cut off from the fruits of the system and aware of their own political impotence. This indeed represents the findings of the empirical "political alienation" studies, such as those conducted by Levin in Boston and by Thompson and Horton at Cornell University. Real psychic loss is experienced by those substantively disenfranchised by the workings of the "total system." It is not for nothing that we believe in "the right to vote," or that overtly disenfranchised groups such as Southern Negroes risk violence in order to obtain the vote. We are dealing here with the difference in imagery between the subject and the citizen. We must ask Parsons what can be done about political alienation insofar as it is real, unless he is prepared to relegate democracy to the status of a rather ingenious gear in his machine.

Summing up briefly, we have observed that Parsons considers the holders of power in industrial society to be those in responsible positions for fostering the achievement of societal goals (and that, by devious implication, the societal goals are being served by those acknowledged to be in power). The holders of power furthermore have access to the mobilization of support and loyalty to themselves and to the institutions which they command through the electoral process; this is true in the United States as well as in the Soviet Union (though Parsons probably would not claim that it is true in both cases to the same degree).

But we recall that Parsons considers the major system goal of an industrial society to be economic development and growth; our entire value system is supposedly integrated around the drive to attain this. We might thus expect Parsons to forge a connection here and to consider economic development as the central preoccupation of the holders of power. This is, in fact, exactly what he does, as he builds economic change into his model of the American political system:

> American society is not static, but dynamically evolving. The political system must be adapted to this fact and must include mechanisms of adjustment to social change. Under American conditions the main autonomous processes

of social change do not operate through government, but largely through the development of the economy. The business element, which is the core of this process of change, tends to be politically conservative because the positive use of the powers of government has been felt, since the early thirties, to imply interference with the process. The left, on the other hand, is relatively residual, tending to gather together those elements in the society on whom the problems and difficulties arising from the dynamic process impinge, and who see in governmental action an opportunity to remedy their situations. (*American Voting Behavior,* p. 95.)

The key phrase here is of course the citation of the "business element" as the "core of the change." There is a strong temptation to believe, at this point, that Parsons has swallowed whole a major part of the American business creed. The corporate managers are here represented to be the most "progressive" element in the society, understandably resisting the efforts of government to interfere with their (farsighted and enlightened) stewardship of the "core of the process of change." Parsons does not consider the possibility that the managers may be strongly interested in profits, dividends, or stock options; that they enter into collusion to restrict output and to suppress innovation; or that they pursue pricing policies which are insane from the point of view of the growth of the economy as a whole, as well as from the standpoint of the sale of their own goods on the world market. As I have remarked before, the American business community seems to be doing a clearly inadequate job in carrying forward the general growth and development of the economy. Were it not for the vast governmental military expenditure, the business community would in fact be hard put to avoid a most severe contraction.

A historical note is also in order: the American business community had been "politically conservative" and opposed to the "Positive use of the powers of government" long before the early thirties. Nor has the record been unambiguous. During the early days of the New Deal, the business community ran gleefully into the arms of NRA, as it was then powerless to save itself and also as it saw the opportunities for short-run financial gain inherent in organized restrictions of output and fixed prices. When business had recovered from the most catastrophic depths of the Depression, NRA appeared as an onerous economic encumbrance, as well as an immoral interference of government in business.

Another characteristic Parsonian touch is the reference to the left as "relatively residual" and composed of elements "on whom the problems and difficulties arising from the dynamic process impinge." Parsons rarely if ever attributes political radicalism or political action movements to direct confrontations of interest within the social structure. Rather, the distressed groups have generally been sideswiped by the major processes of change going on autonomously around them. We will return to this matter later.

But above all, the passage quoted on page 105 indicates to us another entire dimension that is left out of Parsons' discussion of power. This dimension is role-creative ability; which is to say that a major feature of a political role is the ability to do whatever you want to do (within limits). I have certainly overstated this somewhat, but it is clear that the holders of power are not merely exercising authority delegated by the collectivity and grounded in a set of "value-orientations" in order to achieve a set of goals (economic development and growth) already preset by the "total system" itself. Rather, the powerful employ their existing authority and coercive ability to accomplish things and to define and set goals not called for by the "mandate" given to them in the Parsonian system. And aside from whatever worthwhile that may be done with role-creative ability because of any altruistic motives of the powerful, it is to be expected that a great deal of this role-creative ability will be done in the selfish interests of the powerful themselves. Thus, referring back to the situation presented in the passage quoted on page 105, we can readily see that the business community is the center of much of the dynamic change which exists precisely because it has, on the basis of its authority and the coercive pressure it has been able to generate, acquired the freedom—which is to say, the role-creative ability—to block, forestall, delay, hinder, or frustrate many other types of change which would otherwise have been possible but which ran counter to the interests of the business community. This ability is not so great as it once was. The business community is now vulnerable to demands for change emanating from government or labor or other groups (such as "consumers") which it could have easily blocked thirty-five years ago.

An adequate theory of power in a complex and changing industrial society must, in my opinion, consider all three dimensions, authority, coercion, and role-creative ability, as contributing to the capacity of the powerful to act. Parsons' theory accounts adequately for only the first, and thus has great difficulty in assimilating the facts of modern society; it would of course be much more appropriate when applied to the abstract model of the so-called "traditional society," where social change is by definition ruled out. In this model (which is of course never completely realized) "value-orientations" would be so thoroughly internalized, and legitimation so thoroughly grounded in the "value-orientations," that deviance and political opposition would be minimal, and thus the employment of coercion would also be minimized. Political roles would also be so thoroughly delimited that role-creative ability would be near zero (as formerly was the case, for example, with the Yoruba of Western Nigeria, who would order a chief who got out of line to commit suicide by presenting him with a basket full of blue peacock eggs). And furthermore, in such a model, "societal goals" would generally be either routinized (such as the maintenance of an adequate level of economic prosperity) or transitory (such as repulse of barbarians), and therefore the demands made upon the system for the "generation" of power would be neither great nor especially pressing.

Parsons has evidently tried to compensate somewhat for the difficulties of his theory of power by linking "societal goals" and power in industrial society to economic growth and development. But then he is faced with the problem that the values surrounding economic growth are not shared equally by all members of the society, and in fact tend to be class-specific. But he gets around this by what I can only consider a legitimizing rationalization of the positions of those who control the major economic institutions: the values of the "total system" are identified with the activities of the reigning economic directorate, whether or not this directorate can actually be shown to be exerting itself on behalf of growth and change. This implies a further contradiction: if the population is divided into a minority who are considered to embody the "total system" values and a majority who do not share these values, how is the power structure to be understood without giving theoretical primacy to the concepts of domination and the overcoming of opposition?—which Parsons explicitly rejects.

It is not to be supposed that Parsons hews uncompromisingly to the theoretical absurdities which have been cited; if necessary, he can make considerable concessions to reality—which, of course, he never accepts entirely. His article, "The Distribution of Power in American Society," written as a review of C. Wright Mills's *The Power Elite,* is among the most lucid and readable pieces he has done. He begins, of course, by attacking Mills where he is weakest—the conceptualization of power. Parsons is a theoretical conceptualizer where Mills is a polemical conceptualizer, and the Parsonian battleship easily blows the Mills PT-boat out of the water. But Parsons goes on to accept Mills's picture of a self-perpetuating elite within the business community:

> The general tenor of my argument has been that, given the nature of an industrial society, a relatively well-defined elite or leadership group *should be expected to develop* in the business world; it is out of the question that power should be diffused equally among an indefinite number of very small units, as the ideal of pure competition and a good deal of the ideology of the business community itself would have it. (SAPMS, p. 211.)

Among other things, this passage reflects Parsons' intense preoccupation with the necessity for the development of a stable elite in American society. He regards the lack of such an elite as a major source of instability.

But having accepted the notion of a business elite, Parsons now explicitly denies the possibility that such an elite can or does dominate our society. By definition, "In a complex society, the primary locus of power lies in the political system (SAPMS, p. 212)." He then admits that the precise boundaries of this system cannot easily be traced, but he does consider the political system to be vaguely coextensive with governmental organizations. Since the political system is apparently highly differentiated from "other systems" and possesses its own internal structure, Parsons feels safe in locating the "primary locus of power" there (SAPMS, pp. 212-213). He now cites the enormous growth of the political system relative to the economic system in recent times. The polity may have been in a position of great weakness relative to the economy in the latter half of the nineteenth century, but the balance, he believes, has surely been shifted. Parsons next presents a relatively "optimistic" picture of the success of government in regulating the business community:

> Internally, beyond the more elementary provisions for law and order and essential minimum services—much of this, of course, on a local basis—the main focus of the development of our political system has been *control* of economic organization and processes, and coping with some of the consequences of economic growth and industrialization. The process started well before the turn of the century with the Interstate Commerce legislation and the Anti-Trust Act and continued through the New Deal era, not steadily but with waves of new measures and levels of political control. (SAPMS, p. 213.)

Parsons of course ignores the fact that the Anti-Trust Acts have largely been a sham, generally devoid of enforcement, with the government itself often participating in tacit violations; and that such ostensibly regulatory bodies as the Securities and Exchange Commission, the Civil Aeronautics Board, the Federal Trade Commission, and the Federal Communications Commission have throughout most of their existence been mere service agencies for the private organizations they were supposed to police. Parsons rejects Mills's contention that the corporate directorate still holds the balance of control over government, and presents us with a statement which must surely count as a masterpiece of fatuity:

> If genuine and, in some sense, effective controls had not been imposed, I find it impossible to understand the bitter and continuing opposition on the part of business to the measures which have been taken. (SAPMS, pp. 213-214.)

Parsons is, of course, an academic liberal and as such has no qualms about government intervention in the economy. But his underestimation of the power of the business community vis-à-vis government, as manifested in this article, seems to result from his being "had" by his own theory. In the first place he here as elsewhere locates the focus of our value system in the economy. Our primary goals are material and economic. Second, Parsons assigns to the businessman "primary responsibility for production." Thus the businessman is to be primarily understood as custodian of an economic institution participating in the attainment of the central goals of the society; whatever costs he exacts from the community to serve his "sectoral" interests are theoretically secondary. It simply does not occur to Parsons that the structure of the economy has evolved to the point where the corporate directorate should no longer be entrusted with the "primary responsibility for production." His detailed political views as an academic liberal, which lead him to regard the major features of the welfare state as desirable apparently clash [rather sharply] with his theoretical dispositions, which lead him to isolate the polity from the economy—each has its own cell in his diagrams. (Parsons has a vague belief in the increase of "differentiation" as in some way concurrent with the advance of civilization, and in his consideration of the United States he may feel that the assumption by government of responsibility for production might represent "poor boundary maintenance" between his A and G systems.) In the end, it seems, the theory wins out. He castigates Mills for "suggesting that the development of the power elite is bringing [the] capitalist evil to a climax, to a situation which is intolerable for liberals and socialists alike." Since Parsons considers himself a liberal in good standing, he is mortally offended:

> I suggest an alternative view: that, though of course accompanied by a whole range of "abuses," the main lines of social development in America are essentially acceptable to a humanistic ethic which in my case is closer to the liberal than to the other two outlined here (capitalist and socialist). (SAPMS, p. 224.)

But Parsonian liberalism differs from the traditional "individualistic liberalism"; by this time we know that in the Parsonian world the individual doesn't have a chance. He instead advocates a set of assumptions which "assert the desirability [for whom or for what?—D.F.] of positive social organizaton." It is the System that wins. And furthermore, "it can be positively asserted that power, while of course subject to abuses and in need of many controls, is an essential and desirable component of a highly organized society." And very highly organized it is, too. One might say too much so, in fact. Mills is in the end sent packing with an admonition to unlearn his entire education:

> Hence, in my opinion, many of the difficulties of Mills' analysis of a crucial problem in American society arise from his failure to transcend the dilemmas inherent in American and more broadly, in Western thought. It seems to me that he is clearly and, to the degree that he pushes this position, unjustifiably anticapitalist. He is partly pro-liberal and probably even more prosocialist. . . . (SAPMS, p. 225.)

Thus does Parsons contemptuously deal with the central issue raised by *The Power Elite*: the submergence of the individual beneath a bureaucratic world managed by the Establishment. Parsons is supremely confident as to the absence of any threat to the individual in modern society:

My conviction on this point is strengthened by a variety of . . . considerations. . . . First, I am extremely skeptical of Mills' interpretation of what he calls the "mass society," which includes the structural position of the great majority of the American population. In this he ignores kinship and friendship, and the whole mass of associational activities and relationships. One example is the spread of church membership—which I suppose Mills would dismiss as simply an escape from the boredom of white-collar life, but in my opinion is of considerable positive significance. (SAPMS, p. 218.)

We now have every reason to suppose that Parsons simply *does not care* what an individual thinks, feels, or experiences as a result of living in the System.

Parsons' views on social conflict in industrial societies take their cue from his theory of power and are, in fact, easily derivable from the latter. In the first place, a class system, like a set of power relations (which it also is), is viewed as held together largely through *loyalty*. We recall that Parsons defines loyalty as the " 'spilling over' of motivation to conform with the interests or expectations of alter beyond the boundaries of any institutionalized or agreed obligation (*Social System,* p. 98)." Loyalty is one of the prime components of the glue with which the Parsonian edifice is held together. For example, with regard to the expression of affection, "Here the focal problem for the social system is the allocation of loyalties among the different collectivities in which the component individual actors have roles, and the expression of these loyalties." (*Ibid.,* p. 418.) Parsons devises a complete theoretical analysis of the role of loyalty in the integration of a class system in his article, "A Revised Analytical Approach to the Theory of Social Stratification" (1953). We will not go into this article here; rest assured that the place given to loyalty is major.

Such a conception, in which, conceivably, the antagonism of the proletariat toward the bourgeoisie might be considered analytically secondary to the surplus of zeal exhibited by the proletariat in carrying out its tasks on behalf of the bourgeoisie, tends to eliminate from the analysis any consideration of conflict between subordinate and superordinate strata as a major motivating factor in social change. Indeed, such conflict is almost defined out of existence. We recall that Parsons regards the managerial directorate as the core of the dynamic processes of change at work within our society, since the managers are the custodians of those "collectivities" in which are institutionalized the dominant "value-orientations" of our society. In that case, a clash of interests among the various strata would exert only a marginal influence on change. Besides, Parsons considers that the powerful, by definition, are well able to enlist at the very least the "unconditional loyalties" of the subordinate strata. When we add this to Parsons' exaggerations of the integration and unity of our value system (see pp. 99-102 above), we see that Parsons understandably finds no place in his system for a direct confrontation of interests; it would be highly inconvenient at the very least. Thus, in *The Social System*, Parsons asserts that our stratification system is just "loose" enough; any shift in a " 'radical' direction, which would drastically cut down the rewards open to *any* elite elements, would have a seriously disturbing effect." (*Op. cit.*, p. 515.)

Parsons of course does recognize group antagonisms within the social system. But rather than causing change, such antagonisms represent the side effects of it. Processes of social change result in "strains," whereby those groups which receive the backlash of the tail of the change become disaffected, and are thus potentially disruptive of the system. Parsons states this explicitly in *The Social System:*

> It is probable that the strains imposed by these processes [of change] much more than any inherent 'conflict of interest' is the primary factor in the genesis of so-called 'class-conflicts' in modern Western society. In England it was the agricultural laborers who felt their livelihood threatened by machinery who constituted the spearhead of radical movements rather than the 'proletariat' as such. (*Op. cit.*, p. 513.)

It is interesting that Parsons considers the Luddites rather than the Labour Party as typical of English proletarian movements. It is clearly ludicrous to assert either that there has been no social conflict in England since the periods of primitive capitalist accumulation at the beginning of industrialization, or that marginal groups such as dispossessed agricultural laborers are to be considered the typical mass base for radical movements in industrial society. Accordingly, Parsons' choice of an example here, as well as his liberal use of quotation marks, can readily be considered as a desire to avoid the substantive issue of class conflict on the basis of interests.

Pursuing this matter further, we recall that Parsons considers the Left to be residual, "tending to gather together those elements in the society on whom the problems and difficulties arising from the dynamic process impinge." (See pp. 107-108 above.) This of course stems from Parsons' location of the center of change in the business community. Those politically opposed to what Parsons considers to be the major drift of the "value-orientations" of the "total system" are by definition interfering with change; they merely "see in governmental action an opportunity to remedy their situations." It does not occur to Parsons that the left may actually seek substantive structural changes in the economy and society.

What is to be done about the side effects of social strains was suggested in rather grisly fashion in "Propaganda and Social Control," one of the *Essays*. There, the victims of strains were bluntly compared to neurotics whose antics were clearly detrimental to the functioning of the social system. As for therapy, Parsons explicitly compares the role of the propagandist to that of the psychoanalyst. Presumably, the cure is effected when "unconditional loyalties" have been exacted. But we will hopefully assume that Parsons is far too much the academic liberal ever to countenance the consistent application of the logical implications of his position (the mass-manipulation features of the totalitarian state)—except perhaps in wartime.

Fortunately for Parsons, there was a situation in which academic liberalism and theory apparently coincided rather well: the McCarthy period in the United States. The result is a particularly lucid and well-written paper, "Social Strains in America" (1955). Here Parsons, with a good measure of accuracy, ascribes the McCarthy madness to the pyramiding of external strains upon the total society in the form of foreign policy disasters on top of severe internal strains in the form of the aftereffects of industrialization and of status anxieties in both and immigrant and native white Protestant groups. The groups under strain, says Parsons, resorted to "irrational behavior," which he compares to regression in individual neurosis and primitive magic. I feel that this analysis is basically sound; I myself have elsewhere ("The Politics of Delusion and Dream") analyzed the current outbreak of Radical Rightism largely in terms of a threat to the self-conception of subcultural validity held by an affluent segment of the Midwestern-Southern-Southwestern native white fundamentalist Protestant population. But what may be called into question is Parsons' chief remedy for the disease:

> Under American conditions, a politically leading stratum must be made up of a combination of business and nonbusiness elements. The role of the economy in American society and of the business element in it is such that political leadership without prominent business participation is doomed to ineffectiveness and to the perpetuation of dangerous internal conflict. It is not possible to lead the American people *against* the leaders of the business world. But at the same time, so varied now are the national elements which make a legitimate claim to be represented, the business element cannot monopolize or dominate political leadership and responsibility. (SAPMS, p. 247.)

So the Parsonian answer to the problem of the extremist movements deriving from social strains is the creation of a sanctified ruling class, with which there can be no argument, and which can be entrusted with holding in check all opposition, both of the Left and of elements even farther Right. He also again places exaggerated trust in the business community.

Parsons may be substantially right about the genesis of antagonisms in this particular context, but he definitely has no cause for smugly assuming that his notions of "social strains" can adequately explain all forms and occurrences of social conflict.

Our last major topic is Parsons' views on the industrialization of the underdeveloped world. Paradoxically, it seems that here his views most closely approach convergence with the great currents of the time, in the sense that he adopts the viewpoint of the modernizing elites of the underdeveloped nations. He is furthermore led directly to his position on industrialization by the same emphases which rendered much of his theory so grossly unreal when applied to the United States.

In the first place, there is no question but that he wants Production, and lots of it; it is not central to him whether the economic directorate is political or corporate:

> Looked at both in value terms and in organizational terms, the differences between the "public" and "private" modes of structuring the economy are secondary in the sense that preference between them becomes a question of *relative economic efficiency* which, in the nature of the case, will vary with concrete conditions; it is not a simple question of "principle."
>
> In value terms, the striking fact is that virtually the whole world has, within our time, come to assign to economic productivity a very high value indeed. The essential differences are not over productivity as *value*, but over the most effective means of implementing this value. Even the difference between American and Soviet orientations, which some feel is the deepest difference in the world, is not primarily a difference over the value of productivity. (SAPMS, p. 100.)

There is, of course, a certain element of truth here, but Parsons grossly oversimplifies. The value of political democracy seems to have at least marginal significance, but Parsons has already dismissed the question of political democracy (see pp. 106-107 above); for analytical purposes he finds no great difference between what is called democracy in the United States and the forms of "People's Democracy" behind the Iron Curtain.

As for the institutional arrangements of the industrial economy, Parsons holds that differences between the United States and the Soviet Union merely

> concern the *top* levels of the organizational structure, namely whether control should be implemented directly from above by administrative mechanisms or whether there should be heavy reliance on the more "automatic" controls which operate through the market mechanisms. (SAPMS, pp. 100-101.)

Here Parsons appears somewhat blinded by classical economic theory. The bulk of the nongovernmental controls on the American economy are of course the result of the collusive activities of "private governments" such as the automobile and steel industries (and, to a much lesser extent, such segments of organized labor as the UAW and the United Steelworkers), which employ their strategic positions in the economy to protect themselves against the very "market mechanisms" which Parsons believes structurally distinguish our economy from that of the Soviets. In an economy of "administered prices," the role of old-style market mechanisms as controls is distinctly secondary; in order to get an accurate picture of the features which distinguish our economy from that of the USSR, it is necessary to speak in terms of the *profit system,* as well as of organized *extragovernmental* economic power.

Parsons goes on to state that the American and Soviet managerial directorates, as well as their subordinate labor forces, occupy analogous positions in both economies. This is true because the organizational requirements of modern industry are the same everywhere; thus

> at the level of the producing unit or "firm," the differences are decreasingly significant. That the typical large-scale firm must be a "bureaucratic" organization now goes without saying. (SAPMS, p. 101.)

Here Parsons is clearly on firmer ground. The theoretical contention has a hoary respectability (Weber), and is firmly buttressed by empirical evidence (such as David Granick's study, *The Red Executive*). We will not quibble.

Parsons relates the existence in any economy of either public or private ownership to the historical evolution of the industrial system. Those societies bent on getting quick and efficient results are more likely to choose the socialist alternative. "A relatively 'mature' industrial economy of the American type" can, however, be effectively operated in the collective interest, within the capitalistic context. But Parsons also finds good historical reasons for the existence of the capitalist form of the industrial economy in the West.

One of the major contentions in the paper, "Some Reflections on the Institutional Framework of Economic Development" (SAPMS, pp. 98-131), is

> that the *original* development of industrialism in the Western world not only *did* but *had to* take place in "industrialistic" forms. This is because political organization in a pre-industrial situation without outside pressures would put unusually insurmountable obstacles in the way of such economic development, unless there were features in the social structure which could put institutional restraints on the exercise of political power and which *independently* of the political structure would provide special impetus to economic development. (SAPMS, p. 102.)

Parsons attempts to prove his case using the sociological equivalent of back-to-the-womb-and-beyond psychology. Among other things, he throws in Ancient Judaism, Greek thought, the Medieval Church, and, of course, Calvinism. We get here the entire Parsonian theory of history, complete with the linking of increasing "differentiation" with the advance of civilization. ("The keynote of my analysis is consideration of the process of structural differentiation in societies.") Recalling the intense Parsonian emphasis on "value-orientations" such as "instrumental activism" in industrial society, it is not surprising that the major point here is

> that a *primary* orientation to economic productivity on the part of a major sector of the total social structure, which modern industrialism requires, could not emerge until a relatively advanced stage of the process of differentiation had been reached. A variety of institutional and cultural features of Western society have tended to press this process of structural differentiation further and faster than it occurred in other parts of the world. . . . (SAPMS, p. 102.)

An immediate impetus, he says, was supplied by Calvinism, but deeper than this, as we find in another article ("Some Principal Characteristics of Industrial Societies," SAPMS, pp. 132-169),

> The Judeo-Christian tradition has from early times tended, with certain periods of "recession" from it, to be highly activistic in relation to the external environment. (SAPMS, p. 138.)

This is contrasted with the case in China and India. Yet we now find a tendency on the part of some scholars to discover intellectual roots for Chinese communism in the "worldly" character of Confucianism. Intellectual history is a dangerous thing.

But we digress. To return to the topic somewhat, it seems to me that Parsons entertains a fundamental misunderstanding of the history of the industrialization process in the West. It may be quite true that states in the pre-industrial or early industrial-capitalistic periods possessed neither the resources nor the insight for effective over-all planning of a developing economy (as may be inferred from the substantial failures of modernizing attempts by Peter the Great in Russia and Mohammed Ali in Egypt). But this should not prevent the assignment to political institutions of an enormous portion of the credit for the success of industrialism in England, the United States, Belgium, and other pioneers of industrial capitalism. Although the immediate impetus for economic development may have come from the capitalist firms themselves, government played a variety of roles. For instance, banks, canals, railroads, and other enterprises in the United States received a vast amount of financial "breaks" from political institutions at the federal, state, and local levels during the nineteenth century. Much of this financial help was either illegal or quasi-legal (Credit Mobilier). Related to this is the fact that many political measures not specifically designed for the enrichment of business were seized upon by the rising plutocrats for their own advantage. Notably among such measures were the financing of the Civil War and the Home stead Act (the railroads acquired huge amounts of Homestead land and sold it to the settlers at immense profits). Another form of governmental aid was the setting of high import tariffs—to the advantage of the industrial-commercial interest of the Northeast and to the detriment of the agrarian interest of the South. This issue, as we know, stimulated a secession movement in South Carolina (in 1833) which was put down only by the threat of the use of federal troops made by President Andrew Jackson. Still another means of governmental assistance was the use of police and troops representing all levels of political organization to discipline, bully, and coerce the labor force and thereby prevent labor unionization.

In England, the employment of governmental coercion took an interesting turn. As is universally acknowledged, the labor force in early English industry was derived largely from former peasants, agricultural laborers, and other rural dwellers, who were forced out of the countryside and into the cities as a result of the enclosure movement. The impetus for this movement was originally the "rationalization" of agriculture, but the advantages for industry were ultimately perceived. The complicity of government in this took the form, first of all, of Acts of Enclosure passed routinely by Parliament. Where peasants vigorously resisted their expropriation, troops were sometimes used (see *Das Kapital* on this). Once the labor force was accumulated in the cities, governmental force was used to break strikes, smash unions, and quell incipient violence.

Not only did industry never develop "*independently* of the political structure," but indubitably there was a fairly intimate tie-in. It was not for nothing that Marx called the capitalist state of the period of industrialization "the executive committee of the ruling class."

Although complete over-all planning may have been impossible during the period of Western industrialization, there might have been more planning than there actually was. Certainly the amount of unnecessary human misery and economic waste during this period staggers the imagination. Farsighted individuals understood this, but they were politically impotent within their societies and ideologically submerged within their class.

We might sum this up by saying that Parsons' emphasis on the structural differentiation of economic institutions from political ones and their initiative in the industrialization process leads him to minimize the importance of substantive unity between government and business on the level of policy.

Having completed the above digression, we turn to Parsons' ideas on the contemporary industrialization of the non-Western world. Here we find Parsons to be largely sound, intelligent, and not particularly original. He begins by presenting us with an abstract two-class model of the type of traditional society supposedly characteristic of most underdeveloped nations, with, as he sees it, the upper group enjoying prerogatives of political power and usually also religious prestige, and the lower consisting predominantly of peasants and some craftsmen and petty traders. (SAPMS, p. 117.)

The upper class controls, but does not manage, economic production, siphoning off what little surplus there is in order to maintain its traditional "life-style." Parsons notes and emphasizes the "dissociation" between the functions of economic production and other standard upper-stratum functions (such as political leadership) in traditional societies, and cites this as an obstacle to economic development.

Parsons qualifies this description of the upper stratum by noting that "interstitial" elements, which can be readily classified into neither great stratum, often have specialized economic aptitudes. Such groups may be classes (Japanese "chōnin") or ethnic groups (Jews, Parsis, Tamils). Parsons considers them a possible opening wedge for economic development.

The lower classes, engaged in "labor-intensive peasant agriculture," offer two huge blocks to economic development, "traditionalism," and "a strong pressure to reproduce the existing pattern of economic organization wherever opportunity exists for its expansion." These are bound up in a "peasant complex" which must somehow be broken for any development to take place. For this to be done there must be a combination of "favorable circumstances," which may be presented either by "locally meaningful" incentives to increase investment in agriculture and improve methods, or by "locally meaningful" opportunity for non-agricultural employment. But in general, Parsons sees both great indigenous classes, peasants and gentry, as well-nigh hopeless for appreciation of economic development. The situation is made even worse by the fact that the "private enterprise" ideology imported by the colonial power is identified with the "primary negative symbol" of colonialism, and "lacks resonance" (Parsonian for "sex appeal") in either of the two great classes.

But this picture of ironbound resistance to change has been upset, according to Parsons, by the wave of nationalism which has arisen since World War II. He regards the late war as something of a *deus ex machina* which erupted into the scene to transform relations that otherwise would have remained unchanged, and ignores such matters as economic exploitation by the colonial powers, racialism and racial discrimination, political repression often accompanied by military barbarism, economic changes begun under the colonial regimes, and cynical support by the colonialists of corrupt "traditional" rulers.

At any rate, Parsons expects that the national independence movement would bring about a tendency to restore the traditional values of the society, since after independence, "the first responsibility falls on the indigenous upper groups." It is, however, questionable whether this pattern is typical. A substantial number of nationalistic movements, especially in Africa, have been radical from the start. Restorationist movements, such as those of Northern Nigeria and the Ivory Coast, do not seem to be strong in most areas. But given the situation of a restorationist movement on the part of the upper class, Parsons in this instance holds no brief for the status quo, since, "Such restorationism is . . . directly inimical to economic development" (SAPMS, p. 121). He is principally interested in finding the source of the impetus for modernization, and finds it in political *countervalues:*

> It seems clear that the two-class structure I have posited greatly favors the Marxist definition of the situation, and that the restorationist tendency further plays directly into its hands. It is indeed this dominant two-class system, with religion associated with the upper classes as an obstacle to development, which is the primary explanation of the ironical fact that Marxism has appealed in almost directly inverse proportion to the level of a society's economic development. (SAPMS, p. 122.)

Parsons expects that "an organization like the Communist Party" could combine hostility to colonialism with opposition to indigenous restorationism. The Party is also committed to economic development and is able to adduce sufficient incentives to make the idea appealing. Given "outside support," such as "the blundering of Western powers suspected of wanting to restore the old colonialism," the Party's chances are good.

The social source of the new pro-development and socialist values Parsons locates in a new interstitial group: the intellectuals recruited from the old upper class. Taught from birth to disdain manual labor and economic pursuits, such intellectuals fear that the "economic individualism" of the West would lead to the erosion of the "central national community." Since they are Western-trained, they are committed to economic development. Hence, they embrace socialism. It is here that Parsons introduces the notion of the instrumental function of socialist ideology. This is worthy of note because Parsons' contempt for ideology—especially when it is employed by his fellow social scientists—is boundless, and few things give him greater pleasure than the factual disconfirmation of ideological contentions, especially those of Marxism. (Parsons' views on ideology and ideologists would be worth special attention in themselves, but they are not directly relevant to this paper.) But here he states that

> some sort of "socialist" ideology of economic development allows intellectuals to oppose restorationism, precisely from the point of view of national interests because restorationism is unrealistic as a program under the conditions of the modern world. Unless the intellectuals have secular political support which taps nationalistic motivations, it is difficult to see how this argument against fundamentalist restoration could be successful. (SAPMS, p. 124.)

The climate for socialism is favorable, since the society is preoccupied with questions of "its own identity and internal solidarity," and is subject, as a weak nation, to strong external pressures. The result is a concentration upon political problems. Accordingly, Parsons expects that the "primary impetus to change will come from the political sector of the society" (*loc. cit.*). This in turn facilitates a rapid transition to Western bureaucratic industrialism. Since an industrial system is already in existence, Parsons feels that the underdeveloped world should adopt the most modern features of it as soon as possible. He closes his discussion with the pious hope that "the introduction of the inevitable changes will be gradual," by which he means, unaccompanied by the mass extermination of the traditional upper class. Faithful to the notion of the "total system" to the very end, Parsons prefers a situation where the radical government acts as a leverage which exacts contributions to progress from all classes (Indonesia) over one in which it at least temporarily allies with the lower classes against the upper and seeks the total suppression of the latter (China). He points to Israel as an example of the kind of noncommunistic modernization which can be successfully achieved, but this example is fallacious and nonrepresentative for several reasons: the Israeli government is neither radical nor revolutionary; a large percentage of the Israeli population are immigrants from Western Europe and come ready-equipped with the modern attitudes, skills, and education characteristic of Europe (and of the best in Europe, since Jewish educational levels have traditionally exceeded those of the surrounding Gentile population); Israel has been heavily subsidized by West Germany and the New York City Jewish community; and the present Israel has not emerged from the pre-existing traditional society (the Palestinian Arabs); but has instead expropriated it and driven it (violently) out of the country.

In any case, I suspect that while violence may in the concrete case offend Parsons' sensibilities, it is "theoretically secondary," and is thus unimportant. If this is true, it cannot surprise us, since, as we know (pp. 105-106 above), he finds no great analytical difference between elections in the United States and the USSR; nor is he especially concerned why there should be. Parsons has no intellectual defense against the cruel logic of totalitarianism except a primordial emotional protest which, it appears, may easily be squelched by the ineluctable implications of his theory.

Parsons' notions as to the centrality of values in setting the development process in motion have been criticized by professional economists. Albert O. Hirschman, in *The Strategy of Economic Development,* is readily willing to concede the importance of fostering the appropriate values in facilitating economic change (p. 137). But he insists that a change in values is by no means necessary to *development;* indeed, the value shift may be a mere by-product of economic development long since under way. In the first place, he says, economic progress is never an even process within a society; the more favored groups will loudly proclaim their superiority over the others. This self-glorification tends to cause its own perpetuation:

> Even though the initial success of these groups may often be due to sheer luck or to environmental factors such as resource endowment, matters will not be left there. Those who have been caught by progress will always maintain that they were the ones who did the catching; they will easily convince themselves, and attempt to convince others, that their accomplishments are primarily owed to their superior moral attributes and conduct. It is precisely this self-righteousness that will tend to produce its own evidence; once these groups have spread the word that their success was due to hard work and virtuous living, they must willy-nilly live up to their own story, or at the least will make their children do so. In other words, there is reason to think that the 'protestant ethic' instead of being the prime mover, is often implanted *ex post* as though to sanctify and consolidate whatever accumulation of economic power and wealth has already been achieved. To the extent that this happens, a climate particularly favorable to further growth will actually come into existence in the sectors or regions that have pulled ahead. . . . (*Op. cit.,* pp. 185-186.)

This seems to explicitly and flatly contradict Parsons' contention that "a major sector of the social structure" must first be converted to values favorable to economic development (and this in turn requires a "relatively advanced stage of the process of structural differentiation") before industrialism becomes possible.

If we were to classify Parsons' views on industrialization as a political ideology, they might wind up being called "modernizing corporationism." Parsonianism combines nationalism and socialism with the encouragement of national solidarity and the suppression of class warfare. Such a theory is apparently being practiced by the modernizing elites of some of the newly independent nations (Ghana, Tunisia, Indonesia).

In considering Parsons' theories of industrialization, we have observed that they are inadequate and grossly idealized when applied to the evolution of industrial capitalism in the West, largely because of the intellectual difficulties arising from his fixation upon the idea of the structural differentiation between economy and polity (which also bedevils his view of contemporary reality). But on the question of the modernization of the underdeveloped world of today, we find him, if wide of the mark at several points, substantially in tune with the general drift of the times (at least insofar as he accords with the viewpoint of the modernizing elites who are now seeking to transform the underdeveloped nations). I feel that this is true because the question of contemporary modernization affords a possibility for the convergence of several consistent themes in Parsons' ideas: the first theme is the role of "value-orientations" in defining the course of a society's development. The values of traditionalism are here overwhelmed by the countervalues of socialism, nationalism, and economic development.

The second theme is the ability of a minority elite to embody the values of economic development and to mobilize the entire society behind them in their pursuit of the goals of progress. While great currents such as those of nationalism may be safely presumed to pervade an entire society, it is worthy of note that the specific values pertaining to economic growth and development are even more class-bound in the newly-emerging nations of Asia and Africa than in the highly developed societies of the West. (The masses in colonial territories seem to expect that independence will lead to little more than lower taxes and racial equality. There are, of course, dreams of pie-in-the-sky for all, but these are a long way from the "instrumental activism" that Parsons deems requisite to industrialism.)

Third is Parsons' reluctance to deal with the problem of the individual as a focus of value in his own right. We recall that no matter how many times or in how many ways Parsons defends the American business directorate, he never conceives of it as composed of powerful individuals acting in their own interests. They are always considered as members of the business community, or in relation to the institutions they manage, or in relation to the "total system." He cannot understand that they exact a heavy price from the society as individuals and as a group at the same time that they incidentally do a job for it by promoting whatever economic growth they promote. He is moreover skeptical, as he states in his review of *The Power Elite,* of "individual utopianism," whether in its capitalist, liberal, or socialist forms. Instead, as we recall, he favors a set of assumptions "which not only admit the necessity but assert the desirability of positive social organization." He, in fact, by his own admission (see p. 112 above), seems to have broken with (or "transcended") much of "the individualistic tradition in American and, more broadly, in Western thought." Now, however badly they may have been lived up to, the Western tradition has left us with at least the values of the individual apart from and against the system and of political democracy. But modernization in the contemporary underdeveloped world presents none of the aforementioned problems. The managerial directorates, while extremely powerful within their respective societies, are very closely identified with modernization for reasons which are primarily unselfish, except with regard to the perpetuation of their political power. They may accumulate petty luxuries here and there, or live in very marked contrast to the living standards of the masses, or suppress political opposition; but the cost to the societies in question is in the long run not nearly so great, in most cases, as that exacted by the Robber Barons of the early industrial capitalism. Also, the official ideologies, both traditional and radical, which are adopted by the governments of emerging nations, clearly tend to emphasize the primacy of the nation over the individual. Modernizing elites are nothing if not proponents of "positive social organization." And instead of political democracy, single-party states and military regimes are the rule in the underdeveloped world. In short, the pragmatic needs of the times neatly coincide with Parsons' great intellectual blind spot: for reasons which are intellectually respectable, he need not ever come to grips with the problem of the claims of the individual as an individual on the system.

When considering poor nations going through the throes of rapid forced industrialization, it is entirely appropriate, with some misgivings, to countenance the submergence of the individual in the totality. But in the case of the advanced industrial society such as ours, where sufficient resources exist so that the question of further growth can well become secondary, it is monstrous to conceptualize such a society from the central standpoint of further growth. The first questions to be asked are, "What are the valid claims which any individual may make upon the System? What obstacles prevent these claims from being satisfied and what are the deleterious effects of the System upon the individual personality? And how can such obstacles and conflicts be removed through structural change?"

In conclusion, I would say that Parsons exhibits a consistent tendency to gloss over the horrors of industrial society with bland phrases, tricks of definition, thinly disguised clichés, and arrogance; and to abolish all individual values other than those which serve the "total system." The Parsonian world does not provide for any possibility of a discontinuity between the individual's day-to-day life inside the System and its effects upon the inner world of his own personality. This point may be exemplified by Parsons' definition of anomie:

> Anomie may perhaps most briefly be characterized as the state where large numbers of individuals are to a serious degree lacking in the kind of integration with stable institutional patterns which is essential to their own personal stability and to the smooth functioning of the social system. (*Essays,* p. 125.)

The last phrase, "and to the smooth functioning of the social system," of course warps Durkheim's concept out of all recognition. The trouble is that the social Juggernaut can keep functioning all too smoothly at the same time as large numbers of people, who put in their eight hours per day, may be suffering from anomie. If this is true, it is important to take cognizance of the fact and treat it as a matter about which something should be done, despite the fact that the wheels of the social machine may be humming on merrily.

Despite what can only be considered an earnest and highly intelligent effort on Parsons' part, his sociology of complacency is a failure in dealing with the experiential reality of industrial society. It fails to touch upon an entire vast realm of the industrial experience, horror. It fails to comprehend either the collective horrors or the personal horrors which certain features of industrial society almost necessarily involve.

What may be needed is a "sociology of horror" in which social science tries to be honest with the industrial world and with itself.

Selected Bibliography

Parsons, Talcott, *The Structure of Social Action*, Glencoe, Ill.: Free Press, 1949.

——, *The Social System*, Glencoe, Ill.: Free Press, 1951.

——, *Essays in Sociological Theory*, Glencoe, Ill.: Free Press, 1954.

——, *Structure and Process in Modern Societies*, Glencoe, Ill.: Free Press, 1961.

——, "A Revised Analytical Approach to the Theory of Social Stratification," in Bendix and Lipset, eds., *Class, Status, and Power*, Glencoe, Ill.: Free Press, pp. 92-129, 1953.

——, " 'Voting' and the Equilibrium of the American Party System," in Burdick and Brodbeck, eds., *American Voting Behavior*, Glencoe, Ill.: pp. 80-120, 1959.

Williams, Robin M., *American Society: A Sociological Interpretation* (2nd ed.), New York: Alfred A. Knopf, Inc., 1960.

WHAT IS ALIENATION?
THE CAREER OF A CONCEPT

Lewis Feuer

Every age has its key ethical concept around which it can best formulate the cluster of its basic problems. "Duty" summated for Kant the meaning of life in the Prussian bureaucratic and pietistic society; "peace" was the basic longing of Hobbes living in England's time of civil war; "happiness" defined for Bentham the aims of a middle-class England which was challenging the rule of a landed aristocracy. Twenty-five years ago, the concept of "exploitation" was the focus of most socialist and liberal political philosophy. Today many thinkers would replace it with the concept of "alienation," which has indeed become the central one for the neo-revisionist school of Marxism. By "alienation," says Erich Fromm, "is meant a mode of experience in which the person experiences himself as an alien. He has become, one might say, estranged from himself." [1] Thus, neo-revisionism introduces an unusual emphasis into the history of socialist thought. The classical revisionism of Eduard Bernstein aimed to supplant the materialist negation of ethics with a "back to Kant" movement. Where Marx and Engels looked at ethical ideas as the epiphenomenal by-products of class struggle, Bernstein and Jaures sought a universalistic ethic with its formal expression in Kant's categorical imperative.

Neo-revisionism today returns not to Kant but to the youthful Marx who in manuscripts, sometimes unpublished, wrote down an ethical critique of capitalism. Marxism, aged, bureaucratized, and de-ethicized in the Soviet society, is being rejuvenated by young Marxists in Poland and America with the repressed and rejected ethical writings of the young Marx. In the past, the history of socialist thought has shown a certain oscillation between economics and ethics. During times of eco-

"What is Alienation? The Career of a Concept." From *New Politics* (Spring 1962), I, No. 3, 116-134. Copyright © 1962 by *New Politics*. Reprinted by permission of the author and *New Politics*.

nomic depression and distress, the socialist argument has tended to consist primarily of a demonstration that the economic system was beset by contradictions, disequilibria between production and consumption, which were insoluble in a capitalist society. In times of prosperity and rising living standards, on the other hand, the socialist argument has become primarily an ethical one of the disvalues of human life in capitalist society. Classical revisionism thus reflected the betterment in the life of the Western European working class at the end of the last century. Neo-revisionism today is a critique of both communist and capitalist societies, in their age of coexistent affluence, from the standpoint of the ethical aims of all human society.

In the Soviet Union itself, younger philosophers, evidently restive with the received bureaucratized version of Marxism, are turning to the younger Marx, the philosopher of alienation, to express their own disaffection with the bureaucratized world. An act of publication of Marx's writings in the Soviet Union is a political decision. In this sense, the recent publication in Moscow of Russian editions and English translations of Marx's *Economic and Philosophic Manuscripts of 1844* and his and Engels' *The Holy Family* betokens an interest in the underlying ethical source of Marxism, that ethic from which Marx and the Marxists became "alienated" in later years. The recovery of ethical consciousness in Marxist circles tends naturally, as long as Marxism itself is not rejected, to proceed by way of recovery of the forgotten, repressed ethical writings of Marx. It is a devious, tradition-bound avenue to the recovery of ethical consciousness, especially since the socialist ethic emerges with greater purity in the writings of such men as William Morris. Neo-Marxism throughout the world is clearly, however, finding a temporary conceptual halfway house in "alienation."

To evaluate the significance of the revival of "alienation," let us ask the following questions:

1. What was the meaning and use of "alienation" in Marx's thought?
2. What accounts for the appeal of the concept "alienation" among American intellectuals?
3. What does "alienation" signify today? Is it a useful concept for understanding societies?

The concept "alienation" has a lineage which one can trace right back to Calvin, who saw man alienated through all time from God by his original sin.[2] Calvin wrote with eloquence that "spiritual death is nothing else than the alienation of the soul from God, we are all born as dead men, and we live as dead men, until we are made partakers of the life of Christ."[3] Hegel imbibed the concept of alienation from pessimist Protestant theology; and the early Marx, in turn, like his fellow Hegelians, regarded man's history as one of alienation. His youthful *Economic and*

Philosophic Manuscripts depicted alienation as the essence of the capitalist order: "Private property is therefore the product, the necessary result of alienated labor, of the external relation of the worker to nature and to himself." Alienated man experienced himself not as an agent but as patient, not as creator but creature, not as self-determined but other-determined. The products of man's labor were transformed "into an objective power above us, growing out of our control, thwarting our expectations, bringing to naught our calculations. . . ." Because he was alienated from the product of his labor, man also became alienated from other men.[4] This estrangement from the human essence leads, in Fromm's words, to an "existential egotism," or as Marx stated it, man becomes alienated from "his own body, external nature, his mental life, and his *human* life."

Now the evidence is strong that, during the latter 1840's, Marx and Engels came to reject emphatically the use of the concept "alienation" as the foundation for their socialism. Their *Communist Manifesto* ridiculed in scathing terms the German True Socialists who refurbished the economic sense of the French Socialists with their metaphysical nonsense of "alienation": "They wrote their philosophical nonsense beneath the French original. For instance, beneath the French criticism of the economic functions of money they wrote *Alienation of Humanity. . . .*"[5] For the fact of the matter is that "alienation" as first used by Marx, Engels, and their fellow young Hegelians and Feuerbachians was a romantic concept, with a preponderantly sexual connotation. It was the language of a group which made a protest of romantic individualism against the new capitalist civilization, but which soon went on to its post-adolescent peace with bourgeois society. Marx and Engels discarded a concept which became alien to their own aims.

To have developed the concept "alienation" would have meant for Marx and Engels to have taken a direction which Freud later took; they would have had to study the forms of alienation, that is, *neuroses,* of bourgeois society, and, if "alienation" proved to be a universal concept, the modes of alienation common to all societies. "Alienation," however, was too much the catchword of the romantic intellectuals with their personal drama of temporary estrangement in an industrial civilization. Alienation moved a handful of poets and professors, who achieved their therapy with a few poems and treatises. The masses of men, on the other hand, were moved to action by exploitation.

The concept "alienation" expressed the striving of the Romantic movement, the recovery of spontaneous emotional life. There was a revulsion against sexual asceticism, a rediscovery among the German intellectuals of physical pleasure. German philosophy, the product of theological seminaries, had negated the human body; the new philosophers, disciples of Ludwig Feuerbach, affirmed it. The root meaning of "alienation" for Feuerbach was, it must be emphasized, sexual; the alienated man was one who had acquired a horror of his sexual life, and whose whole way of thinking was determined by this repression of sexuality. The critique of religion was so important for Feuerbach precisely because religious dogma was the manifestation of this sexual alienation. We might cite a few passages in which Feuerbach states the primary, sexual meaning of "alienation":

> The more man alienates himself from Nature . . . the greater the horror he has of Nature, or at least of those natural objects and processes which displease his imagination, which affect him disagreeably. . . . That which does not please him, which offends his transcendental, supranatural, or antinatural feelings ought not to be. . . . Thus the idea of the pure, holy Virgin pleases him; still he is also pleased with the idea of the Mother. . . . Virginity in itself is to him the highest moral idea, the *cornu copiae,* of his supranaturalistic feelings and ideas, his personified sense of honour and of shame before common nature. . . . Even the arid Protestant orthodoxy, so arbitrary in its criticism, regarded the conception of the God-producing Virgin as a great, adorable, amazing holy mystery of faith, transcending reason. . . .
>
> Now if abstinence from the satisfaction of the sensual impulse, the negation of difference of sex and consequently of sexual love,—for what is this without the other?—is the principle of the Christian heaven and salvation; then necessarily the satisfaction of the sexual impulse, sexual love, on which marriage is founded, is the source of sin and evil. . . . The mystery of original sin is the mystery of sexual desire.[6]

Alienation in a philosophical sense, that is, the denial of the reality of the material world, was the consequence of the religious alienation from sexuality. As Feuerbach stated it: "Separation from the world, from matter, from the life of the species, is therefore the essential aim of Christianity." Sexual asceticism was the source of the idealist metaphysics: "Pleasure, joy, expands man; trouble, suffering, contracts and concentrates him; in suffering man denies the reality of the world . . ." [7]

To overcome alienation signified for Feuerbach the overcoming of the Christian heritage of masochism and the emotions and thought-ways of clerical celibacy. To Marx, writing in 1844 as a Feuerbachian, the sexual meaning of "alienation" was still central. The ultimate human relationship which provided the criterion for the evaluation of societies was for the young Marx the sexual:

> The direct, natural, and necessary relation of person to person is the *relation of man to woman.* . . . In this relationship, therefore, is *sensuously manifested,* reduced to an observable fact, the extent to which the human essence has become nature to man. From this relationship one can therefore judge man's whole level of development . . . ; the relation of man to woman is the most natural relation of human being to human being.[8]

The alienation of man from himself signified that his natural human emotions had been distorted. *Alienation signified a mode of life in which man was being compelled by social circumstances to act self-destructively,* to cooperate in his own self-mutilation, his castration, that is, the destruction of his own manhood. The economy which men had created presumably to satisfy their needs was finally warping their deepest instincts. Repeatedly the young Marx and Engels characterized the bourgeois society in metaphors and actualities of sexual alienation. Economic exploitation eventuated in the mutilations of sexual alienation. Thus Engels wrote in his *The Condition of the Working-Class in England* how bourgeois society "unsexes" the human being:

> And yet this condition which unsexes the man and takes from the woman all womanliness, this condition, which degrades, in the most shameful way, both sexes, and through them, Humanity, is the last result of our much-praised civilization . . . ; we must admit that so total a reversal of the position of the sexes can have come to pass only because the sexes have been placed in a false position from the beginning.[9]

In these early writings, Marx and Engels, as Freudian forerunners, regarded love, not work, as the source of man's sense of reality. They wrote in *The Holy Family* against the idealistic subjectivists who could not recognize "love, which first really teaches man to believe in the objective world outside himself, which not only makes man an object, but the object a man!" [10]

The German idealistic intellectuals, whom Marx called the "Critical Critics," were estranged from reality, precisely because they repressed the natural sexual senses of love and tried with all sorts of metaphysical devices to spiritualize its reality: "Critical criticism must first seek to dispose of *love*. Love is a passion, and nothing is more dangerous for the calm of knowledge than passion." The alienated intellectuals use linguistic tricks to transform love into "a theological thing":

> by making *"love"* a being apart, separate from man and as such endowed with independent being. By this simple process, by changing the predicate into the subject, all the attributes and manifestations of human nature can be Critically transformed into their opposite and *estrangements.*[11]

Underlying the philosophers' misuse of language, according to Marx and Engels, were psychological motivations to repress the world of flesh and material reality. Socio-psychological analysis, in psychoanalytical fashion, established when a linguistic estrangement from reality was taking place. Critical Criticism eventuated in alienation because its masochistic motivation sundered man from himself and the external world: Critical Criticism was thus "a Moloch, the worship of which consists in the self-immolation and suicide of man, and in particular of his *ability to think.*" "But love is an un-Critical, unchristian materialist," continued Marx and Engels. Sexual repression led to the impairment of the sense of reality, and consequently to ideological devices which substituted abstractions for things; the liberation of love led to a renewed sense of citizenship in the universe.

With heavy-handed humor, Marx and Engels satirized the critical ideologists who substituted the idealistic category of Dancing for the frank sensuality of the cancan:

> The reverend parson [Szeliga] speaks here neither of the *cancan* nor of the *polka,* but of dancing in general, of the *category* Dancing, which is not performed anywhere except in his Critical cranium. If he saw a single dance at the Chaumière in Paris his Christian-German soul would be outraged by the boldness, the frankness, the graceful petulance and the music of that most sensual movement.

The dancers "give the spectator the inspiring impression of frank human sensuality"; they "can and must necessarily be frankly sensual human beings!" The antisensual Critic substitutes an essence for existence: "The Critic introduces us to the ball for the sake of the *essence of dancing.*" [12]

Marx's tribute to the cancan would have outraged Khrushchev, who with Bolshevik virtue railed at Hollywood for the cancan immorality.

The idealistic metaphysicians, according to the young Marx and Engels, aim to deprive love of its bodily reality:

> As soon as there is no more nervous current and the blood in the veins is no longer hot, the *sinful body,* the seat of sensual lust becomes a corpse and the souls can converse unhindered about "general reason," "true love," and "pure morals." The parson debases sensuality to such an extent that he abolishes the very elements which inspire sensual love—the rush of the blood, which proves that man does not love only by insensitive phlegm; the nervous current which connects the organ that is the main seat of sensuality with the brain. He reduces true sensual love to the *mechanical secretio seminis* and lisps with an ill-renowned German theologian: "Not for the sake of sensual love, not for the lust of the flesh, but because the Lord said, increase and multiply." [13]

Eugene Sue, the author of *Les Mystères de Paris,* had similarly mystified over the sexual attraction of one of his characters, Cecily, a slave. Marx and Engels saw no point in mystifying about this attraction: "The mystery of Cecily is that she is a *half-breed.* The mystery of her sensuality is the *heat of the tropics.*" [14] Behind every religious and philosophical mystery was an alienation of man's sexual nature from himself. Thus Marx and Engels rail against the "puritan sermon" which spins its unreal web of "the mystery of the mystery, the essence of the essence" of love.[15]

At this time Marx and Engels did not regard class struggle as humanity's lever for the achievement of communism. Their definition of communism omitted any reference to class struggle. Communism, they defined as the "complete return of man to himself as a social (i.e., human) being—a return become conscious . . . it is the *genuine* resolution of the conflict between man and nature and between man and man—the true resolution of the strife between existence and essence, between objectification and self-confirmation, between freedom and necessity, between the individual and the species." [16]

Communism for Marx and Engels constituted at this time the overcoming of all alienation. The sexual overtones of "alienation" persisted as they tended to generalize the concept to signify the subjective state which accompanies any situation of emotional frustration which is the outcome of man's own misconceived social behavior and social arrangements. They expressed the hatred of commercialism common to the Romantic School, which regarded bourgeois society as having alienated man from his sexuality; money, in Shakespeare's words, was the "common whore of mankind." "Money is the alienated ability of mankind," and it enables the ugly man, contrary to nature, to secure the loveliest woman: "I am ugly, but I can buy for myself the most *beautiful* of women. Therefore I am not *ugly*, for the effect of *ugliness*—its deterrent power—is nullified by money." [17] Money is an "overturning power," a destroyer of "individualities." Money makes man's love impotent: "Assume *man* to be *man* and his relationship to the world to be a human one: then you can exchange love only for love, trust for trust, etc." But, "if you love without evoking love in return . . . then your love is impotent—a misfortune." [18] In short, when love is transformed into a self-destructive experience which gives masochist traits to the character, man has been alienated, self-estranged from his essence, by the rule of money. For in bourgeois society, "you must make everything that is yours salable"; the tyranny of the competitive market crushes "all sympathy, all trust." Political economy wars with human nature, "the ontological essence of human passion." Political economy castrates both capitalists and workingmen. The workingmen are asked by bourgeois economy to give up sexuality altogether. The Malthusian ideologists with their antisexual motivation propose that the workingmen "prove themselves continent in their sexual relations . . . Is not this the ethics, the teaching of asceticism?" [19] Bourgeois political economy and a humanist ethics are at loggerheads. Political economy becomes the antihuman ideology of asceticism:

The science of marvelous industry is simultaneously the science of asceticism . . . Self-denial, the denial of life and of all human needs, is its cardinal doctrine. The less you eat, drink and read books; the less you go to the theater, the dance hall, the public-house; the less you think, love, theorize, sing, paint, fence, etc., the more you *save*—the *greater* becomes your treasure, which neither moths nor dust will devour—your *capital*. The less you *are*, the more you *have*; the less you express your own life, the greater is your alienated life—the greater is the store of your estranged being.[20]

Alienated from his own activity, the worker's life is "activity as suffering, strength as weakness, begetting as emasculating, . . ." [21] The worker is transformed, as one would say, into a masochist.

As Marx and Engels drew closer to the realities of working-class life and social struggle, they became disenchanted with the friends of their first circle, the Young Hegelians and the Feuerbachians. Their erstwhile philosophical associates seemed to them to make their preoccupation with "alienation" the basis for ridiculous gestures against society—an adolescent sowing of philosophical wild oats. The revolutionary activity of the Young Hegelians in the Society of the Free consisted of buffoonery, wild processions in the streets, "scandalous scenes in brothels and taverns," the taunting of a clergyman at a wedding.[22] They tended to be indifferent in 1844 to the revolt of the Silesian weavers; not so Marx, who was stirred by their song of protest, and saw the emergence of the proletariat to the dignity of a self-conscious class. Arnold Ruge, spokesman of the Young Hegelians, mocked at the "meager handful of artisans" in the workingmen's club, the League of the Just, and was appalled by their communist ideas, but this group moved Karl Marx into an intensity of thought and action he had never experienced in the literary-philosophical circle. The workingmen's leaders impressed Marx and Engels as "three real men," and Marx pondered their ideas deeply.

There are scholars who maintain that Marx and Engels came to their socialist standpoint and materialist conception of history through a study of Hegelian and Feuerbachian texts. The truth is rather that they imbibed a certain terminology from the philosophers, but the impelling force was their own sensitivity to social movements and their own deep sympathies for the workingmen. Engels did not learn the significance of economic reality from an internal criticism of Hegelian texts. Rather, he tells us, "while living at Manchester, I was made painfully aware that economic factors, hitherto assigned an insignificant role or no role at all by historians, were, at least under modern conditions, a decisive power in the world." [23] And Marx was led to considering communist ideas by his experiences as editor of the *Rheinische Zeitung*. He had to write editorials in 1842 on the encroachments of rich landowners against the peasants' common lands and the peasants' recourse to wood theft from the landowners' forests. In this pre-industrial situation, Marx undertook to plead the cause of "the unpropertied masses without political and social rights," the dispossessed peasants and pre-proletarians. In the course of this controversy, he announced that he planned to study the communist ideas of Leroux, Considérant, and Proudhon. "There was no provision in Hegel's ideological system," said Marx, for dealing with such socio-economic problems.[24] This was a journey the Young Hegelians did not make; Bruno Bauer, their leader, ridiculed the masses as in everlasting opposition to intellect, that is, the intellectuals. Logic follows on emotion, and where the social emotion was absent, the Young Hegelians wallowed in the masochistic joy of their "alienation." Marx and Engels finally discarded the vocabulary of the school, and spoke in the direct language of social realities which needed no romantic metaphor.

With their abandonment of the concept of alienation, Marx and Engels made central in their political philosophy the concept of struggle. German ethical socialists, with their humanistic talk of love, seemed indeed to Marx and Engels akin to masochist ascetics with their lack of aggressive vitality and energy. Moses Hess, the "communist rabbi," who, besides introducing Marx and Engels to communist ideas, was their precursor in using "alienation" as the ground for the criticism of capitalist civilization, was a saintly figure. To Marx and Engels, however, his compulsion to undo justice which led him to marry a prostitute, must have seemed guilt-tormented and self-immolating.[25] The workingmen of the League of the Just looked with suspicion upon the "humanism" of such intellectuals.[26]

What emerged in Marx was a socialism founded on aggression, not on love. It must not be forgotten that force, not love, was for Marx "the midwife of every old society which is pregnant with the new," and Engels wrote eloquently of the therapy of violence, which, in Germany, "would at least have the advantage of wiping out the servility which has permeated the national consciousness. . . ." To reject violence, according to Engels, was the "parsons' mode of thought—lifeless, insipid, and impotent. . . ."[27]

This insistence on the primacy of hatred, aggression, for the socialist movement was a reiterated theme in Engels' writing. To Lavrov, the Russian Populist sociologist, Engels wrote in 1875: "In our country it is hatred rather than love that is needed—at least in the immediate future —and more than anything else a shedding of the last remnants of German idealism. . . ."[28] He and Marx feared that the entry of ethical intellectuals into the workers' movement would "castrate" the Party. One must avoid the mood, they said, which makes for "humble submission and confession that the punishment was deserved."[29] Not talk of " 'true love of humanity' and empty phraseology about 'justice' " but class struggle was required.[30] There was a concern always for the maintenance of the masculinity of the movement, a fear that a dwelling on concepts such as "alienation" would indeed masochize the workers' movement as it had the intellectuals.

Engels in later years regarded the writings on alienation as philosophic juvenilia which scarcely warranted the interest of the developed socialist movement. When a young Russian Socialist in 1893 asked about them, "Engels was embarrassed," he later recalled.[31] Both Marx and Engels still continued to entertain great hopes for a basic transformation of the character of work and the family; nevertheless, they did not make use of the concept of alienation to formulate these hopes.[32] The word "alienation" was absent from Marx's mature analysis.

Thus Marx and Engels veered to an opposite extreme as they extirpated "alienation" from their ideas and made "struggle" central. They left a tremendous gap in their theory of socialism by simply ruling out ethical ideas as "modern mythology." They made it all the easier for the Stalinist perversion of their philosophy to justify itself with appeals to technological necessity, the historical mission of hatred, and the meaninglessness of absolute justice. Whether the basis for a liberal ethic, however, can be provided by a return to the Calvinist-Hegelian concept of alienation seems doubtful. Its root-metaphor, as we shall see, is not a helpful one for the understanding of the world's problems.

Engels' reluctance to publish Marx's and his early writings has called forth contrary explanations from various scholars. A few years ago, I called the attention of Mr. Daniel Bell to these passages, and he made extensive use of them in his well-known essay "Two Roads from Marx." Then Robert Tucker, in his erudite study *Philosophy and Myth in Karl Marx*, tried to explain Engels' embarrassment at the mention of these early works. Marx and Engels, according to Tucker, always continued to hold to their youthful concept of alienation, but felt constrained to be "secretive" about their early writings because to publish such philosophical material "would confuse and disorient the always unsufficiently class-conscious workers." [33] Tucker's theory seems to me singularly unconvincing. For Marx and Engels never hesitated to follow what seemed to them the scientific course, and to publish the most technical and abstruse analyses. The proletariat had to struggle the best it could with the volumes of *Capital* and *Anti-Dühring*. No, "Engels was embarrassed," as the young Narodnik Voden put it, because he was being reminded as an old man of youthful writings which were filled with sexual and romantic language and yearnings. His paragraphs on cancan dancing, tropical love, sexual secretions, and his sexual invective against money were juvenilia which embarrassed him. Moreover, as he told his translator, Florence Kelley Wischnewetzky, in 1886, "the semi-Hegelian language of a good many passages of my old book is not only untranslatable but has lost the greater part of its meaning even in German." [34] To have put them forward seriously, and to have had them therefore taken by naïf disciples and hostile critics as the philosophical basis of the socialist movement probably seemed to him to run a needless risk of exposing Marx, himself, and the movement to considerable ridicule. So Engels classified these writings in the same category with the love lyrics Marx wrote as a student.

II

Let us turn now to the varieties of usage of "alienation" in contemporary social analysis.

The great problems of contemporary society have all been described as arising from different modes of alienation. We can distinguish six different principal modes in which, from the sociological standpoint, alienation is said to characterize the experience of modern people. These modes of alienation are:

(1) the alienation of class society
(2) the alienation of competitive society
(3) the alienation of industrial society
(4) the alienation of mass society
(5) the alienation of race
(6) the alienation of the generations.

These modes of alienation are independent of each other. A class society need not be a competitive one; there have been competitive economies which were founded on handicrafts, and mass societies, such as the Indian and Chinese, which were pre-industrial. A strict class society, carried to caste extremes, brings with it relief from competitive tension, but it aggravates the frustrations of initiative and choice of one's own work; in addition, the man of the lower class must internalize feelings of inferiority, and cultivate a degree of self-hatred and contempt. In this sense, he is internalizing feelings and attitudes towards himself of self-destruction.

A competitive system makes for a mode of alienation distinct from that in which classes are more fixed. In the United States during World War II, the men in the Air Force were found to be more discontented with their rank than were the men in the Military Police. This, despite the fact that the Air Force was full of corporals and sergeants, whereas the Military Police were mostly privates. Indeed, the very plentifulness of opportunity in the Air Force deepened the sense of disappointment, personal inadequacy, and resentment in the minds of those defeated in the competitive struggle for stripes. On the other hand, the M.P. felt less relatively deprived, since most of his friends shared his own lowly status.[35] Competition exacts this toll; from the standpoint of the deepest feelings, there is no "good loser."

Industrial society brings its characteristic mode of alienation to the man on the assembly line. Ely Chinoy found that nearly four-fifths of his sample of automobile workers cherished the dream of leaving the factory forever. Mostly they longed for the independence of small business men.

As he approached middle age, the worker sadly renounced his dream, and resigned himself to the assembly line.[36] This alienation of man from the machine, which stands against him, imposing its rhythm on him so that he is a satellite to its motions, is something which is common to all industrial societies, whether they be capitalist or socialist. As automobile workers told Walker and Guest:

> The work isn't hard, it's the never-ending pace . . . The guys yell "hurrah" whenever the line breaks down. . . . You can hear it all over the plant.
> The job gets so sickening—day in and day out plugging in ignition wires. I get through with one motor, turn around, and there's another motor staring me in the face. It's sickening.[37]

The different segments of modern industry vary greatly in the extent to which their work processes give their respective workers a sense of alienation. Where the worker has a greater measure of control over the pace of his job, where he is relatively freer from the overseeing eye of a supervisor, where, above all, the character of the job makes possible the mutual aid, solidarity, and friendships of an on-the-job working group, to that extent job satisfaction rises.[38] Manual workers of all kinds, however, derive far less satisfaction from their work than men in the professions. Labor still remains for the bulk of mankind affected with the curse of alienation from nature which Adam and Eve sustained when they were ousted from the Garden of Eden: "Cursed is the ground for thy sake; . . . In the sweat of thy face shalt thou eat bread, . . ." No wonder that a neglected socialist classic is entitled *The Right to Be Lazy*.

The alienation of race is distinct and irreducible to the other modes. Negro writers have told of the Veil which exists between them and white men. "Within the Veil was he born, said I; and there within shall he live,—a Negro and a Negro's son," wrote W. E. B. Du Bois of his firstborn.[39] This racial alienation could coexist with a planned socialized economy; it has found its place in socialist parties and labor movements. The alienation of generations appears especially in the gerontocratic societies of the Far East. The youth in the Japanese Zengakuren, for instance, find little to admire in the older generation; they must look for their inspiration to persons outside their national history or create their own ideas.

Is "alienation," however, a useful concept for the analysis of these modes of human unhappiness and frustration? Is it more than a dramatic metaphor which for reasons peculiar to intellectuals' experience has become their favorite root-metaphor for perceiving the social universe? Is it less, however, a tool for understanding than a projection of the psychology of intellectuals disenchanted with themselves?

It would be a major blunder to regard alienation as characteristically a phenomenon of modern society.[40] For what stands out from an historical and comparative standpoint is the omnipresence of alienation; it takes different guises in all societies. There are modes of alienation in small, egalitarian, cooperative, and agricultural societies. The countries of New Zealand and Sweden have achieved a high egalitarian standard of living, but qualified observers have complained of the drab and dull character of their lives. Margaret Cole, doing research on *Democratic Sweden* for the New Fabian Research Bureau, couldn't wait to leave the Scandinavian social democratic tedium, while Leslie Lipson found an oppressive "like-mindedness" among the New Zealanders, a "cultural homogeneity," the offspring of equality and security, which led New Zealanders to be suspicious and intolerant of intellectuals, foreigners, and freethinkers, in short, a world "made safe for mediocrity" in a "small and culturally homogeneous milieu." [41]

The agricultural cooperative societies of Israel, the *kibbutzim,* inspire their own corresponding mode of alienation; a typical novel of kibbutz life depicts the "interminable vacuity" of its existence, and portrays characters who, becoming desperate in this collective microcosm for a sense of their own individualities, flee to their tents which shut out a world, "Petty, noisy, full of shadow and darkness." "He reacted to communality by going off by himself, by standing aloof. . . . Then people show up as petty, ludicrous, selfish, malicious, cruel: you fall into an attitude of general contempt; you hate and become still further alienated from your fellows. It is a closed circle, a squirrel cage from which there is no release. . . . Pettiness and selfishness creep in, even into the midst of their community based on equality and fraternity." [42] Carol Kennicott in Sinclair Lewis' *Main Street* discovered the tyranny of the disanonymous small society, while in lonely hamlets in Vermont, farmers built their houses on hills to catch a glimpse of a neighbor; living in individualistic outposts, far from mass societies, they became ridden with incest and neurosis.[43] Those who think alienation was born with modern technology might ponder the picture of the peasant which La Bruyère gave in the French traditional society of the seventeenth century:

> Certain wild animals, male and female, are scattered over the country, dark, livid, and quite tanned to the sun, who are chained, as it were, to the land they are always digging and turning up and down with an unwearied stubbornness; their voice is somewhat articulate, and when they stand erect they discover a human face, and, indeed, are men.[44]

If alienation then is so multiform, can it be given a precise operational meaning which would be useful in social analysis?

Able social scientists have tried in recent years to define the dimensions of alienation, and to construct scales which would enable one to measure statistically a person's degree of alienation. Melvin Seeman, for example, has tried to distinguish between five variants in "alienation"—powerlessness, meaninglessness, normlessness, isolation, and self-estrangement. Seeman wishes to remove "the critical, polemic element in the idea of alienation," and to translate what it has to say into the language of the psychological theory of learning. But the will to criticize and polemize is precisely the essential intent behind the idea of alienation, and a multitude of alienated persons would be dissatisfied equally with conditions of power-possession, meaningfulness, norm-orientedness, involvement, and self-acknowledgment.

Alienation has a way of eluding a fixed set of dimensions because it is as multipotential as the varieties of human experience. Seeman, for instance, gives an operational definition of "meaninglessness"; it is a mode of alienation which is characterized "by a low expectancy that satisfactory predictions about future outcomes of behavior can be made"; the person senses that his ability to predict behavioral outcomes is low.[45] But, contrary to Seeman's standpoint, a great deal of contemporary thought finds a state of alienation precisely in those ideologies which profess to predict with high confidence the outcome of people's behavior. What is "historicism" in modern terms if not a theory which aims to foresee the broad social resultant of the sum of individual actions? Historicism is assailed by thinkers such as Karl Popper and Isaiah Berlin exactly because they find themselves alienated in a world of social determinism; they wish for a world in which the degree of social predictability would be low. In such a world, they would feel less alienated.

Again, the alienated man is a person, according to Seeman, who finds himself at odds with popular culture. He does not read *Reader's Digest,* and like many intellectuals, attaches a low value "to goals or beliefs that are typically highly valued in the given society." Yet the plaint is often precisely in the other direction. The artist, the writer, the poet, complain how quickly they become successful, how rapidly the public now accepts them. The avant-garde cannot now long enjoy the pleasures of the vanguardian: *Holiday, Mademoiselle,* and *Esquire* compete for the most experimental poems, and stories. Peter Viereck has spoken eloquently of how the artist finds quickly the accolades of popular culture, and he has protested against the very loss of loneliness and pride in isolation which was once the artist's.

Today the forces of mere prestige—the Rotarianism of the highbrows—have a more effective method than the stake. They make him chic.

Every new philosophical, literary, or religious insight (emphatically including the new conservatism) soon finds itself adopted, adulterated by the Overadjusted Man. . . . Today the lonely crowd rushes to buy an abridged pocketbook of *The Lonely Crowd* or, easier still, to read the still more abridged abridgment that appeared in a popular weekly.[46]

The avant-garde is separated now only by a few issues of a little magazine from acceptance into the big. But the artist then voices an altered mode of alienation. He dislikes acceptance even on his own terms. In retrospect, he finds values in isolation which are lacking in acceptance and identification. Whichever direction one takes on the social compass, one finds alienation.

The alienation of self-estrangement is equated by Seeman with the notion of "other-directedness" made famous by David Riesman. Yet here, too, we find that directions go awry, and that inner-directed and other-directed both share the alienated status. The child, says Riesman, is conditioned to other-directedness when it learns that whatever it does must not be valued for itself, "but only for its effect on others," and this Seeman translates as making one's behavior dependent upon anticipated future rewards; the person becomes self-estranged because he enjoys nothing for its own sake. There is a sound insight in this formulation, but it has nothing to do with other- and inner-directedness. For a Calvinist, inner-directed person, who serves his conscience and not public opinion, can be every whit as alienated as the other-directed person.

When the young John Dewey found an "inward laceration," a sense of "divisions and separations," which were "a consequence of a heritage of New England culture, divisions by way of isolation of self from the world, of soul from body, of nature from God," he was defining exactly the inner-directed mode of character from which he sought liberation.[47] The person with a strong internalized superego can feel alienated from himself, and long, as a matter of fact, for more "other-directedness" as a way of overcoming his inner tension. Thus Dewey looked to "shared experience," to "social" experience as the highest, as an almost mystical deliverance from alienation.

Indeed, it soon becomes evident that the categories "inner-directed" and "other-directed" are limited in clarifying the modes of alienation. For what is omitted is the quality of the feeling experienced toward the self, others, family, God, nation, or tribe. To describe an emotional vector, the kind of feeling and its intensity are dimensions as well as its direction. A man who follows the Golden Rule is, from one standpoint, other-directed; if he does so from dictate of conscience, he is inner-directed; but if he acts from motives of calculation, probably it would be most accurate to call him narcissistic. For whatever warm feelings he has are directed toward his self.

Dale Carnegie in his tract for the times *How to Win Friends and Influence People,* which sold five million copies, proposed some excellent precepts: "Be a good listener. Talk in terms of the other man's interests. Make the other person feel important." If this "other-directedness" were the outcome of a genuine affection for others, it would not signify alienation. But where it is simulated behavior, where the underlying motive is hatred and aggression toward others, then this behavior, even when successful, gives rise to alienation. For the person is then repressing his deeper feelings, and acting in ways which run contrary to what he would express. The schematic terminology of means and ends fails to state clearly the crucial significance of the underlying emotion. What matters is not that you are using others as a means but rather that your basic emotion toward others is one wishing to debase them, to use them in order to degrade them. You may treat a person as an end because of your stern conscience; you will still remain alienated because the underlying emotion remains one of hostility toward him. In any case, Riesman's terms, with their directional emphasis, do not clarify the emotional source of alienation.

In another noteworthy effort to measure alienation, Dwight Dean has devised several scales to measure three components—powerlessness, normlessness, and social isolation.[48] Yet his attempt, too, fails as a measure of "alienation" precisely because that experience can be found in every direction of human experience—among the powerful as the powerless, the normful as the normless, the socially involved as well as the isolated. For instance, consider the item in the measurement of powerlessness:

"We are just so many cogs in the machinery of life."

The human switch or lever can, however, be as alienated as the human cog. A power-driven Stalin, aware of his own tyrannical power, but caught and haunted by never-ending anxieties, in a domain of paranoid self-aggrandizement, is an alienated man, estranged from the mankind around him and the socialist aspiration which once had partially moved him. The superpotent man is complementary in his alienation to the impotent.

Or consider again the items designed to help measure normlessness:

"The end often justifies the means."
"I often wonder what the meaning of life really is."

Leon Trotsky felt that the Bolsheviks gave meaning to their lives because they pursued an end which at least partially justified their means. By the sociologist's standards, the Bolsheviks, however, were normless.[49] Again, what of the philosophical individual who is agnostic as to norms and ultimates? Is he more an alienated man than the person who is indifferent to such questions? Many persons, however normless in an ultimate sense, find fulfillment in their human affections and their own chosen loyalty to a job. Life can provide the identification of provisional, pre-ultimate goals. "And pursue the unknown end," said Justice Holmes in his final aphorism of life, and one would hesitate to place him, therefore, among the alienated. Ignorance as to the meaning of life can be the basis for a cultivation of human experiences which become their own justification; indeed, the world of human facts may then be all the more closely sought. John Dewey, as he turned from religious metaphysics to agnosticism, found a more effective device against alienation ("dualism" and "separation" he called it) in political, social, and educational activities.

To measure the extent of social isolation, Dean proposes such items as:

"Sometimes I feel all alone in the world."

The image of "the lonely crowd" is most influential in social criticism today. The child deprived of affection or threatened with its loss finds an inner emptiness within himself, and sometimes, as he sees the world pervaded with hostility, wishes to have it all over with. At the same time, however, we have the revolt against the cult of "togetherness," against what Whyte calls the "social ethic." The right to privacy, as Brandeis named it, becomes rediscovered in a society which emphasizes collectives, committees, and cooperative achievements. If there is an alienation in loneliness or anomie, there is a corresponding alienation in togetherness and overidentification. The Hegelian philosophers reduced the individual into an adjective of the Total; there was no loneliness here, only an oppressive perpetual absorption in which the individual longed to become an independent noun.

This recovery of the sense of one's individuality, as distinct from the roles which party, class, organization, or group imposes, is what lies behind what is often called "the quest for identity." Alienation lies in every direction of human experience where basic emotional desire is frustrated, every direction in which the person may be compelled by social situations to do violence to his own nature. "Alienation" is used to convey the emotional tone which accompanies any behavior in which the person is compelled to act self-destructively; that is the most general definition of alienation, and its dimensions will be as varied as human desire and need.

Why, however, should the word "alienation" be used to describe the subjective tone of self-destructive experience? The metaphor of "alienation" overlays this experience with a quality which is peculiar to the drama of contemporary intellectuals in their most despondent mood. The contemporary intellectuals' experience of alienation is concretely one of his withdrawal from political movements; he has disavowed identifications. The existentialist's insistence on a chosen individuality which will not partake of any class, group, or party identification involves necessarily a sense of alienation. Alienation is the dramatic metaphor of the intellectual who has left the Political Garden of Eden and projects his experience as the exemplar of all human frustrations. The frustrations are immense and universal, but are they not misdescribed in the projective metaphor of a very small section of humanity?

The fondness of the contemporary intellectual for the concept "alienation" has little to do with the modes of alienation associated with mass, class, competitive and industrial societies. The intellectual's alienation was in part a self-alienation which arose as he discovered the character of his own underlying aims. Self-discovery brought the reproaches of conscience; there was also the realization that the movement, class, or party with which he had identified himself could become evil-ridden as the society which he had hoped to help redeem. The sustaining sense of the intellectual's mission all but vanished during the last two decades; the disruption of the labor-intellectual alliance has left the intellectual, at least for a time, without the sense of a supporting identification which gives meaning to his efforts. The words "meaninglessness," "powerlessness," "normlessness," which are used to characterize the dimensions of alienation, have a special application to the experience of the contemporary intellectual; the meaninglessness of his life is its lack of a social goal; his powerlessness reflects the intellectual's self-description: "we have no social class with which to work"; his normlessness is the fact that his socialist ethic is gone, and the recognition that it's all careerism.

Every movement of social reform has been characterized by a "back to the people" ethos; correspondingly, the end of such a movement has always been accompanied by an "away from the people" mentality. During the thirties, the American intellectual experienced an identification with the working-class movement, and regarded himself as united with labor to achieve a more just and civilized society. A few years after the Second World War, however, he was alienated from a working class which seemed to him devoid of a sense of historic mission; "we disaffiliate, we disinvolve, we disengage," said the intellectuals frankly. "We were right, but they [the masses] wouldn't listen," writes Dwight Macdonald. "Nothing is more frustrating for an intellectual than to work out a logical solution to a problem and then find that nobody is interested." [50] Another writer described this experience of alienation in the sexual idiom of contemporary fiction:

> This gentleman, and others like him, decided they'd been stood up by history for the last time. They're through with her; she seemed attractive, but has proven to be a bitch. No respectable girl would turn down clean, handsome Marxists who love her for herself, then go to bed with triflers. . . . The logic of the clean, handsome Marxists of the 1930's demands that they renounce such a promiscuous slut, and search for a good virgin. . . .[51]

Prosperity came to the generation of leftist intellectuals. Thirty years ago Walter Weyl spoke of his generation of "tired radicals." The alienated intellectuals, however, were not tired; they were filled with creative energy and helped to research and work by the unprecedented Research Revolution in the universities and the efflorescence of magazines and television. The alienation was not weariness but a sense that they themselves were not as fine persons as once they had been, that love had left their hearts. There were those intellectuals who discovered that power, possessions, and status were what they had wanted all along, but their newfound narcissism and reconciliation with their selves did not banish completely the self-reproach they call "alienation." And like a true metaphysician, the intellectual projects his "alienation" upon every facet of discontent in the social universe. A universal indictment, however, provides no lever for social action; it expresses the mood of disaffiliation. The most remarkable film of the fifties was thus a drama of high alienation, *High Noon,* in which the former leftist intellectual, speaking through the allegory of a western story, expressed his disillusionment and ultimate rejection of every aspect of American society.

"Alienation" thus lends a distinctive emotive-dramatic metaphor to experiences of social frustration. It imposes on them the metaphor of the prophets who failed. It conveys a mood of pervasive tragedy rather than the possibility of effective action. The socialist movement proposed to eliminate economic exploitation and to abolish the class system. These were relatively definable goals. A movement cannot, however, very well propose to alienate the alienators as it did to expropriate the expropriators, for the alienated mood is so multiform in its expression, so unlocated in any specific social form, that it does not delineate the clear goals and foci for action which a political movement requires. The career of this concept, from Calvin's depiction of man, the original sinner, alienated from God for all time, to the modern notion of man alienated somehow in every form of social organization, indicates indeed that its dominant overtone is social defeat.

One sympathizes with the effort of such thinkers as Erich Fromm to restore the full ethical consciousness to the socialist philosophy. For Stalinist sadism found its theoretical apology precisely in the repression of ethics from the Marxist standpoint. The life history of the concept "alienation" suggests, however, that what it says can be better said without it; human self-destructive behavior is better dealt with without this metaphor. Some writers indeed seem to have a "will to alienation," and to revel in their perpetual alienation. An irreverent humorist indeed proposed some time ago the organization of "Alienated Anonymous."

From another standpoint, the emphasis on "alienation" is an indication how the politics of the superstructure has in the last decade replaced the politics of the economic foundation. The advent of prosperity has meant the shelving of any mood for basic economic reconstruction. The concern shifts from the production and distribution of wealth to the question of the ends and goods to which wealth shall be devoted. Whether "alienation" however provides an adequate basis for the definition of human good seems to me doubtful. "Alienation" remains too much a concept of political theology which bewilders rather than clarifies the direction for political action.

NOTES

1. Erich Fromm, *The Sane Society*, New York, 1955, pp. 110, 120.

2. Erich Fromm in his stimulating *Marx's Concept of Man*, New York, 1961, mistakenly says that "the thinker who coined the concept of alienation was Hegel." Cf. p. 47.

3. John Calvin, *Commentaries on the Epistles of Paul to the Galatians and Ephesians*, transl. Rev. William Pringle, Grand Rapids, 1948, p. 219; *Commentaries on the Catholic Epistles*. transl. Rev. John Owen, Grand Rapids, 1948, p. 162.

4. See the various passages from Marx cited in Erich Fromm, *Marx's Concept of Man*, pp. 52-53.

5. Karl Marx and Friedrich Engels, *Basic Writings on Politics and Philosophy*, ed. Lewis S. Feuer, New York, 1959, p. 33.

6. Ludwig Feuerbach, *The Essence of Christianity*, transl. George Eliot, reprinted, New York, 1957, pp. 136-138, 311.

7. *Ibid.*, pp. 161, 185. Feuerbach, the precursor of Freud in the psychology of religion, probed into the origin of religious dogmas in sexual ascetiscism. Cf. William B. Chamberlain, *Heaven Wasn't His Destination: The Philosophy of Ludwig Feuerbach*, London, 1941, pp. 60-61. Engels, in his old age, wrote energetically against Feuerbach's philosophy of "self-love." Cf. *Basic Writings*, pp. 216 ff.

8. Karl Marx, *Economic and Philosophic Manuscripts of 1844*, transl. Martin Milligan, Moscow, p. 101.

9. Frederick Engels, *The Condition of the Working-Class in England*, transl. Florence Kelley Wischnewetzsky, in Karl Marx and Frederick Engels, *On Britain*, Moscow, 1953, p. 179.

10. Karl Marx and Frederick Engels, *The Holy Family, or Critique of Critical Critique*, transl. R. Dixon, Moscow, 1956, p. 32.

11. *Ibid.*, pp. 31-32.

12. *Ibid.*, pp. 91-92.

13. *Ibid.*, 88-89.

14. *Ibid.*, p. 93.

15. *Ibid.*, pp. 86-88.

16. *Economic and Philosophic Manuscripts of 1844*, p. 102.

17. *Economic and Philosophic Manuscripts*, pp. 136-138.

18. *Ibid.*, pp. 138-141.

19. *Ibid.*, p. 121.

20. *Ibid.*, p. 119.

21. *Ibid.*, p. 73.

22. Franz Mehring, *Karl Marx*, transl. Edward Fitzgerald, New York, 1935, p. 72. Several generations later, in the Greenwich Village of the twenties, Joseph Freeman observed, from a Marxist viewpoint, the philosophy of the Villager was that of Feuerbach, that "sex love was the highest activity of man, . . . a philosophy of life." Alienation was conceived as having basically a sexual referent. Joseph Freeman, *An American Testament*, New York, 1936, p. 286.

23. Frederick Engels, *Germany: Revolution and Counter-Revolution*, New York, 1933, p. 126.

24. Otto Rühle, *Karl Marx: His Life and Work*, transl. Eden and Cedar Paul, New York, 1929, p. 40.

25. Isaiah Berlin, *The Life and Opinions of Moses Hess*, Cambridge, 1959, p. 10. Auguste Cornu, *The Origins of Marxian Thought*, Springfield, 1957. pp. 70-71.

26. Boris Nicolaievsky and Otto Maenchen-Helfen, *Karl Marx: Man and Fighter*, Philadelphia, 1936, p. 76.

27. Frederick Engels, *Herr Eugen Dühring's Revolution in Science*, transl. Emile Burns, New York, undated, pp. 209-210.

28. Karl Marx and Frederick Engels, *Selected Correspondence*, Moscow, Ed. 1953, pp. 367-368. Also, *The German Ideology*, ed. Roy. Pascal, New York, 1939, p. 69.

29. Marx and Engels, *Selected Correspondence*, p. 395.

30. *Ibid.*, p. 392.

31. *Reminiscences of Marx and Engels*, Moscow, undated, p. 330.

32. Frederick Engels, *Anti-Dühring*, pp. 329, 346. Karl Marx, *Capital*, Modern Library Edition, Vol. I, p. 534.

33. Robert Tucker, *Philosophy and Myth in Karl Marx*, Cambridge, 1961, p. 173.

34. Karl Marx, *Letters to Americans: 1848-1895*, New York, 1953, p. 151.

35. Cf. Samuel A. Stouffer, "A Study of Attitudes," *The Scientific American*, Vol. CLXXX, 1949, 13. Samuel Stouffer, *The American Soldier*, Princeton, 1949, Vol. I, p. 251.

36. Cf. Ely Chinoy, *Automobile Workers and the American Dream*, Garden City, 1955.

37. Charles R. Walker and Robert H. Guest, *The Man on the Assembly Line*, Cambridge, 1952, pp. 51, 52, 55.

38. Robert Blauner, "Work Satisfaction and Industrial Trends in Modern Society," *Institute of Industrial Relations*, Reprint No. 151, Berkeley, 1960, pp. 346-350.

39. W. E. Burghardt Du Bois, *The Souls of Black Folk*, reprinted, New York, 1953, p. 209.

40. Nathan Glazer once described "alienation" as "an omnibus of psychological disturbances having a similar root cause—in this case, modern social organization." "The Alienation of Modern Man," *Commentary*, Vol. IV, 1947, 380.

41. Margaret Cole, *Growing Up into Revolution*, London, 1949, pp. 177-178. Leslie Lipson, *The Politics of Equality: New Zealand's Adventures in Democracy*, Chicago, 1948, pp. 491-493.

42. Lewis S. Feuer, "Leadership and Democracy in the Collective Settlements of Israel," in *Studies in Leadership*, ed. Alvin W. Gouldner, New York, 1950, p. 375. David Maletz, *Young Hearts*, transl. Solomon N. Richards, New York, 1950, pp. 43, 46.

43. Harold Fisher Wilson, *The Hill Country of Northern New England: Its Social and Economic History, 1790-1930*, New York, 1936.

44. *The Characters of Jean de la Bruyère*, transl. Henri van Laun, London, 1929, p. 318.

45. Melvin Seeman, "On the Meaning of Alienation," *American Sociological Review*, Vol. XXIV, 1959, 786.

46. Peter Viereck, *The Unadjusted Man: A New Hero for Americans*, Boston, 1956, pp. 16, 52.

47. John Dewey, "From Absolutism to Experimentalism," in *Contemporary American Philosophy*, ed. G. P. Adams and W. P. Montague, New York, 1930, Vol. II, pp. 13, 19.

48. Dwight G. Dean, "Meaning and Measurement of Alienation," *American Sociological Review*, Vol. XXVI, 1961, 735-758.

49. Leon Trotsky, "Their Morals and Ours," *The New International*, Vol. IV, 1938, 164.

50. Dwight Macdonald, *Memoirs of a Revolutionist*, New York, 1957, p. 24.

51. Calder Willingham, "Politics and the Artist," *The New International*, Vol. XIII, 1947, 222. Irving Howe, "Intellectuals' Flight from Politics," *ibid.*, p. 241.

By way of addendum, we might note that in 1899 the American philosopher, Alfred A. Lloyd, made the concept of "alienation" the basic one in his *Philosophy of History*. Lloyd was indeed the first American philosopher of man's alienation.

Part IV

THE REDISCOVERY OF SOCIOLOGY: SOME STRAWS IN THE WIND

SOCIOLOGY AS AN ART FORM
Robert A. Nisbet

I admit readily that both by temperament and academic background I have always been more interested in the nonuses of our discipline than the uses. I admit further to believing that theories should be tested as much by their reach as their grasp, their importance as their validity, and their elegance as their congruence with such facts as may be at hand. It is my major contention that the science of sociology makes its most significant intellectual advances under the spur of stimuli and through processes that it largely shares with art; that whatever the differences between science and art, it is what they have in common that matters most in discovery and creativeness.

Nothing I say is intended to imply that sociology is not a science. I am quite willing, for present purposes, to put sociology on the same line with physics and biology, applying to each of these the essence of what I say about sociology. Each is indeed a science, but each is also a form of art, and if we forget this we run the risk of losing the science, finding ourselves with a sandheap empiricism or methodological narcissism, each as far from science as art is from billboard advertisements.

My interest in sociology as an art form was stimulated recently by some reflections on ideas that are by common assent among the most distinctive that sociology has contributed to modern thought. Let me mention these:

"Sociology as an Art Form." From the *Pacific Sociological Review* (Fall 1962), 5, No. 2, 67-74. Copyright © 1962 by the *Pacific Sociological Review*. Reprinted by permission of the author and *Pacific Sociological Review*.

mass society, alienation, anomie, rationalization, community, disorganization. I will have more to say about these ideas and their contexts a little later. Here it suffices to note that all of them have had lasting effect upon both the theoretical and empirical character of sociology. And all have exerted notable influence on other fields of thought, scientific and humanistic.

It occurred to me that not one of these ideas is historically the result of the application of what we are today pleased to call scientific method. If there is evidence that any one of these ideas as first set forth in the writings of such men as Tocqueville, Weber, Simmel, and Durkheim, is the result of problem-solving thought, proceeding rigorously and self-consciously from question to hypothesis to verified conclusion, I have been unable to discover it. On the contrary, each of these profound and seminal ideas would appear to be the consequence of intellectual processes bearing much more relation to the artist than the scientist, as the latter tends to be conceived by most of us. Apart from processes of intuition, impressionism, iconic imagination (the phrase is Sir Herbert Read's), and even objectification, it seems unlikely that any one of these ideas would have come into being to influence generations of subsequent thought and teaching.

For a few, no doubt, this conclusion, if believed at all, may seem like throwing vile suspicion on trusted ancestors: like a child's discovery that his father is a member of the John Birch society or his mother a descendant of the Jukes or Kallikaks. It may smack of an anthropologist's gratuitous demonstration to a pentecostal communicant of the totemistic origins of Christianity. But let us withhold further comment on this aspect of our subject, turning instead for a few moments to a more fundamental and inclusive matter—the habit of treating science as though it were substantively and psychologically different from art.

It is a deeply rooted habit, but by no means universal in the history of modern thought. We need go back no further than the Renaissance to discover a time when art and science were universally regarded as but different manifestations of the same form of creative consciousness. We know that Leonardo da Vinci thought of his paintings and his ingenious works in physiology and mechanics as, equally, art and science. The type of thought and even the outcome in each did not seem significantly different from the other. And, three centuries later, Goethe seems to have felt the same way. He did not suppose that one type of thought operated while he was writing *Faust* and another during his remarkable inquiries in geology and botany. In both the Renaissance and Enlightenment a radical distinction between art and science would have been incomprehensible.

When, then, did the change take place that produced self-consciousness in the scientist and the artist, so like that of Adam and Eve after the Fall? Like a few other things that plague us, it was, I think, in the nineteenth century. Beginning with social movements generated by the French Revolution, and closely connected with processes of division of labor introduced by the industrial revolution, we find a growing tendency in the nineteenth century to assume that the artist and scientist work in ways that are alien, even antagonistic to one another. Gilbert and Sullivan were but giving lyric expression to what everyone knew when they wrote that the scientist is "a matter-of-fact young man, an alphabetical, arithmetical, every-day young man" whereas the artist is "a crotchety, cracked young man, an ultra-poetical, super-aesthetical, out-of-the-way young man."

In art there had developed, by the end of the nineteenth century, the view that creation works through some inscrutable process called genius or inspiration, never through technique and experimental work. We see this vividly in Romanticism and especially in the *fin de siècle*. Associated with this stereotype was the equally fundamental one that the artist is not concerned with reality or truth, but only beauty—timeless supra-terrestrial beauty. And, forming the context of both of these, was the fateful view of the artist's role in society. Far from admitting any continuity with, or dependence on, society, the Romantic artist emphasized instead the gulf between him and society, seeking in solitary escape the anodyne that his medieval and Renaissance forebears had found in fellowship and social purpose. His rejection of the world that was being created by the industrial revolution was total.

But while art was becoming mythicized in this fashion, science was succumbing to another myth, one of reverse character and of equal influence on the popular mind. This was the myth, not of inspiration, but of method. Here, as in the case of art, we are dealing with something related to the industrial revolution. But, whereas art was generally repelled by the new industrial society, science was virtually absorbed by it. Just as industry began to dominate technology, technology dominated science, making it not what it had been for centuries, primarily a pursuit of the reflective mind, but a profession governed by rules and by criteria of service, all of a piece with law, engineering, and medicine.

The new universities in both Europe and America gave immense impetus to science but, to a very large extent, it was science of the applied type. In the United States the rise of the Land Grant colleges, based in their earliest years on an unrelieved vocationalism, was a major step in the union of science and industry and in the cultivation of the stereotype that science, like industry, is practical, the very opposite of art. The "mechanic arts" became, for several generations, the prime conception of everything scientific, placing their stamp upon the type of science done and respected at large. It was Thomas Edison who became the archetype of the scientist in the United States. A Willard Gibbs was simply overlooked.

Gradually the idea spread that science, unlike art, flows along the same methodical and systematic channels that business or law or medicine does. What is crucial, it was felt, was not free reflection, intuition, and imagination but rigorous adherence to procedure. The machine in the factory was proof that skill could be transferred from man to technology, making human ingenuity an expendable item. Could not method be the analogue of the machine? Several generations of Americans thought that it could, and schools and colleges were filled with students doggedly learning what was thought to be scientific method—not, alas, as an aid to ratiocination but as a substitute for it.

It is little wonder, given the overwhelmingly practical and methodical character of American science that Europeans looked for a long time with scant respect upon American science. It is a safe generalization that had it not been for the European institutes to which Americans in rising number went for advanced work, thus acquiring a truer conception of science, American science would never have burst forth from its shell of useful mediocrity. To be sure, there were those of like mind in Europe, especially England; those for whom science was profession, subject to and limited by rules and techniques. But in Europe, where the humanistic tradition was stronger as the result of a much older predemocratic, preindustrial past, and where a mind of the stature of Faraday's could reject for himself the title of physicist, preferring that of philosopher, and be understood and honored for it, there was less likelihood of science becoming mired in unrelieved method and technique.

II

The worst result of the nineteenth-century separation of art and science is not one of historical interpretation. It is the continuing belief in many classrooms and laboratories that the objectives as well as thought processes are different. At its worst, this view tells us that science alone is concerned with reality; that art's function is simply to titillate the senses in a kind of aimless quest of the decorative and eye-pleasing.

Nothing could be further from the truth. Any art form that is serious, be it the novel, poem, or painting, is concerned first and foremost with reality. It is interested in throwing light upon reality, and in somehow communicating this light to others. And this, basically, is what science—as contrasted with technology—is concerned with. I venture the judgment that there is more in common between Picasso and Einstein—in objective, in inspiration, and mode of fulfillment—than there is between Picasso and, say, Norman Rockwell or between Einstein and any of the stolid practitioners of what A. N. Whitehead once called "dustbowl empiricism." Both the artist and the scientist are driven by the desire to understand, to interpret, and to communicate their understanding to the rest of the world.

The artist, let it be trumpeted, is *not* interested in decoration, and it is only because Non-Artists have worked as though decoration, fatuous reminiscence, and eye titillation were the highest ends of art that many persons still find themselves accepting or rejecting an art work largely in terms of whether it is beautiful to the eye. Of course art can be beautiful, but not if it seeks beauty as its chief end. So, let it be remembered, can science be beautiful though no one would suppose that even a mathematician is actuated fundamentally by the goal of beauty.

"The essential nature of art," writes Sir Herbert Read, "will be found neither in the production of objects to satisfy practical needs, nor in the expression of religious or philosophical ideas, but in its capacity to create a synthetic and self-consistent world: a world which is neither the world of practical needs and desires, nor the world of dreams and fantasy, but a world compounded of these contradictions: a convincing representation of the totality of experience: a mode therefore of envisaging the individual's perception of some aspect of universal truth. In all its essential activities art is trying to tell us something: something about the universe, something about nature, about man, or about the artist himself. . . . It is only when we have clearly recognized the function of art as a mode of knowledge parallel to the other modes by which man arrives at an understanding of his environment that we can begin to appreciate its significance in the history of mankind." [1]

The artist's interest in form is the scientist's interest in structure. In each the desire for vision and understanding is dominating. Each works empirically; each strives to communicate what it finds through a pattern or formal structure requiring technique for its mastery. It is worth noting that the word "theory" comes from the same Greek root as the word "theater." It means, basically, looking fixedly at, contemplation. It is allied with the word imagination—that is, literally, internalizing the outer world to an image that the mind holds tenaciously. Both art and science, in short, depend upon the capacity for detachment and upon the ability to hold back from commitment. The essence of each, wrote Santayana, "is the steady contemplation of things in their order and worth."

In truth, science and art have had a profoundly important cultural relationship for the greater part of the history of man. Eugene Rabinowitch, distinguished chemist and science editor, has recently written some words that might fittingly hang in every hall of learning.

The evolution of the human mind is a single process, revealed with different intensity, different clarity, and different timing—in its various manifestations—in art, science, philosophy, social and political thought. It is like a fugue, or an oratorio, in which different instruments or voices enter in turn. The voice of the artist is often the first to respond. The artist is the most sensitive individual in society. His feeling for change, his apprehension of new things to come, is likely to be more acute than of the slower-moving, rational, scientific thinker. It is in the artistic production of a period, rather than in its thinking, that one should search for shadows cast in advance by coming events, for prophetic anticipation. I do not mean the forecast of future events, but rather the revelation, in the framework of artistic production, of the mental attitudes which only later will become apparent in other fields of human endeavour. Thus the impending breakdown of the existing order of things, of the generally accepted system of values, should be—and often is—first recognizable in a revolt against the values and canons that had dominated artistic creation; a revolution in art precedes the revolution in society.[2]

Repeatedly, the history of the West has shown these words to be true. Historians of both ancient and modern European culture have emphasized the directive role played by the artist's mind: how philosophical and scientific images of man were preceded by those to be seen first in the drama, the sonnet, and in painting or sculpture. This first became a vivid truth for me several years ago while going through the great Uffizi gallery in Florence. Here it is possible to trace, in hall after hall, standing for age after age, the historically evolving images of man in Western Europe: from the spiritual, almost mystical and transcendent representations of man to be found in the Italian Primitives, through transitional manifestations that are both divine and human in appearance, to the frankly human, self-contained, and overwhelmingly terrestrial men and women of the Renaissance and Baroque. It is a development that plainly precedes the analogous transitions of image in philosophy and science. It was art with its swift, encompassing, and iconic vision that formed the bridge from medieval asceticism and corporatism to modern humanism; from organism to the obsessing problem of man's relation to society and values.

It was indeed in the Renaissance—and what else was the Renaissance but the conception of man and society as works of art?—that the whole modern view came into existence. This is a view that has since been modified in countless ways—now enhanced, now vulgarized; now made tragic, now trivial; sometimes ennobled, sometimes debased—but never really changed after the late fourteenth century in Italy. Whether the objective was the building of a cathedral or a bridge, the planning of a tapestry or a voyage to the Indies, the forming of a guild or the state itself, Renaissance man saw the world around him from the vantage point of the artist-scientist; not as something to worship or to manipulate but to understand and master even as Michelangelo mastered the marble he worked or Marco Polo the route to Cathay.

The problems and answers that form the core of modern culture are the work, not of the Usefuls in society but of the Visionaries, those who are lost in wonder and who, not knowing where they are going, go therefore the farthest. The same impulse to reality and its communication drove Michelangelo and Machiavelli alike—the one to the majestic *David*, the other to the Renaissance state—each a product of the artist-scientist.

The basic affinity between the artist and the scientist is, as the mathematician Marston Morse has told us, psychological and spiritual. "The first essential bond between mathematics and the arts is found in the fact that discovery in mathematics is not a matter of logic. It is rather the result of mysterious powers which no one understands, and in which the unconscious recognition of beauty must play an important part. Out of an infinity of designs a mathematician chooses one pattern for beauty's sake, and pulls it down to earth, no one knows how. Afterward the logic of words and of forms sets the pattern right. Only then can one tell someone else. The first pattern remains in the shadows of the mind." [3]

These are important words, burning words. They might hang over the entrance to every methodology seminar as a prophylaxis to pedantry. Too many sociologists have assumed that because scientific thought is by definition rational and logical in expression, its psychological roots must therefore be limited to strictly empirical and logical processes. Only that is scientific—so runs the folklore of scientism—that proceeds from an unambiguous and precisely delimited problem, drawn from statistically aseptic data, to a carefully tailored hypothesis. All else is, by definition, art or philosophy. It is hard to think of a better way to apotheosize the routine and insignificant.

Of course science is concerned with problems, with questions rooted in empirical observation as well as reflection. Like the artist, the scientist is interested in understanding the world around him and in discovering significant relationships. But from the large and incontestable truth that scientific thought is ultimately rooted in a preoccupation with the unknown, in a gnawing desire to reduce the tensions of uncertainty, it does not follow that scientific discovery is wholly, or even largely, the simple consequence of problem-defining and problem-solving thought. Such a conclusion has done much to drive sociology into areas of study chosen not because of their intrinsic intellectual importance, but because in them quantitative methodologies can work frictionlessly.

The late Florian Znaniecki foresaw, a generation ago, the trend that things are taking. He was referring to the already manifest influence of methodology courses. "This influence consists in substituting tabulating technique for intellectual methods, and thus eliminating theoretical thinking from the process of scientific research . . . A condition can be foreseen—indeed, it has almost been reached—when anybody who has learned by heart the various technical rules and formulae of statistics, with no other education whatsoever and no more intelligence than a moron, will be able to draw from a given material all the conclusions which statistical problematization makes possible. . . . The role of creative thinking in science, according to this conception, will be reduced to the function of formulating hypotheses which are to be tested by technical means. But we have seen that the only hypotheses statisticians ever have formulated, and ever can formulate, in view of the unavoidable limitations of their method, are no more than superficial generalizations of common-sense practical reflection. There is little place for creative thought and even for scientific progress in this kind of problematization."[4]

Despite the candor of many distinguished scientists in telling about their work, and despite what we are on the way to learning about processes of creativity in general, there is still a great deal that we do not know about how scientists arrive at their problems, do the really crucial work on them, and draw their basic insights. But this much is clear. Such problems and ideas, from all that we can presently learn, seem to come as often from the unconscious as the conscious mind; from wide and extraneous reading, or from buried experience, as from the data immediately in view; from the "left-handed" processes of feeling and intuition as from the "right-handed" imperatives of logic and reason. Therefore, may we not draw this conclusion?: Anything that shrinks the field of experience and imagination, that in any way diminishes the sources of inspiration, that routinizes the workings of the intelligent mind, is to be regarded with suspicion.

MARVELOUS

III

It is time to return to the ideas in sociology I referred to at the outset of my paper. Let me describe them briefly again, for they are indubitably the most distinctive and illuminating contributions of sociology to the study of culture and society. There is, first, the view of human association as containing endemic processes of disorganization, dysfunction, call them what we will. Second, there is the view of the individual as alienated and anomic. Third, there is the perspective of community—in contrast to rationalistic and contractual forms of relationship—involving the key concepts of hierarchy and status. Fourth, we have the great theme of rationalization as a process in history and in the whole structure of modern society.

We know where these ideas came from: from the writings of four or five remarkable minds in the late nineteenth century: Tocqueville, Weber, Simmel, Tönnies, and Durkheim. I need not enlarge upon their formulations of the ideas. I am more interested in the processes by which the ideas came into being: that is, the contexts in which the ideas were uttered, the traditions they came out of, and, if it were possible, the mental states behind the ideas. Obviously, we are limited in what we can say positively, but I believe certain points are clear.

There is, first, the manifest discontinuity of these ideas in the history of modern social thought. Not one of them could have been deduced from the propositions of rationalism on human behavior that flourished in the Enlightenment. The true heritage of the Enlightenment is to be found, not in sociology, but in classical economics, individual psychology, and utilitarian political science. What we find in sociology—that is, in its distinctive currents—is a revolt against the rationalist view of man and society.

The second point is this. Not only are the key ideas of sociology unrelated to prior "scientific" ideas; they have their closest affinity with an art movement, Romanticism. In the same way that the Renaissance image of man proceeded from prior currents in art, so, I argue, the sociological image arises in the first instance from visions which had their earliest and most far-reaching appeal in Romantic art.[5]

Weber has somewhere likened his own concept of rationalization to the poet Schiller's earlier view of the "disenchantment of the world." He was candid and accurate. Tocqueville, Simmel, and Durkheim might well have done likewise. From the first burst of the Romantic spirit in the late eighteenth century—rising to do battle with the classicist-rationalist view—we find luminously revealed two central visions: (1) the estrangement of the individual from a growingly impersonal and disorganized society (and the consequent spiritual inaccessibility of modern institutions—city, factory, mass society); (2) a celebration of status and community—whether rural, religious, or moral—in contrast to the individualistic and contractual society of the *philosophes*.

Third, and most important, even if most elusive, are the psychological affinities between the Romantic artists and the sociologists. It is impossible, as I have already suggested, to entertain seriously the thought that these major ideas were arrived at in a manner comparable to what we think of as scientific methodology. Can you imagine what would have happened had any one of them been subjected, at the moment following its inception, to a rigorous design analysis? Can anyone believe that Weber's vision of rationalization in history, Simmel's vision of metropolis, or Durkheim's vision of *anomie*, came from logico-empirical analysis as this is understood today? Merely to ask the question is to know the answer. Plainly, these men were not working with finite and ordered problems in front of them. They were not problem-solving at all. Each was, with deep intuition, with profound imaginative grasp, reacting to the world around him, even as does the artist, and, also like the artist, objectifying internal and only partly conscious states of mind.

Consider one example: the view of society and man that underlies Durkheim's great study of suicide. Basically, it is the view of the artist as much as that of the scientist. Background, detail, and characterization blend into something that is iconic in its grasp of an entire social order. How did Durkheim get his controlling idea? We may be sure of one thing: he did not get it, as the stork story of science might have it, from a preliminary examination of the vital registers of Europe, any more than Darwin got the idea of natural selection from his observations during the voyage of the *Beagle*. The idea, the plot, and the conclusion of *Suicide* were well in his mind before he examined the registers. Where, then, did he get the idea? We can only speculate. He might have got it from reading

Tocqueville, who could certainly have got it from Lamennais who could have got it from Bonald or Chateaubriand. Or, it could have come from personal experience—from a remembered fragment of the Talmud, from an intuition born of personal loneliness and marginality, a scrap of experience in Paris. Who can be sure? But one thing is certain. The creative blend of ideas behind *Suicide*—a blend from which we still draw in our scientific labors—was reached in ways more akin to those of the artist than to those of the data processor, the logician, or the technologist.

It is not different with the ideas and perspectives of Simmel—in many ways the most imaginative and intuitive of all the great sociologists. His treatment of fear, love, conventionality, power, and friendship show the mind of the artist-essayist, and it is no distortion of values to place him with such masters as Montaigne and Bacon. Remove the artist's vision from the treatments of the stranger, the dyad, and the role of secrecy, and you have removed all that gives life. In Simmel there is that wonderful tension between the aestheically concrete and the philosophically general that always lies in greatness. It is the esthetic element in Simmel's work that makes impossible the full absorption of his sociological substance by anonymous, systematic theory. One must go back to Simmel himself for the real insight. As with Darwin and Freud, it will always be possible to derive something of importance from the man directly that cannot be gleaned from impersonal statements in social theory.

This leads to another important fact. Our dependence upon these ideas and their makers is akin to the artist's dependence upon the artists who precede him. In the same way that the novelist will always be able to learn from a study and restudy of Dostoevski or James—to learn a sense of development and form, as well as to draw inspiration from the creative source—so the sociologist can forever learn from a rereading of such men as Weber and Simmel.

It is this element that separates sociology from some of the physical sciences. There is, after all, a limit to what the young physicist can learn from even a Newton. Having once grasped the fundamental points of the *Principia,* he is not likely to draw very much as a physicist from rereadings (though he could as a historian of science). How different is the relation of the sociologist to a Simmel or Durkheim. Always there will be something to be gained from a direct reading; something that is informative, enlarging, and creative. This is precisely like the contemporary artist's return to the study of medieval architecture, the Elizabethan sonnet, or the paintings of Matisse. This is the essence of the history of art, and why the history of sociology is so different from the history of science.

IV

That such men as Weber, Durkheim, and Simmel fall in the scientific tradition is unquestioned. Their works, for all the deep artistic sensitiv-

ity and intuition, no more belong in the history of art than the works of
Balzac or Dickens do in the history of social science. The conclusion we
draw is not that science and art are without differences. There are real
differences, as there are among the arts and among the sciences.[6] No one
asks a Picasso to verify one of his visions by repeating the process; and,
conversely, we properly give short shrift to ideas in science that no one
but the author can find supported by experience. The ideas of Durkheim
may, as I have suggested, be dependent upon thought processes like those
of the artist, but none of them would have survived in sociology or become fruitful for others were it not for criteria and modes of communication that differ from those in art.

The conclusion, then, is not that science and art are, or should be,
alike. It is the simpler but more fundamental conclusion that in both art
and science the same type of creative imagination works. And everything
that impedes or frustrates this imagination strikes at the source of the discipline itself. This unhappily is what is happening today in large areas
of sociological instruction and research. It is a recurrent phenomenon in
philosophy and science.

All too often in the history of thought we find techniques, methods,
and doctrines becoming puny earthworks, hiding the view of the Olym-
pian heights. How many mute, inglorious Simmels, how many village
Cooleys lie today buried in required sequences of curriculum and in the
computer rooms, their talents occupied not by development of ideas and
insights but by the adaptation of trivial or well-worn ideas to the language of the machine or by the endless replication of studies that often
shouldn't have been done in the first place? Such servitude is justified
on the false and appalling ground that the student can thus be taught
the "method" of science. One may observe cynically that he sees no Simmels and Durkheims walking the campus today. I venture the statement
that there would have been none in their day had certain curricular requirements and terminological fashions been then in existence.

Which leads me to my final observations. I have stressed the art element in sociology not because I think the villain is the machine—any
more than it is the machine tender who occasionally walks like a social
scientist. The danger, if I may indulge myself in the presidential preroga-
tive of the sermon, is nontechnological; it is sociological; it is the system-
atics and the dogmatics that always threaten to seep into the cellars of
intellectual disciplines, thus driving out the art elements. For art's war is
with system building, not with science. I know of no better way of expressing this than in the form that Francis Bacon chose three centuries
ago. That is, in the form of the Idols of the Mind. Let us call them the
Idols of the Profession.

There are, first, you will remember, the Idols of the Tribe. These are
the inclinations, perspectives, and modes of perception that are common
to all; they are unavoidable, but must nevertheless be allowed for. The

mere fact that we are sociologists—instead of biologists or economists—means that there are certain endemic, uniting ways of seeing the world around us. They are valuable and unavoidable, but not final.

Second, there are the Idols of the Cave—those that come, not from the character of the profession as a whole, but of that small part of the profession each of us lives in. Here we have the idols of specialization; the human but nevertheless dangerous tendency to reduce the richness and variety of the whole to the specialized perspectives and techniques that each of us operates with and that always threaten to become as rigid and fixed as the skills of technicians.

Third, we have the Idols of the Market Place—words, phrases, and neologisms that become substitutes for ideas. Who among us has not learned to his advantage or disadvantage of the hypnotic fascination that is exerted upon foundations, research committees, and certain editors, by phraseology? And who does not know of the ease with which the words conveying the concept become the thing itself—with resulting inability to go beyond the words?

But, the greatest and most formidable of the Idols are those of the Theater. Here Bacon had reference to systems of thought, systems which become, like bureaucracies, their own reason for being; where original goals have become displaced, leaving only the goals of systematic survival and self-maintenance. It seems to be the mark of all systems that their very degree of initial success leads before long to an almost ritualistic conclusion. We have all laughed at the teacher of classics who saw in the *Antigone* "a veritable treasure house of grammatical peculiarities." And for this teacher's students the classics were indeed killed. But why do we not laugh also at the teacher of sociology who introduces his students not to the rich and endlessly diversified field of social and cultural experience but to dull and potentially alienating analyses of fashionable systems and methodologies. Is not at least part of the attraction today of the natural sciences for the gifted student the assurance that he will be introduced immediately to the materials and problems of science and not to the locutions of systems? Systems so easily become bureaucracies of the spirit, subject to the same pettifogging rules and regulations.

Art abhors systems, and so does all creativity. History is the graveyard of systems, and this is precisely why Simmel and Cooley and Sumner remain fresh and valuable for us today and why few read Spencer or Ward. How often do system-builders produce students who are themselves creative and viable? The system killeth, the insight giveth life. What remains today of nominalism, realism, sensationalism, pragmatism, and all the other systems that once paraded over the landscape of Europe? Dead, all dead. God lives, Blake wrote, in the details. I amend this to say he lives in the insights, the intuitions, the imaginations of the artist. I cannot better conclude than with one final excerpt from Marston Morse:

The creative scientist lives in "the wildness of logic" where reason is the handmaiden and not the master. I shun all monuments that are coldly legible. I prefer the world where the images turn their faces in every direction, like the masks of Picasso. It is the hour before the break of day when science turns in the womb, and, waiting, I am sorry that there is between us no sign and no language except by mirrors of necessity. I am grateful for the poets who suspect the twilight zone.

The more I study the interrelations of the arts the more I am convinced that every man is in part an artist. Certainly as an artist he shapes his own life, and moves and touches other lives. I believe that it is only as an artist that man knows reality. *Reality is what he loves, and if his love is lost it is his sorrow.*[7]

NOTES

1. Sir Herbert E. Read, *Art and Society*, London: William Heinemann, Limited, 1937, pp. x-xii.

2. Eugene Rabinowitch, "Integral Science and Atomized Art," *Bulletin of the Atomic Scientists*, 15 (February, 1959), 64. The entire issue is organized around the theme, science and art, and contains a number of highly perceptive pieces by both scientists and artists. Particularly valuable are those by Rabinowitch, Marston Morse, Carl Holty, and Martin Kamen and Beka Doherty.

Some prolonged, if unsystematic, personal questioning of scientists suggests to me that there is a stratification of acceptance of the art element in creative science. Mathematicians and theoretical physicists, currently high in the status system of modern science, are prone to accept immediately the reality of intuitive and nonlogical elements in scientific discovery. So, for the most part, are those working in such relatively new and highly creative areas as biophysics and biochemistry. Geologists, today low in the pecking order of science, appear least likely to accept or understand the art element in science, although they have much company in the more established and formalized areas of other disciplines, including biology and physics and chemistry. In the behavioral sciences generally there is a greater insistence upon rigor and logic of method—and preoccupation with method itself—than is true of the physical sciences. There are differences, of course, by field. Thus the educationists are more likely to fluff their scientific feathers than are the anthropologists in whose number unabashed artists have always flourished and who have, on the whole, spent least time on matters of abstract methodology. Similarly, my experience indicates, acceptance of the art element in science seems to follow the curve of personal distinction. I am told that one Nobel laureate, a chemist, dismissing method, describes scientific discovery as "rape followed by seduction."

3. Marston Morse, "Mathematics and the Arts," *Bulletin of the Atomic Scientists*, *op. cit.*, 56-57. Two recent literary studies have shown, with impressive imagination and learning, how unreason and reason, unconscious and conscious, hunch and hypothesis, have worked together historically. See Wayne Shumaker, *Literature and the Irrational*, Englewood Cliffs, N.J.: Prentice-Hall, Inc., 1960, and Ernest Tuveson, *Imagination as a Means of Grace; Locke and the Aesthetics of Romanticism*, Berkeley: University of California Press, 1960.

4. Florian Znaniecki, *The Method of Sociology*, New York: Holt, Rinehart & Winston, Inc., 1934, pp. 234-235.

5. I have discussed this at greater length in an article "Conservatism and Sociology," *American Journal of Sociology*, 134 (September, 1952), 167-175. See also Leon Bram-

son's interesting discussion in his *The Political Context of Sociology*, Princeton, N.J.: Princeton University Press, 1961, Chap. 1.

6. Charles Morris, the philosopher, has suggested that the major difference is this: although both science and art communicate by the use of ideas and representations not completely describable in terms of sense experience, science typically seeks to make its communications capable of identification or verification by the largest number of individuals, whereas art tends to insist that each individual translate the original vision into something peculiarly his own creation.

There are probably also interesting role differences between artists and scientists, though this is, so far as I can discover, a relatively unexplored area of study. Martyl Lansdorf, an artist, and Cyril S. Smyth, a scientist, in a joint article in the *Bulletin of the Atomic Scientists* already cited, say: "In many contacts with humanist and scientific friends we have noticed only one consistent difference of professional attitudes—the scientists are jealous of their ideas; the humanists do not seem to mind if someone appropriates their ideas but are outraged by a plagiarism of form." This is an important insight, but I judge that it has more relevance to painters and sculptors, and possibly poets, than to novelists and playwrights who are certainly as jealous of ideas, and as secretive, as are the scientists. Legal battles over plots are not unknown.

One commonly alleged difference between scientists and artists deserves critical comment. It is an old stereotype of the scientist, sedulously cultivated in many a seminar, that the scientist, simply because he is scientist and not artist, is preconditioned to a willingness, even a desire, to be displaced by the work of students and others. But this stereotype says more about the ideal world of science than it does about actual scientists. The desire for self-preservation is surely as strong among scientists as among artists, and the evidence suggests that in such matters as protection of personal theories, hoarding of data, and secretiveness of intent, there may not be very significant role differences.

Passion for self-preservation may be more functional in scientific thought than is commonly supposed. Marston Morse, in the article referred to above, is of this view so far as mathematics is concerned. He cites the famous feud between Poincaré and his young colleague Lebesque, suggesting the similarity of conflict and outcome to the revolt of Philipp Emanuel Bach against the work of his father, Johann Sebastian. In each case the reactions were dictated by instincts of self-preservation which, as Professor Morse points out, were clearly to the advantage of posterity.

On one point the evidence is clear. Scientists have a far higher sense of priority—though not of competitiveness—than artists. This would seem to follow from the broad differences of context. It is highly unlikely that anything in the history of art resembles what Robert Merton has emphasized in his studies of priority in science or what Frederick Reif has described as prevailing practice among physicists in an article, "The Competitive World of the Pure Scientist," *Science*, 134 (December 15, 1961), 1957-1962.

7. Morse, *op. cit.*, p. 58.

SOCIAL THEORY IN FIELD RESEARCH

Joseph Bensman and Arthur Vidich

In the last fifteen years a central concern of both sociology and anthropology has been the relationship between theory and research. One of the turning points in this discussion was Merton's comment on the position of sociological theory,[1] in which he calls for more attention to "theories of the middle range"—"theories intermediate to the minor working hypotheses evolved in abundance during the day-by-day routines of research, and the all-inclusive speculations comprising a master conceptual scheme from which it is hoped to derive a very large number of empirically observed uniformities of social behavior." [2] Other studies addressed to issues in the relationship between theory and research are represented in the work of Mills, Blumer, Becker, Abel, A. K. Davis, Becker and Boskoff, Znaniecki, Borgatta and Meyer; Coser and Rosenberg; and Goode and Hatt, to mention only a few. All these authors have criticized the hiatus between low-level theory dealing with factually exact minutiae and the world-sweeping generalizations of theorists who appear to fail to appreciate the time-consuming task of systematically gathering and interpreting data. In addition, the older classical theorists have been explicitly criticized for being more interested in probing specific problems than in developing theoretical systems, independent of specific cases. This has led to a movement to construct a general theory that can be independent of specific data, but for the most part the authors mentioned have joined the issue on the disparity between generalized theory and low-level theory.

Two methods have been developed to provide a link between empirical observations and higher theory:

1. Closed logical-deductive models which presuppose that *coordinates* can be established which will make possible linkages between the models and the

"Social Theory in Field Research." From *The American Journal of Sociology* (May 1960), LXV, No. 6, 577-584. Copyright © 1960 by The University of Chicago Press. Reprinted by permission of the University of Chicago Press.

open systems of the empirical world.[3] When the general dimensions of elements or units of systems have been specified, the investigator can develop complex models of systems based on the various combinations and relationships of the elements in them. It may be a personality system, a terminological system, a social system, a cultural system, a kinship system, a motivational system, etc. A fundamental method in the construction of such systems is the comparison of specific empirically open systems with the abstract, common elements necessary to any social system.

2. The "codification of theoretical perspectives," [4] in which the researcher-theorist attempts to state systematically the relationship of existing theories to each other. Specific and discrete theories which have been used in the past on specific problems are examined, and the investigator attempts to discover the fundamental dimensions, implicit and explicit, of each, after which he compares them.[5] In making comparisons, the codifier discovers overlapping areas, convergences, different levels of generality and generalization, and different vectors of observation and perspective. He constructs paradigms and models of the various theories so as to offer a complete theoretical point of view which points to the data necessary to answer theoretical problems. The net product is a heuristic model which serves as a basis for future research.

Both these approaches to theory have been offered as corrections of the unsystematic uses to which theory has been put in the past. It is useful, however, to inquire what the older "unsystematic" and "specific" theory purports to do and how it focuses on the relationship between theory and research. Blumer has indicated that adherence to unsystematic theories sensitizes the theorist and the researcher who is familiar with a wide range of theories to a plurality of possibilities—to wide ranges of data.[6] Shils has specifically shown how the older, unsystematic theorists have helped him to locate and define one of the major problem areas in modern society, and he provides a vivid description of their part in the evolution of his own research and his perspective on society.[7] Blumer and Shils both show that the researcher-theorist can probe and check his data against a number of perspectives in theory and then discern the theoretical possibilities of them.[8] The researcher discovers novel and previously unspecified relationship in his data. Unsystematic theory, in this way, can lead to creative work.

To explore systematically one way in which unsystematic theories have been used, we will confine ourselves to specific research problems in which we have recently been engaged:[9] How is a small rural community related to the large-scale mass society? How does the mass society affect the public and inner life of the individuals of the community? How does the mass society affect the social structure of the town, particularly its class structure and the character of its institutional arrangements? What is the response of the small town institutionally and individually, to the institutions and agencies of the mass society that affect it?

EVOCATION OF THEORY FROM OBSERVATION

In response to the research organization's inquiry into possible sources of creativity among members of the community,[10] the observer's attention was directed to the locally owned and operated telephone company, whose management was considering a program of expansion. A newspaper's announcement of a proposed plan to install a new telephone system, with underground cables, dial phones, and an automatic central switchboard, offered an example of creative activity in community life which seemed ideal for investigation.

It was discovered that the force behind the drive for expansion was not the local operator but the state telephone company. In fact, the elderly local owner and policy-maker would have preferred to keep the installation as it was, since he had neither the stamina nor the capital to undertake the expansion. However, he could not resist the expansion program because he was dependent on the state company.

The local system was linked to the state system, through connecting trunks and long-distance lines, to all neighboring towns and the state and the nation at large. In addition, the local company's installations and finances bound it closely to the state company, which provided it with an auditing service, engineering consultants, advertising layouts, etc. The responsibilities of the local company were for maintenance, collections, and ownership. The state company was interested in promoting the expansion program because it found the local installation cumbersome and awkward; incoming calls could not be handled easily or automatically, and much attention from outside specialists was required. All these irritants could be removed, and service could be improved, by modernization.

The state company did not want to buy the local company. It appeared that it wanted to retain this and other independents as "competing independent companies." The local owner could not close down, though he might have liked to, because the state Public Service Commission would not permit termination of a public service. Since the company existed and since some improvements had to be made, the local company announced and undertook the expansion program. Almost nothing about the expansion, however, could be attributed to local action.

When the various external influences in the local "spontaneous" action were noticed, the attention of the authors was directed to an entirely different range of problems from those which led to the original inquiry. Not only were state agencies, other bureaucracies, and a whole range of experts decisive in the case of the telephone company, but similar connections and influences were at work in politics, education, religion, and the cultural life of the community. Local educational policy, religious affairs, public policy and politics—all were intimately related to policy-determining groups far removed from the town. The question then was:

How is it possible to comprehend and interpret the relationships between local and external action in a way that is true to the basic facts and elements observed? We turned our attention to various unsystematic and unsystematized theories developed in the past to handle similar data and problems: those of Redfield, Weber, Tönnies, Veblen, Merton, Lynd, Warner, Mills, Sapir, and Tumin. In each case we applied their perspectives to our data. In effect, we asked: "What in their theories would permit us to comprehend our data?"

In the case of each theory which our initial finding made salient, we had a directive for data which could be elicited by further field research. Thus, for example, Veblen's study of the country town makes the point that the political conservatism of rural life rests in the rural village because economically it dominates the surrounding agricultural area. We did not find this to correspond with our observations and could only account for the difference by noting that Veblen wrote in a day when rural banks were strong and apparently autonomous agencies. While many things in Veblen's study of the country town rang true, it did not provide us with a basis for further investigation of our particular problem. On the other hand, Sapir's analysis of spurious culture, which emphasizes the role of cultural imports, directed us to view all phases of the cultural life of the community as a successive series of imports made at different times since 1890. In short, existing theory gave our field work a focus, and we could conduct it along the lines thereby suggested.

Theories were helpful in opening our eyes to specific facts about our problem. For example, Sapir called our attention to the agencies of cultural penetration; Mills and Selznick, to the agencies of institutional penetration and organizational co-optation. In some instances a theorist's minor point became a central point to us, while his central point seemed irrelevant. In no case did we view any theory as offering us a solution to our problem, nor did we use any one theory exclusively to direct our observations. Research, for us, did not demonstrate, document, or annotate theory, but rather it exhausted the theories that came to our attention. Sapir's theory of the genuine culture was exhausted when nothing was found in the cultural life of the community that was indigenous to it—when everything cultural could be traced to an external source. In our procedure a theory was exhausted if and when it either yielded little follow-up data or if the data suggested by the theory were not forthcoming.

The Exhausting and "Destruction" of Theories

If a theoretical perspective does not yield the expected data, the question to be raised is: What facts and what theories are necessary to account for the gaps left by the specific theory? When one set of theories does not exhaust the potentialities of the data, other sets can be employed to point to and to explain the facts which remain unexplained. Thus for any initial statement of the field problem a whole series of theories may be successively applied, each yielding different orders of data and each perhaps being limited by the special perspectives and dimensions on which it is predicated.[11]

The relationships between theories and levels, orders and vectors of analysis, are not resolved a priori, but rather on the basis of the contribution of each perspective to the solution of the research problem. The order achieved (if the research is successful) is not the logical order of concepts but the order of uniformities in the social structure of the community. The value of these unsystematic theories is not in their formal order but in their heuristic usefulness.

Each of the theories provides a set of questions asked of the data, and the data lead to the continuous destruction of unproductive theories whenever the theories no longer yield new data or fail to solve the original problem. The reverse is also true: the theory may lead to the evocation of new data by focusing observation and its assessment.

THE SUBSTITUTION OF THEORIES

However, it has been our experience that, when new data are evoked by a theory, they lead quite frequently to the reformulation of the research problem, sometimes in a way that leaves the original theories (in this case dealing with penetration, external influences, etc.) inadequate. This is the case in which the data evoked by the observation forces such a radical shift in perspective that new theories must be called forth. For example, in tracing both the impact of the mass society on the community and the response of the community to agencies of the mass society, it was relatively easy to discover that different social and economic classes responded in different ways. Farmers as a class, for example, were the only group directly protected and aided by federal legislation, but not all farmers responded similarly to the benefits it brought them. A farmer's reaction to federal legislation had an important effect on his local class position. Small businessmen had lost their monopoly of the local market to the large urban chains, and they responded to the loss in a psychologically and economically defensive manner. The connections of the professional class to the outside world were almost exclusively cultural, but these enhanced their prestige in the local community, etc. In examining the problem of penetration, we could not look at the town as a unified whole but had to examine how each class was related to the outside world.

As a result of these observations it was necessary to recast our problem as a consideration of class. Class had to be considered, however, in terms not only of the specific problem of mass society but also of the general theories of class. In posing our problem as a class problem, again a whole range of new theories was evoked, including those of Warner, Lynd, Kaufman, Hollingshead, Weber, and Marx. However, again, theories of class were not considered *sui generis* but rather as pragmatic devices which would bring us to a solution to the original problem; that is, the alternative data which would be selected by different theories were considered initially only in terms necessary to solve the problem of the relationship of the local class structure to the mass society, using as many dimensions as theory would allow. The new focus meant making an examination of all relevant class data.

When the data had been re-examined and additional research had been conducted on class, theory was used in an additional way. The conception of the class structure of the community which we had developed in our research was criticized in the light of the class theories with which we were working.

THEORIES IN THE CRITICISM OF FIELD WORK

The procedure we followed was to take various theories of class and to postulate them as hypothetically fruitful and, then, to ask what would the hypothetical yield of each be toward exhausting the data then locally available. Some data that should have been elicited by certain of the theories were not present in the initial field work. The question was then raised: Is this a deficiency of the theory or of the field work? It was necessary to reanalyze the data already gathered and to make additional observations in order to make sure the fault was not the researcher's in these theoretical respects. This does not mean that all theories were equally productive or, in fact, productive at all.

We found that the prestige associations reported in Warner's work were not to be found in the initial analysis of our data. We postulated Warner as a critic of our analysis and then found that we had to ask ourselves why our analysis had not revealed socially exclusive local groups based on prestige. However, while Warner's system forced us to find groups of the type he describes, the class system we had discovered and described did not appear in most other respects to fit his model.[12] This does not prove or disprove the validity of Warner's work, which might in other communities be more meaningful; however, it did not cover the whole range of our data. In the same way, the theories of Hollingshead yielded valuable data, but again the phenomena were not entirely the same.

Theories of class led to another refocusing of the problem, this time in the area of politics.[13] It became apparent that members of different classes played different roles in local political life. Accordingly, we considered the political theories of Weber, Centers, Marx, V. O. Key, Mosca, Neumann, Michels, and Mills.

Each successive application of theory, derived in each instance from stimulation given by the immediately preceding investigation, caused us to take into account new orders of data which in turn forced us to select different types of theory. Thus the method compelled us to consider not only politics but the relationship between political and nonpolitical leadership, between the public ideology of the town and the private lives of its members, the role of religion in local life, and modes of personal adjustment to the social system. Our original starting point turned out to be merely a starting point for an examination of the major institutional and psychological problems of the community.

Thus successive modifications of our problem followed from the interplay of new data and new points of view. Only a portion of this process took place during the field phase; some was a result of the re-examination of field records, and some occurred during the writing-up of the data.

Let us summarize the functions that unsystematic theory can serve and the conditions under which it can be employed in research:

1. The specification of possible areas of field work as the researcher leans upon the educated perspective of his predecessors to guide him to important and significant areas of investigation.

2. The criticism of field work while doing it. Alternative perspectives in theory yield alternative perspectives in field observation.

3. The discovery of the limitations of one's original statement of the problem; the continuous discovery of new data compels new formulations of the problem.

4. The discovery of the limitations of one's own theory by its continuous confrontation with empirical observation.

5. The discovery of new dimensions of the problem.

6. The reconstruction of one's problem, field work, and past theory into a further limited and discrete theory to handle the problem. Such a theory is not final or general but adequate only to the specific problem in the specific field. However, this type of theoretical solution, in turn, provides raw materials for other research posing new problems, and these new problems as they are studied by other investigators in other settings contribute to the continuous cultivation of new theories.

THE RELATIONSHIP BETWEEN HEURISTIC AND SYSTEMATIC THEORY

Heuristic theory as outlined above is operative at every level of research: the statement of the problem, the gathering of the field data, the analysis and evaluation of the findings, and the analyzing and reporting of the results. However, heuristic theory is highly limited in that it does not produce generalized findings valid beyond the statement of the specific original problem. The generalization of the findings after observation, analysis, and interpretation must depend on other types of theory. Theorists of systematic theory have assumed the function of generalization.

As an enterprise, systematic theory can integrate new research findings with established theory and findings, thus accomplishing a continuous evaluation and assessment of research and heuristic theory. However, this can be accomplished only if general systematic theory pays attention to the differences in the problems, in the levels of heuristic theories, and in the field situations in which the problem and the theory are specified. The attempt to seek the common features of all social systems or of a hypothetical "the social system" overlooks the specific validity and the specific character of most heuristic theory and all research. If systematic theory is at all possible as an aid to scientific research, it must reach out and establish its empirical coordinates to the empirical world. It can do this only if it takes into account the limited and specific character of heuristic theory.

The Codification of Theory and the Heuristic Approach to Theory

There is relatively little difference between the theoretical enterprise that codifies theoretical perspectives and heuristic theory as described above. The major difference—and it is very important—is in the timing of the integration of the theoretical perspectives brought up for consideration. Codification of theory attempts to bring together and relate the various theoretical dimensions that can be brought to bear on a problem by the rigorous logical analysis of received theory in terms of the theories themselves. All these theories are considered in one analytical operation; ideally, the composite perspective derived from them is applied as a unit to a field situation.

Contrary to codified theory, heuristic theory allows past theory to remain as a residue of latent possibilities which the research worker can bring to bear on his specific field problem. He cannot know in advance exactly what orders of theory are relevant to his problem until he discovers its nature in the field and what resistances to his preconceptions emerge as his field work progresses. Totally new perspectives emerge as he discovers these resistances. New perspectives, new levels, new orders, and new dimensions of data become salient, regardless of what level of codification he has considered in the past; in the field, in the encounter with the world, the press of the data is manifold, continuous, and not easily amenable to preconceived selection. Moreover, the level of detail of data, the precision of analysis, and the concepts employed are functions of the emerging perspectives of the field worker in the field. It can thus happen that whole areas, codified in the past, may prove worthless for coping with a specific problem, though the past codificatons may be valuable for other problems. However, there is no level of codification sufficiently precise to be applicable when empirical data become the focus of attention.

To exhibit all possible dimensions of a problem in advance, codification would have to be extremely complex, cumbersome, and unworkable (e.g., in one problem the authors reached 256 formal logical possibilities of the data without ever reaching its substantive level) and, because of the complexity, one is, in effect, forced to work with heuristic concepts rather than with the full range of logically deducible possibilities. One deals with five or six major cells in a logical matrix and ignores a host of others which, for purposes of social science, are conceived of as logical but irrelevant. As a result, the researcher-theorist must continuously refine his theoretical analysis in terms of his problem and data.

LIMITATIONS OF HEURISTIC THEORY

Heuristic theory, as subjected to the rigors of specific substantive problems, has a number of limitations:

1. It cannot work if the research worker on a priori grounds is unwilling to entertain the possibility of using or seriously considering all or a variety of the available theories. Commitment to one school or theory means, in most instances, commitment to selected levels of data. These forms of commitment prevent the research worker from criticizing his findings from alternative points of view and may blind him to the exhausting of his own favored theoretical approach. In the heuristic approach there is no guaranty that such standards of open-mindedness will prevail or that self-criticism can and will be made. Science, then—particularly social science—must depend not only on self-criticism but on the criticism made by others, willingness to accept which then becomes the basis of social science.

2. The *ad hoc* rotation of theoretical perspectives does not in itself guarantee the exhaustion of the empirical data if it is only ritual eclecticism. The only purpose in considering many perspectives is to solve or to redefine the problem. The listing of the alternative possibilities of different theories is not a solution, since listings are not a structural relationship of data. The end objective of the procedure is not only to find what data are relevant to the problem but also to determine how they are functionally related. The only point that needs emphasis is that the functional relationships are products of the research and not of a priori theorizing.

3. These procedures of exhaustion and rotation of perspectives are dependent on the contingencies of field work, the investigator's background, and his sensitivity to his data; hence there is no guaranty that their use will assure success. There is no immutable deductive procedure which automatically guarantees the production of new concepts, theories, or findings. The research worker must face the possibility of failure in the knowledge that it may be due to the way in which he handled the problem.[14] Scientific inquiry means living an intellectually dangerous existence.

4. The method outlined here is amenable to not all types of research. Experimental studies assume that causes can be postulated in advance and that the problem in research is simply one of determining their conditions and efficiency. Large-scale surveys frequently telescope all the procedures of research described above into a single operation which does not and cannot allow for the continuous modification, substitution, and

refinement of hypotheses and problems on the basis of field experience. The survey worker, in the absence of these intermediate checks on his thinking, may be forced to pose all at the same time a wide range of theoretically possible alternatives resulting from a priori formulations and hunches, hoping that one or more of his theoretical dimensions will be productive after the field work is done and analysis is completed. He frequently finds that a limited number of areas are highly productive, but, since in the beginning he had to consider on a priori grounds a variety of alternative areas, time and funds limit the depth to which he can analyze those variables which finally proved productive. This is the familiar phenomenon of knowing better how to make a survey after it is done than at the beginning.

It is apparent from this discussion that in no case can the research worker feel that he has fully solved his problem. He must recognize that new levels of theory and new theories of which he may not have been aware at the time might have required new levels of data and further exhaustion of theory. At best, he can feel that he has advanced his problem along an infinite path so that his work need not be repeated. One must recognize that there is no final accumulation of knowledge and no final solution, in the usual meaning of these terms.[15]

NOTES

1. Robert K. Merton, "The Position of Sociological Theory—Discussion," *American Sociological Review*, XIII (1949), 164-68, republished in substantially the same form in Robert K. Merton, *Social Theory and Social Structure* (rev. ed.; New York: Free Press of Glencoe, Inc., 1958), pp. 4-10.

2. *Social Theory and Social Structure, op. cit.*, pp. 5-6.

3. Edward Shils has described this process in a similar way as follows: "The role of general theory consists of a general systematic scrutiny of particular facts: then the theory is either disconfirmed by the facts and is replaced by one more adequate to them, or the hypothesis and corresponding theory are confirmed and the problem is settled" ("Primordial, Personal, Sacred, and Civil Ties: Some Particular Observations on the Relationships of Sociological Research and Theory," *British Journal of Sociology*, VIII, No. 2 [June, 1957], 130-45).

4. Merton, *Social Theory and Social Structure, op. cit.*, p. 12. Also see James Olds, *The Growth and Structure of Motives* (New York: The Free Press of Glencoe, Inc., 1956), pp. 21-22, on "the limited theory viewpoint" in which the position of H. G. Birch and M. E. Bitterman (in "Sensory Integration and Cognitive Theory," *Psychological Review*, LVIII [1951], 355-361) is used as an illustration.

5. Best exemplified by Robin M. Williams, Jr., *The Reduction of Intergroup Tensions: A Survey of Research Problems of Ethnic, Racial, and Religious Group Relations* (Social Science Research Council Bull. 57 [New York: Social Science Research Council, 1947]), esp. chap. III. Similar studies are Merton, "The Sociology of Knowledge," in *Social Theory and Social Structure*, pp. 217-245; R. Sarbin, "Role Theory," in Gardner Lindzey (ed.), *Handbook of Social Psychology* (Cambridge, Mass.: Addison-Wesley Publishing Co., Inc., 1954), pp. 223-258.

6. Herbert Blumer, "What Is Wrong with Social Theory?" *American Sociological Review*, XIX (1954), 3-10.

7. Shils, *op. cit.*

8. Shils's article *(ibid.)* is a case history of this procedure. He has shown how the interplay between his research experience and received theory has led him to discard, revamp, and reinterpret the different theorists with whom he has been concerned, accordingly as his experience with different sets of data has called forth and brought into perspective different elements and segments of the theorists with whom he has been concerned—mainly Tönnies, Cooley, Mayo, Schmalenback, Lenin, Weber, Parsons, and Sorel.

9. The analysis of these problems is reported in the authors' *Small Town in Mass Society: Class, Power and Religion in a Rural Community* (Princeton, N.J.: Princeton University Press, 1958).

10. Cornell Studies in Social Growth, sponsored by the Department of Child Development and Family Relationships, New York State College of Home Economics, Cornell University, with the aid of funds from the National Institute of Mental Health, the United States Public Health Service, and the Social Science Research Council. The present study, as well as the original one upon which this one draws, is an independent by-product of Cornell studies and does not represent the authorized viewpoint of the project.

11. Similarly, Robert Redfield, in *The Little Community* (Chicago: University of Chicago Press, 1955), takes five different societies, each studied from a different perspective, and demonstrates how the perspective limits the data.

12. The ladies' book clubs, card-playing groups, men's clubs and associations, and "old American" families resemble groups found by Warner, but other classes in our study did not; e.g., "Old American" families, or what we called the "Old Aristocracy," occupied symbolically important positions but could not be called an "upper-upper" class.

13. In our first work politics received only scant attention; only the role of the lawyer as an intermediary between local government and state agencies had been examined by us (Bensman and Vidich, *op. cit.*, chap. iv).

14. John Dewey, *The Quest for Certainty: A Study of the Relation of Knowledge and Action* (New York: G. P. Putnam's Sons, 1929).

15. The following studies point to a similar conclusion: Max Weber, "Science as a Vocation," in *Essays from Max Weber,* trans. and ed. H. H. Gerth and C. Wright Mills (New York: Oxford University Press, Inc., 1946), pp. 129-156; Homer G. Barnett, "Comment to Acculturation: An Exploratory Formulation," *American Anthropologist,* LVIII, No. 6 (December, 1954), 1000-1002; Robert Redfield, "The Art of Social Science," *American Journal of Sociology,* LIX, No. 3 (November, 1948), 181-190; Herbert Blumer, *An Appraisal of Thomas and Znaniecki's "The Polish Peasant in Europe and America"* (New York: Social Science Research Council, 1939); Dewey, *op. cit.;* Allen H. Barton and Paul F. Lazarsfeld, "Some Functions of Qualitative Analysis in Social Research," *Sociologica,* I (1955), 321-361; Maurice R. Stein, *The Eclipse of Community* (Princeton, N.J.: Princeton University Press, 1960); Barrington Moore, Jr., "The Strategy of Social Science," in his *Political Power and Social Theory* (Cambridge, Mass.: Harvard University Press, 1958, pp. 111-159); and C. Wright Mills, *The Sociological Imagination* (New York: Oxford University Press, Inc., 1959).

THE POETIC METAPHORS OF SOCIOLOGY

Maurice R. Stein

Anyone trained in the methods and theories of modern sociology has been taught about the many respects in which sociology is definitely not a form of poetry. Our research tools have been carefully designed to maximize "objectivity" and to conceal, if not eliminate, any disfiguring marks that the "personal equation" of the investigator may have left on his work. Our vocabularies for interpreting and reporting findings have been screened by experts to eradicate all traces of value judgments other than the ineradicable judgment about the undesirability of making judgments. We are all well versed in the various techniques for eliminating verse from sociological inquiry.

Such antipoetic militancy can only be understood by recognizing that it is actually a defense of a particular poetic metaphor. This metaphor glorifies images of system in various forms ranging from systematic theorizing to systematic research and finally to the study of social systems. With due allowance for poetic license, the root metaphor of modern scientific sociology is clearly the notion of system. It embraces at least two clusters of associated meanings. Viewed as an observational attitude, system implies orderliness, certitude, objectivity, detachment, neutrality, and mechanical reproducibility. Viewed as a quality of objects being studied, it suggests interconnectedness, comprehensiveness, generalizability, and impersonality. It smothers all consciousness of the terrors and the thrills, the heights and the depths that mark the concrete life of man in human society.

Systematic sociology opens itself to encouraging the return of repressed nonsystematic metaphors when it tries to enter into a dialogue with classical sociology. The great classical sociologists from Marx to Veblen, Weber, Simmel, Durkheim, and Mannheim were inveterate sociological po-

"The Poetic Metaphors of Sociology." This essay is a condensation of several chapters in a forthcoming book, tentatively called *Styles of Social Inquiry*. Some of the themes are also discussed in greater detail in the epilogue to the author's book, *The Eclipse of Community*. The author is grateful to Daniel Foss and Arthur Vidich for help in formulating some of the ideas in this essay.

ets. While they each gave system its due, they each also responded to the demonic quality of history. The spectrum of sociological poetics over which they had command ranged through the search for meaningful patterns in the history of urban-industrial society to the search for dramatic consequences and dramatic choice between evolving alternatives and finally to the search for systematic propositions and techniques. Throughout this essay, history, drama, and system will be used as shorthand designations of these three root metaphors from which sociological inquiry can spring.

The most potent attack against the intellectual quicksand of "system" thinking was expressed by C. Wright Mills in his *The Sociological Imagination*. No one could mistake him for a neutral observer. He criticizes our profession as sharply as he did the higher immorality of the power elite or the fatal thrust of the forces heading toward World War III. He shows that the official languages of structural functional sociology and of survey methodology select only a narrow and bloodless range of social phenomena for attention while projecting an aridly complacent attitude toward those phenomena which neutralize effective choice. Mills dramatizes the limitations of academic sociology by renaming it Grand Theorizing and Abstracted Empiricism, while reserving the labels Liberal Scatter and Illiberal Practicality for its applied counterpart. His own program stresses the desirability of historical interpretation applied to the pressing problems of war and peace, although his practice seems actually to have been increasingly driven in the direction of dramatic and even melodramatic presentations of an immediate drift toward war.

THE POETICS OF SYSTEMATIC SOCIOLOGY

Since the metaphorical impetus of classical theory and of contemporary critical theorists like Mills and Riesman remains open and obvious, a few words must be said about the metaphors disguised as nonpoetry or as objective science in systematic sociology. These metaphors receive compellingly lucid expression in the writings of Robert Merton. Let me first quote some selected passages from the Introduction to his *Social Theory and Social Structure* and then comment briefly upon them.

Like the social scientist who errs in thoughtlessly comparing himself with the *contemporary* physical scientist because of the accident that they both happen to be alive at the same instant of history, so the informed public, and strategic decision-makers in that public, often err in appraising social science, once and for all, on the basis of its present capacity to solve the large and urgent problems of society which press in on all of us. The misplaced masochism of the social scientist and the inadvertent sadism of the public both result from the same fault: failure to see that social science, like all civilization, is continually in the process of development and that there is no providential dispensation providing that, at any given moment, science must be adequate to the entire array of problems confronting men at that moment (pp. 7-8).

Contributing to this tendency of sociological exposition to become lengthy rather than lucid is the received tradition—inherited slightly from philosophy, substantially from history and greatly from literature—which holds that sociological accounts would be written vividly and intensely, conveying all the rich fullness of the human scene with which they deal. The sociologist who does not disavow this handsome but alien heritage becomes more intent on expressing the full individuality of his "response" to the sociological case in hand than on seeking out the generalizable, objective and readily transmissible concepts and relationships pertinent to that case. In place of using objective concepts—the very core of science as distinct from the arts—the sociologist who depends on his heritage from the humanities searches for the exceptional constellation of words which best express the particularity of his experience. Too often, he is confirmed by the misplaced use of his genuine artistic skills by the plaudits of a lay public, gratefully assuring him that he writes like a novelist and not like an overly domesticated and academically henpecked Ph.D. Not infrequently, and of course not always, he pays for this popular applause, for the closer he approaches eloquence, the farther he retreats from sense (pp. 13-14).

Thus it is that ostensibly scientific reports become obscured by the inclusion of the irrelevant. In extreme cases, the hard skeleton of fact, inference and theoretic conclusion becomes overlaid with the soft flesh of stylistic ornamentation. Yet other disciplines—physics and chemistry are here in company with biology, geology and statistics—have escaped this misplaced concern with the literary graces. Anchored to the purposes of science, these disciplines prefer brevity, precision and objectivity to exquisitely rhythmic patterns of language, richness of connotation and deep-felt verbal imagery. Because one does not subscribe to the unthinking doctrine that sociology must in all respects hew to the line laid down by chemistry, physics, or biology, one need not subscribe to the contrary doctrine that it must emulate history, discursive philosophy or literature. Each to his last, and the last of the sociologist is that of lucidly presenting claims to logically interconnected and empirically confirmed propositions about the behavior of man in his relations with other men, and the social consequences of that behavior (p. 14).

These quotations taken from Merton's defense of middle-range theorizing and research obviously have many implications, and it is true that they are qualified in many ways in the original essay so as to render their implications densely ambiguous. One might notice, even in the passages quoted, the rejection of comparison with other sciences at one point when the question of sociology's capacity to study significant problems is raised, and the acceptance of such comparisons when discussing the appropriate language for sociology. But more important, the language used here and the imagery employed certainly departs widely from the stated goal of value neutrality.

For poetic purposes, three themes can be extracted from these passages which are amplified in Merton's other writing and which have become the dominant metaphors of most systematic sociologists:

A. *The Position of Modern Sociology*

Diagnosis: We are in a very early stage of the development of our Science and therefore can hardly hope to deal with large-scale social problems like nuclear war.

Prescription: Energy should be concentrated upon reliable middle-range empirical studies and upon orderly middle-range theories in the expectation that these will eventually accumulate to yield more satisfactory sociological thinking.

B. *The Form of Sociological Theory*

Diagnosis: Most earlier theorizing in sociology has consisted of pre-scientific speculative general orientations which do little more than name the kinds of variable that sociological analysts must take into account.

Prescription: Genuine sociological theories should consist of logically interconnected propositions based on confirmed empirical generalizations.

C. *The Language of Sociology*

Diagnosis: Sociologists have paid too much attention to developing richly personalized, evaluative descriptions of the particularities of social processes.

Prescription: The ideal language for sociological discourse at the theoretical level is structural functionalism, while the ideal language of research is constituted by reports of representative survey studies.

This set of assumptions, stated baldly, becomes visibly metaphoric and obviously open to serious disagreement. Even among systematic sociologists, the assumptions of middle-range sociology are questioned by such general theorists as Talcott Parsons. Merton's position acquires its peculiar power from the fact that it offers itself as a scientific compromise between several extremes. It offers to mediate between Parsonian general system theories and nontheoretical survey research. It also claims to mediate between research that is reliable but trivial and research which is significant but unreliable. These claims to mediation are symbolized in the image "middle range." Rather than compromise, it actually tends to discard the baby with the bath water. It does achieve a tepid certainty, but only at the price of abandoning the great potentialities of generalization which lie in heightened perspective on historical processes. It also often abandons the great opportunity for direct involvement in the con- • crete processes of social life that are achieved by the best empirical studies.

The middle-range assumption that its theories and its studies will provide the building blocks for some future Newton to use in his synthesis is even more debatable than Parsons' assumption that he is the future Newton. One would have to ask what kind of sociological building could be erected out of these blocks. Since the mixture discards most of the central facts of political and social life, future synthesizers, having any interest in sociological substance, seem at least as likely to pass over prod-

ucts of the present formalistic phase as they are to find them of constructive use.

Merton's defense of neutral language defeats itself by the partisan vigor
with which he repudiates opposing conceptions. The real issue remains
one of encouraging a plurality of languages. We need the vivid description prose of the community sociologist. How valuable would *Middletown* have been had the Lynds been confined to structural functional
jargon? Yet we also need Mills's passionate indignation. Riesman's subtle
discursive essays, Erving Goffman's keen eye for the underside of everyday
life, and certainly the lucid propositions of Robert Merton. When a given
language or mode of presenting theories is taken as the *only* correct mode,
the presenter runs the risk of cutting himself off from fruitful alternatives.
The recent emphasis on system in American sociology has almost succeeded in cutting off American sociologists from the great American med-
itative social theorists of an earlier generation. We hardly know how to
respond to the writings of Robert Park, Charles Cooley, or W. I. Thomas,
because they employ spacious tones that we have ascetically denied ourselves. Perhaps we can discuss some middle-range problems in impersonal
tones, but the problems of urban immigrants or the causes of World War
III may well evoke more passion.

It is exactly this passionate concern that characterizes the classical sociologists. This is not to say that they cannot also display profound objectivity. Weber commanded several disparate tones and languages ranging from the ascetic lucidity of his reflections on concepts to the rather
dull, detailed summaries of historical processes to occasional passionate
outcries against the limits of specialization and the dangers of bureaucracy. When we let middle-range theorists legislate the tone appropriate to
sociological thought, we also let them place the classical theorists in the
category of authors of pre-scientific general orientations, and therefore
allow them to elevate their own narrow theories above the massive con-
structions of classical theory. By consigning the figures of classical theory
to that peculiar limbo reserved for Hero-Founders, they are paid brief
ritualistic tribute, but then are quickly seen to be superseded by the realities of a more complex age. By erecting a Berlin wall between the older
theory seen in terms of polemics, naïveté, or mysticism and the newer
theory, seen in terms of easily testable functional propositions and ultimately testable mathematical models, this generation has ignored the
structural insights and moral power of such men as Marx and Weber.

The issue then is not to ignore the claims of system but rather to align
them with the claims of history and of drama, according to the special
demands of the problems that one elects to study. A full sociological vision must include the following concerns: (1) concern with the interpretation of the history of modern society; (2) concern with interpreting
major modern crises; (3) concern with developing decisive value judgments leading when possible to effective action; and (4) concern with

systematic ordering of concepts, propositions, and techniques to stimulate further inquiry. Systematic sociology, perhaps more so as it becomes more professionalized, tends to elevate the last concern far above the others. In doing so, it has permitted sociology to become a victim of the very forces —bureaucratization and alienation—that the classical sociologist was trying to understand.

ALTERNATIVES TO SYSTEMATIC SOCIOLOGY

Despite the discontinuites imposed by preoccupation with system in sociological theorizing and research, the task of diagnosing the modern situation proceeds on the margins of academic social science. A group of intellectuals, among whom Riesman and Mills may be included, has continued to work in the tradition of classical sociology. This group also includes Lewis Mumford, Hannah Arendt, Paul Goodman, Marshall McLuhan, Harold Rosenberg, Herbert Marcuse, Norman Brown, Raymond Williams, and Erik Erikson, to mention only the more prominent names. These authors focus on emerging social problems which systematic sociology can neither identify or interpret. They all avoid the pose of value neutrality when it comes to interpreting problems or recommending solutions, but they all display enormous intellectual discipline and objectivity within the context of the body of material that they cover. These authors resemble the classical sociologist in that they synthesize the resources of system, history, and drama to develop interpretations of the threats to individuality in modern life.

The body of work they have produced is already so extensive and so individuated as to defy simple paraphrase beyond an effort at suggesting something of its scope, its substance, and its significance. Each book, like all serious projects in social science or the arts, must be seen against the background of an evolving personal vision which underlies and strengthens the particular statement. Since these books are not as well known to sociologists as they should be, and since the titles tell much about the themes, a listing of selected works is one way of introducing them. Lewis Mumford ranges from *Technics and Civilization* through *The City in History* to *The Transformations of Man* and *The Conduct of Life.* Hannah Arendt starts with *The Origins of Totalitarianism,* proceeds to *The Human Condition,* then to *Between Past and Future* and *On Revolution.* Paul Goodman's books include *Growing Up Absurd, Utopian Essays and Practical Proposals,* and *The Community of Scholars.* Harold Rosenberg has written *The Tradition of the New* and *Arshile Gorky.* Norman Brown's important sociological essay is *Life Against Death,* while Herbert Marcuse ranges from *Reason and Revolution* through *Eros and Civilization* to *Soviet Marxism.* M. McLuhan's two books are *The Mechanical Bride* and *The Gutenberg Galaxy,* while Raymond Williams has written *Culture and Society* and *The Long Revolution.* Erik Erikson is the author of *Childhood and Society* and *Young Man Luther,* along with many articles on the problem of identity. The words in the titles announce the range of concerns—civilization, technics, community, reason, revolution, transformation, culture, life, death, childhood, eros, and Utopia. These titles lead one to expect a fundamental reconsideration of the human condition in our time and no reader will be disappointed.

For most of these authors, Marx and Freud are central figures, although Arendt, Mumford, and McLuhan reflect this double influence the least. Marcuse and Brown set out to restore the radical cutting edge to psychoanalytic thought, and thereby broaden the sociological approach to human behavior. Men not only live up to role expectations, become socialized to cultural values and respond to the internal and external pressures exerted by mechanisms of social control, but, in addition, they also dream, fantasize, play, create myths, create works of art, recall their childhood powers, and repress their childhood wishes. This multidimensional Freudian image of man allows these authors to ask the question, "Why worry about socialization if the society in which we are being socialized frustrates fundamental human impulses?" and "Why worry about social control if the purpose of such control is repressive domination by inhuman forces?" These questions are exactly the kind that value-neutral sociology ignores, but which serious thought in a world of concentration camps and nuclear power must inevitably confront.

Marcuse and Brown criticize the principles that shape conventional reality in our society, and try to show that conformity to this reality principle means repressing one's genuine humanity. Both advocate greater sensuality as opposed to abstract reason, but neither denies the significance of man's rational powers when used for appropriate purposes. These theorists employ the psychoanalytic approach to dramatize vital human faculties which get severely repressed in the lives of modern adults but which could find manifold forms of expression in a society that used the power of technology in a life-affirming rather than a life-negating fashion.

This double orientation to both the Apocalyptic and the Utopian potentialities of technology appears in the work of all authors mentioned. They avoid simple promodern or antimodern formulations in favor of dialectical thought of a more complex kind. Mumford, for example, supplements his sharp criticism of megalopolis with his poetic vision of a bio-technic civilization that is already manifest in several aspects of contemporary life. Paul Goodman is especially effective in cutting through cultural rationalizations with direct suggestions for immediate transformation, while Harold Rosenberg shows how to stay alert and alive in a situation where both diagnoses and remedies quickly change from sensible prescriptions to fixed poses.

All of these authors bridge social science and the humanities. Mumford, McLuhan, Brown, Goodman, Rosenberg, and Williams have written critical essays in the arts, while Goodman and Williams have written

novels as well. Erikson and Rosenberg approach the study of identity
through biography, the former writing about Martin Luther and Freud,
while the latter draws a powerful parable for our time from the life of the
great abstract expressionist painter Arshile Gorky. All show serious interest in the origins of modern industrial society during the Reformation;
and McLuhan, Arendt, Erikson, Mumford, Brown, and Williams offer
especially valuable commentaries on the familiar Weberean hypothesis
about the relation between Protestantism and capitalism. Above all, they
show real interest in placing Western history in the context of world
history.

It should be clear that these writers establish continuity with the substantive side of the classical tradition in sociology. They pick up the historical themes and the dramatic concerns of this tradition and extend
them into our own epoch. Perhaps the most grievous loss that the dominance of systematic concerns could occasion for professional sociology is
its tendency to denigrate this substantive tradition through such epithets
as "speculation," "journalism," or "social philosophy." The only weapon
against such verbal warfare is better poetry of our own.

CONCLUSION

Comprehensive theorizing about a society or a world of societies as complicated, as far-flung, and as rapidly changing as the ones in which we
happen to live, calls for a quite different attitude from that ordinarily
adopted by modern systematic sociology. The new attitude includes as
broad-gauged a sense of total world processes as can be gained from a
careful daily reading of that ever-changing collage, the front page of *The
New York Times*. Despite inevitable nationalist and class biases, *The
Times* assembles a configuration of reports from widely scattered places
of a sort that should become the subject of regular meditation by working sociologists. It provides information about the latest phases of the
"long revolution" which is sweeping the countries of the world into the
urban-industrial fold at an unprecedented rate. This secular trend pervades all aspects of modern life, and constitutes the larger setting within
which the various national dramas and histories must be placed.

Since thinking on this broad plane involves synthetic assimilation of
multiple generalizations, it must assume a flair for discerning hidden
transformations as well as an eye for the more obvious continuities. Such
sensitivity to broad world trends is hard to develop, but we can console
ourselves that we share these difficulties with all thinking men.

Just when the evidence from widely scattered sources suggests that important "norms" are becoming obsolete, that most "role expectations" are
subject to instant redefinition, and that "social systems" change kaleido-
scopically before our very eyes, we find "norm," "role," and "social system" becoming the primary concepts of systematic sociology. Though
these concepts may be helpful for teaching introductory sociology courses,

they can no more arrest the processes of rapid change than can conserva-tive political ideologies. Concepts like these can only encourage the illu-sions of detachment and certainty at a time when we desperately need to recognize that we are participating victims as well as participant observ-ers of the forces that we study.

Restoration of integrative social theorizing and research rests upon recognizing that professionalization currently accelerates fragmentation of thought. The dominant stress on systematic metaphors obscures the vital potentialities of history and of drama. Fortunately, there is a coun-tercurrent which includes Mills, Riesman, and the marginal intellectuals mentioned earlier. But this countercurrent will never become the main-stream because no society, not even the society of professional sociolo-gists, can embrace radical criticism as its central tradition. We should be thankful that there is still room on the margins as well as at the top.

Enlarging the metaphoric range of sociological subject matters and thought styles places a new burden on the practitioner. He must accept responsibility for helping to clarify the conditions for a humane world order. Since the threats to humanity are extreme, the thought forms for comprehending these threats must be radical. We need inclusive synthe-ses that become both more personal and more objective; more abstract and more concrete; more historical and more contemporary; more critical and more constructive; more realistic and more utopian; and finally, more useful and more joyful than the professional advocates of moderation, system, and neutrality will be able to bear. However, we cannot afford to let their rage for order set limits on our imaginative efforts, since doing so would render us collaborators in the very processes that our theories tell us are likely to destroy us all.

Bibliography

Arendt, H., *Between Past and Future* (New York: The Viking Press, Inc., 1961).

———, *The Human Condition* (Chicago: University of Chicago Press, 1958) .

———, *On Revolution* (New York: The Viking Press, Inc., 1963).

Brown, N., *Life Against Death* (Middletown: Wesleyan University Press, 1959).

Erikson, E. H., *Childhood and Society* (New York: W. W. Norton & Company, Inc., 1950) .

———, *Young Man Luther* (New York: W. W. Norton & Company, Inc., 1958).

Goffman, E., *Asylums* (Garden City, N.Y.: Doubleday & Co., Inc. [Anchor Books], 1961).

Goodman, P., *The Community of Scholars* (New York: Random House, 1962).

———, *Growing Up Absurd* (New York: Random House, 1960).

———, *Utopian Essays and Practical Proposals* (New York: Random House, 1962).

Lynd, R., and H. Lynd, *Middletown* (New York: Harcourt, Brace & World, Inc., 1929).

Marcuse, H., *Eros and Civilization* (Boston: Beacon Press, 1955).

——, *Reason and Revolution* (New York: Oxford University Press, Inc., 1941).

——, *Soviet Marxism* (New York: Columbia University Press, 1958).

McLuhan, H. M., *The Gutenberg Galaxy* (Toronto: University of Toronto Press, 1962).

——, *The Mechanical Bride* (New York: Vanguard Press, 1951).

Merton, R. K., *Social Theory and Social Structure* (New York: The Free Press of Glencoe, Inc., 1957).

Mills, C. W., *The Power Elite* (New York: Oxford University Press, 1959).

——, *The Sociological Imagination* (New York: Oxford University Press, Inc., 1959).

Mumford, L., *The City in History* (New York: Harcourt, Brace & World, Inc., 1961).

——, *Technics and Civilization* (New York: Harcourt, Brace & World, Inc., 1934).

——, *The Transformations of Man* (New York: Harper & Row, Publishers, 1956).

Reisman, et al., *The Lonely Crowd* (New Haven: Yale University Press, Hardcover, 1950, Paper, 1961).

Rosenberg, H., *Arshile Gorky* (New York: Horizon Press, Inc., 1962).

——, *The Tradition of the New* (New York: Horizon Press, Inc., 1959).

Stein, M. R., *The Eclipse of Community* (Princeton, N.J.: Princeton University Press, 1960).

Williams, R., *Culture and Society* (New York: Columbia University Press, 1958).

——, *The Long Revolution* (New York: Columbia University Press, 1961).

About the Contributors

MAURICE R. STEIN is Associate Professor of Sociology at Brandeis University, has written *The Eclipse of Community*, and is co-editor of *Identity and Anxiety*.

ARTHUR J. VIDICH is Associate Professor of Sociology and Anthropology at The New School for Social Research. He is a co-author of *Small-Town in Mass Society* and a co-editor of *Identity and Anxiety*.

JOSEPH BENSMAN, co-author of *Small Town in Mass Society* and *Class, Mass, and Bureaucracy*, is manager of consumer research at William Esty and Co.

LOUIS FEUER, professor of philosophy and social science at the University of California, Berkeley, is author of the recently published *The Scientific Intellectual*.

DANIEL A. FOSS is a sociologist currently working on problems of power and authority, at Brandeis University.

HANS H. GERTH, professor of sociology at the University of Wisconsin, is a foremost student of Max Weber and wrote, with C. Wright Mills, *From Max Weber: Essays in Sociology* and *Character and Social Structure*.

ALVIN W. GOULDNER, professor of sociology at Washington University in St. Louis, is the author of *Patterns of Industrial Bureaucracy* and many other essays and books.

SAUL LANDAU is a historical sociologist, an editor of *Studies on the Left,* and author of a C. Wright Mills memoir published in *Root and Branch.*

KARL MANNHEIM, distinguished sociologist, is best known for his *Ideology and Utopia.*

C. WRIGHT MILLS provided us in his books *White Collar, The Power Elite,* and *The Sociological Imagination* with a major analysis of American Institutions.

BARRINGTON MOORE, JR., professor of political sociology at Harvard, is author of several books on Soviet Russia and most recently has published *Political Power and Social Theory.*

ROBERT A. NISBET is professor of sociology and dean at the Riverside Campus, University of California, and author of *The Quest for Community.*

JOHN SEELEY teaches sociology at York University in Toronto and is author of a number of books, including *Crestwood Heights, Community Chest,* and numerous essays.

Spectrum Books in Sociology